Psychology in Practice

with Young People, Families and Schools

Edited by
Allan Sigston, Paul Curran,
Alan Labram and Sheila Wolfendale

David Fulton Publishers
London

David Fulton Publishers Ltd
2 Barbon Close, London WC1N 3JX

First published in Great Britain by David Fulton Publishers 1996

Note: The right of Allan Sigston, Paul Curran, Alan Labram and Sheila Wolfendale to be identified as the editors of this work has been asserted by them in accordance with the Copyright, Designs and Patents Act 1988.

Copyright © David Fulton Publishers Ltd

British Library Cataloguing in Publication Data

A catalogue record for this book is available from the British Library

ISBN 1-85346-390-6

Typeset by The Harrington Consultancy Ltd London N1 6DL
Printed in Great Britain by the Cromwell Press Ltd., Melksham

Contents

Preface

A welcome to the book

The editors and authors of *Psychology in Practice with Young People, Families and Schools* extend a warm welcome to readers. Whether you are an undergraduate student of psychology seeking applications of psychology in the real world, developing clinical skills in professional training as an educational or clinical psychologist, a teacher or a health service practitioner, or an experienced member of one of these professions updating knowledge and experience, we hope that you will find the book useful.

The aims of the book

No professional concerned with the meeting of people's needs can avoid the responsibility of influencing decisions that have long-term consequences: a choice of treatment approaches, a placement in a family or school, the focus and methods of intervention to help a failing institution, etc. While it is rare, perhaps impossible, for theory and research to give absolute answers, it is unforgivable for professionals to make or contribute to these decisions without regard to current evidence.

It is our firm belief that the discipline of psychology has a prime duty to promote people's welfare and our aim as editors has been to illustrate its use in relation to a number of thought-provoking contemporary social issues. The chapter authors were invited to contribute because they had gone some way to bridging the research and practice divide through practising and publishing in their areas. The chapter authors' remit was to review research, outline frameworks and key issues for professional practice and offer casework illustrations.

The structure of the book

The book has four themed sections. The introductory section discusses some pervasive issues that impact upon practice. The second, third and fourth sections focus on young people, families and schools respectively. The first chapter in each of these sections is intended to be a broader review of research and intervention while those that follow progressively concentrate on more distinct themes. Chapters have been designed to 'stand alone' but readers may find some benefit in reading them in the order they appear in a given section.

The introductory section (Chapters 1 and 2)

In the first chapter Allan Sigston looks at a central tenet of the book, that research can (and should) inform practice. He identifies difficulties on the academic and professional sides of the relationship that impede this link. These could be partially overcome by choosing more relevant methodological approaches, the wider adoption of action research and, most importantly, a common objective for researchers and practitioners of developing protocols that describe most effective practice.

   All work in the helping professions requires problem solving. The second chapter, also by Allan Sigston, examines both the need and the means by which professionals can work with clients or other professionals to solve problems. It draws on theory and research from counselling, cognitive and occupational psychology to build a framework for helping groups of people to arrive at solutions that they feel committed to seeing through.

The section on young people

The four chapters (3, 4, 5 and 6) in the section address some of the topical and controversial areas of life experience that provide a context for most children and young adults in modern-day society. For many psychologists, particularly those working within settings such as education, these are topics that are frequently raised as concerns by parents and carers. These issues clearly have a major impact on all aspects of a young person's existence, not the least of which are educational progress and employment prospects. Despite the crucial nature of these issues, however, psychologists and other professionals may feel themselves unprepared to provide soundly based practice, having to resort to little more than general knowledge and 'common-sense' responses.

   Health risks arising from alcohol, drugs and sexual behaviour are considered in Debi Roker's chapter, while Joyce Iszatt and Randa Price focus on the plight of refugees. Neither chapter underestimates the enormity of the issues but both have clear pointers for ways forward and good practice. In his chapter, Alan Labram enters the debate about the influence of the media and whether current concerns are justified. The chapter by Chris Iveson is geared very much to solutions and outlines a therapeutic approach which seems of general applicability in working with young people and which is gaining in reputation. In accordance with the book's aims the authors have attempted not only to highlight these serious issues but to offer an insight into practical means of offering help and support.

The section on families

The five chapters (7, 8, 9, 10 and 11) in the section on families each exemplify a different facet of what has been described by the United Nations as 'the smallest democracy at the heart of society'. Since all of us are affected by existence in, or being deprived of, a family – whether a small, intact unit, or a larger, more sprawling network, 'original' or reconstituted – we all have views about the influence families have upon our lives.

The section as a whole aims to explore perspectives on the family, which illuminate the family in all its complexity. There is often undue focus on the notion of dysfunctional families, wherein families are perceived to be failures and negative influences upon growth and development.

These chapters aim to do the following:

● show how resilient families can be, even where there is stress within and breakdown of the family unit (Andrea Pecherek);
● demonstrate how families can be helped to review and restore themselves (David Jones);
● inform us of the by now well-established (but admittedly not always effective) procedures for identifying and intervening with child abuse (Anna Harskamp);
● provide an overview of contemporary approaches to parent training and support (Sheila Wolfendale);
● describe a range of approaches to and issues within adoption and fostering (Alan and Andrée Rushton).

In this section authors have attempted to bring together and synthesise research and practice and to inform readers of a number of inherent concerns and issues within each sphere. Within the title of the book, the overarching and pervading theme in the section is that of the applications of psychology to the family domain – that is, each author draws together the relevant body of psychological research and thinking (be it in educational or social contexts), and attempts a match with practice. Reciprocally, we can see how practice may be influenced by findings from surveys and theoretical frameworks, which inform current, emerging and future directions of work with families.

The section on schools

The four chapters in the schools section (12, 13, 14 and 15) each address key areas that applied psychologists working in educational contexts with schools and education authorities currently face. All the authors offer practical solutions based on relevant research findings to assist problem resolution in schools.

Irvine Gersch (Chapter 12) reviews the now extensive body of school effectiveness research and the implications for psychological practice giving examples of action research projects psychologists are currently involved with in schools.

Tony Booth (13) redefines the integration or inclusion education debate by examining recent research and practice and the conceptual difficulties with research on the 'inclusion' for young people at school labelled as having special needs.

Chris Best and Charlie Mead (14) show through practical examples how applied psychology can contribute to the support and management of pupils, teachers and schools after traumatic events.

Finally, Michael Hymans, Trevor Bryans and Alison Pinks (Chapter 15) focus on special educational needs and describe how psychology informed an extensive audit undertaken to improve the quality of educational and social experiences of pupils in schools.

The design, writing and editing of this book has offered us many opportunities to reflect on our practice as applied educational psychologists and professional trainers. We hope that it will engage and stimulate you as it has us.

Allan Sigston, Paul Curran, Alan Labram and Sheila Wolfendale
University of East London, January 1996

Contributors

Chris Best

Chris Best has worked as an educational psychologist with Birmingham LEA for the last 12 years. She has worked particularly as part of a team providing crisis response to schools.

Tony Booth

Tony Booth worked as a teacher and an educational psychologist before joining the Open University where he is a senior lecturer in education. He has written and researched widely on special education and integration or 'inclusive education'. He is currently completing research on the inclusion of students with Down's syndrome and an eight country comparative project on inclusion and exclusion.

Trevor Bryans

Trevor Bryans has been a secondary school and remedial teacher and educational psychologist in several LEAs. Until 1994 he was principal educational psychologist in the London Borough of Brent where he is now Director of SEN Policy. He is author and co-author of a number of books, booklets, chapters and articles on aspects of special needs, behaviour management, parental involvement, and equal opportunities.

Paul Curran

Paul Curran is an Associate Tutor to the Doctorate Programme in Educational Psychology at the University of East London's Department of Psychology; and Senior Educational Psychologist responsible for Professional Development in the Essex Service. Paul trained on the 4-year postgraduate professional training course at University College Swansea. He has presented at national conferences most recently on transferable skills for applied psychologists.

Irvine Gersch

Irvine Gersch has worked as a teacher, lecturer and educational psychologist. He is Principal Educational Psychologist for the London Borough of Waltham Forest. He has published widely on school systems, pupil involvement as well as co-editing the book *Meeting Disruptive Behaviour in the Classroom*. He completed a doctoral thesis on school leadership and pupil behaviour. He is currently chair of the British Psychological Society's Training Committee for Educational Psychology.

Anna Harskamp

Anna Harskamp is a Senior Educational Psychologist in the London Borough of Newham. She has developed an interest in child protection issues as part of her clinical work in a local Child and Family Consultation Service, as well as from her school-based work as an educational psychologist. Anna is Chair of the Prevention Sub-Committee of the Newham Area Child Protection Committee and she has developed, along with her colleagues, child protection training materials for a variety of groups.

Michael Hymans

Michael Hymans has been an educational psychologist for the past 11 years and has taught for 9 years. He has worked as a recognised inspector on behalf of the Office for Standards in Education. Michael has written various papers on delinquency, thinking skills, and educational psychologist induction. He has been an Open University Course Tutor and is a regular provider of in-service training for teachers, parents and other professionals.

Joyce Iszatt

Joyce Iszatt is a Senior Educational Psychologist in Enfield Child and Family Service and Associate Tutor on the MSc Educational Psychology Course based at the Tavistock Clinic. Joyce's professional interest is in developing relevant and accessible models of practice to meet the needs of children from all communities. She is currently involved in refugee outreach work at the Tavistock Clinic.

Chris Iveson

Chris Iveson is co-founder of the Brief Therapy Practice, a training and counselling organisation working throughout Britain and Europe. He has been a teacher, social worker and family therapist and now divides his time between doing, teaching and writing about brief therapy.

David Jones

David Jones is a Senior Lecturer in Psychology at Birkbeck College, University of London. He is also a Clinical Psychologist and a Family Therapist and is an Honorary Member of the Institute of Family Therapy. He is a Course Director for the joint Institute of Family Therapy/Birkbeck College MSc in Family Therapy.

Alan Labram

Alan Labram has worked as a secondary school teacher. For the last 9 years he has been a Senior Educational Psychologist with the London Borough of Newham and an Associate Tutor for the (now) Professional Doctorate in Educational Psychology. He has authored and edited a number of articles, chapters and books in the area of educational psychology.

Charlie Mead

Charlie Mead is an educational psychologist with Birmingham Education Department. For the past 10 years he has worked extensively with children experiencing emotional difficulties, both as a headteacher and in his present job. His current work in this field centres on how schools may best respond to the emotional and psychological needs of their pupils. He was a contributor to *Counselling in Schools*, also published by David Fulton.

Andrea Pecherek

Andrea Pecherek works in Sheffield as a Senior Educational Psychologist. Her main professional brief relates to the Children Act which places her in direct contact with the issues and concerns of vulnerable children. She is co-author with Professor Helen Cowie of *Counselling: Approaches and Issues in Education* (published by David Fulton) and has written for the Distance Learning Programme at Sheffield University.

Alison Pinks

Alison Pinks was a teacher in Islington and then trained as an educational psychologist at the Tavistock Clinic. She worked as an educational psychologist in Brent and had responsibility for the audit of special educational needs and for under fives. She is now an educational psychologist in Ealing and is currently involved in a project to raise self-esteem through small group work in primary schools.

Randa Price

Randa Price is a specialist Senior Educational Psychologist in the Enfield Child and Family Service. Randa has studied the responsiveness of existing services to the needs of new communities in Britain from a black professional perspective. Her chapter (written with Joyce Iszatt) was written in acknowledgement of the creative ways communities have developed self-help projects with a strong sense of grass-roots connectedness.

Debi Roker

Dr Debi Roker is the Senior Research Psychologist at the Trust for the Study of Adolescence, an independent applied research organisation based in Brighton. During the past ten years Debi has been involved in research into key areas of young people's lives, including education, training, politics, drugs, sexuality and health.

Alan Rushton

Alan Rushton is Director of the MSc programme in Mental Health Social Work at the Maudsley Hospital and is Senior Lecturer at the Institute of Psychiatry, London. Previously he has been a specialist mental health social worker and lecturer in the UK and Canada. He is involved in a series of prospective studies of disturbed children late placed in permanent new families.

Andrée Rushton

Andrée Rushton is a civil servant writing in a personal capacity. She was formerly a social worker, and a political researcher. She has published articles and research papers and has collaborated in writing textbooks in social work.

Allan Sigston

Allan Sigston has been a primary school teacher and an educational psychologist in several local education authorities. He is Assistant Principal Educational Psychologist in Essex and an Associate Tutor on the Professional Doctorate in Educational Psychology at the University of East London. He is chartered both as an educational and as an occupational psychologist. He has authored and edited a number of articles, chapters and books in the area of educational psychology.

Sheila Wolfendale

Sheila Wolfendale has been a primary school and remedial teacher, an educational psychologist in several local education authorities and is currently Director of the Doctorate in Educational Psychology training programme at the University of East London. She has authored and edited many books, chapters, articles and handbooks on aspects of special needs, early years, and parental involvement. She was awarded a Professorship in 1988 and in 1995 gained a PhD by published works.

PART ONE: Introduction

Chapter One

Research and practice – Worlds apart?

Allan Sigston

This book looks at a number of contemporary issues about young people's growth and development and the family and school systems of which they are a part. It has been the remit of chapter authors to make a connection between research and practice. If psychology is a significant force for good then it should have clear implications for the helping professions. If it does not then we are all in some difficulty, for it will mean that psychology has spiralled off to a region of only academic interest and practising professionals have no basis, beyond intuition and/or their increasingly dated initial training, for their practice. In this chapter I will consider the relationship between research and practice before highlighting some of the reasons why the relationship is not as satisfactory as it might be. Finally I will propose and describe four strategies that may help to bridge the gap.

The relationship between research and practice

I wish to be deliberately polemical in examining the relationship between research and practice. You may feel that some of the points are overstated but progress in this area probably depends on a careful appraisal of our assumptions. I wish to argue that all professional intrusions into other people's lives should have some foundation in research evidence. If they are not then we are at the mercy of our prejudices and fantasies. Questions about, say, whether we should fine or imprison or offer probation to delinquent teenagers are moral but are also practical – what are the different outcomes associated with each of the options? One might offer better rehabilitation in terms of employment and re-offending but another could deter more potential offenders. Research is not a substitute for addressing moral and social questions about the desirability of these options but it must be part of the currency for informed debate.

I would like to take this reasoning a step further and pose the question, 'What right do we have to intervene in the lives of children, families and schools without having good reason to suppose (and demonstrating) that what we are doing is likely to change things for the better?'

Many professionals would retort that each situation encountered is unique and is interpreted through accumulated professional experience. It is a comfortable position because it allows everything to be treated idiosyncratically and differentially. If it is done convincingly complacency need never be stirred. It is this reasoning that led to bleeding and leeches being offered as 'remedies' for centuries. Some may see the argument as a naive, empirical way of viewing complex problems. Certainly I would not wish to underestimate the inherent difficulties of conducting research into social issues but this does not detract from the professional responsibility, even a moral imperative, to base practice on best available knowledge, in so far as it is possible.

Is this a 'straw man' in these modern times? Have not professions all moved in this direction, particularly with the pressures of litigation and quality assurance? I do not believe that this is so, for professionals are more likely to fall foul of litigation if they exceed deadlines or failed to consult with others (maladministration) than because they are not conversant with contemporary research. Let us take an example from education where I think educational psychologists, my own profession and that of all the editors of this book, are particularly vulnerable.

Educational psychologists are centrally involved in the process of assessment of special educational needs. Under the 1993 Education Act educational psychologists in England and Wales must be one of the providers of advice, in the form of a written report, about children who may require special educational provision. While specific laws vary a similar role is undertaken in most of the economically rich countries. It follows that educational psychologists are intimately involved in the placement of young people in special schools.

What evidence is available that educating children in segregated schools is either to their own or to their peers' benefit? You may come to your own conclusions after reading Tony Booth's chapter in this book. Apart from a distinctly sparse literature about the effectiveness of special education (see Slee, 1993) there are a number of researchers who take the view that avoidance of special education enhances success. For example, some have suggested that the long-term effects of pre-school education are at least in part due to avoiding early gateways into special education where children would be the subject of much lower expectations (Lazar *et al.*, 1982; Woodhead, 1988).

The educational psychologists and special educators I know are dedicated people who would be mortified that others might think that they did not have children's best interests at heart, but how can we be reassured that we are not involved in a twentieth-century educational equivalent of blood purging with leeches? The example is dramatic and specific but it is not that difficult to identify key roles in other helping professions that are equally uninformed by research. In two respects the helping professions are victims rather than perpetrators of this problem.

Firstly, the investment of public resources determines the choices available. If a child is encountering difficulties in school there is rarely a finely graded continuum of support to tap into, very often it is stark choice of a minor variation of the present arrangements or a special school. Research evidence falls into insignificance in the face of overriding individual considerations and, to compound things, these decisions serve to confirm and conserve the way resources are organised. Organisations responsible for educational, health and welfare provision tend not to value research by their employees that highlights mismatches between needs and provision. Readers working for education and social services departments are invited to review their job descriptions for indications of responsibilities for research and professional inquiry.

Secondly, there is a malaise in research in applied psychological fields. As has already been mentioned, often research has not been done that could help to support practice in many of the most contentious areas of practice. Where there has been research in related fields it has it has not been effectively disseminated to those that could use it – a problem that we hope that this book goes some small way to redress. In the remainder of this chapter I will consider three reasons for this gulf between research and practice and four strategies that may help to bridge it.

Reasons why research and practice fail to connect

Researchers do not connect theory and practice

There is a common stereotype of researchers as academics in ivory towers who have lost touch with every-day living. Taking a lead from the physical sciences, they see the advancement of knowledge as evaluating theory through hypothesis testing. Finding applications for research findings would be a happy coincidence but these are not required.

If readers were to peruse the major journals on say, cognitive psychology they would find a large number of articles that seem to fit this pattern. Interestingly, the converse criticism has been levelled at much applied research such as the literature on 'school effectiveness' (see Chapter 12). It is argued that it is atheoretical, descriptive or correlational but bereft of assumptions and relationships that offer an understanding of how or why the observable variables interrelate. Hence we know quite a lot about what 'poor' schools are like but we have few ideas about how one goes about changing them (Reynolds, 1994)!

There is a place for both abstracted theoretical inquiry and analysis of applied issues. The problem is that there is very little done to build a bridge between the two through theoreticians *applying* and applied researchers *developing* theory.

Research methods are designed to show statistical rather than practical significance

Barr (1986) reviewed the content of the journal *Reading Research Quarterly*. On the basis of its title one would expect it to be of special interest to teachers. She found that only 25% of articles were concerned with instructing children in reading. Taking a closer look at these she found that 80% followed an experimental design with group comparisons and rigorous control over the conditions to which the groups were exposed. The limited parallels between the contrived conditions and 'real' classrooms meant that any marginal, though statistically significant, differences were difficult to generalise to situations where issues to do with the use of teacher time and manageability are primary considerations.

Researchers are apt to look at what they can measure rather than that which it is important to understand. Undergraduate psychologists yearn and are encouraged by their tutors to seek for statistical significance in their lab reports and the predominant content of psychology journals comprises articles that have yielded such results.

This ethos has been challenged in recent years by 'new paradigm' (Reason and Rowan, 1981) and qualitative research approaches (Bryman, 1988). If we wanted to learn more about the experience of bereavement then we are unlikely to find out much by comparing a bereaved group to a non-bereaved group on a scored test. Qualitative methods build theory *inductively* by an accumulation of coherent evidence rather than *deductively* through the testing of hypotheses. Problems of validity centre on remaining true to the perspective of the participants rather than the careful manipulation of variables.

The point being made here is that there is a range of methodologies available to conduct research and that the types that have been traditionally adopted, and valued, may often be flawed in their ability to generate findings of usefulness to practitioners.

Practitioners filter research evidence to hear what they want to hear

Professions are a social construction. They have at least two purposes: one as a vehicle for the provision of specific services to clients, another is to offer a corporate and exclusive identity for their members – most obviously through their representative bodies. In their second guise professions have their own aspirations, values and ideologies which immunise their members against the intrusion of 'heretical' ideas.

Research done as part of 'Project Follow Through' in the USA showed strong evidence for the effectiveness of Direct Instruction in accelerating the progress of children in basic educational skills (Becker, 1977). Direct Instruction involves scripted group lessons, prompting and orchestrated responses of children. Whether it should be widely adopted or not may be another question but given the numbers of children involved and the size of the effects reported it is surprising that it is virtually unheard of in the UK. I believe that this is because it is so alien to the orthodox view of what a 'good' post-Plowden primary classroom should be like.

Compare this with the high profile of recent debates about 'Real Reading' approaches to the teaching of reading. This eschewed the use of 'contrived' books in reading schemes in favour of real texts deemed to be of intrinsic interest. Many of the ideas underpinning 'Real Reading' have intuitive support from cognitive psychology (Smith, 1988) but there is a paucity of evidence to show the relative effectiveness of this teaching approach, either in terms of attainment or later motivation to read.

Professions selectively attend to research that fits rather than challenges current practice.

Four strategies for bridging the gap between research and practice

In the last section I identified three problem areas for researchers and practitioners to resolve: linking theoretical research to practice, using research methodologies geared to practical implications and the receptiveness of professions to research findings. The four strategies that follow illustrate some important ways in which these can be overcome. The fourth of these, 'Protocols describing effective practice', seems to me to be especially promising as a means of focusing the efforts both of researchers and of practitioners.

Improving the dialogue between practitioners and researchers

A significant way of bridging the gap between theory and practice could be through improving the dialogue between researchers and practitioners. Given an infinite range of study many researchers would welcome enlightenment on those questions of greatest significance to the quality of services for people. Bloom (1980) described a '...new direction in educational research' characterised by a focus on variables that are alterable rather than static. If we wish to study non-school attendance then it will be much more productive to consider school processes, that can be changed, than the socio-economic backgrounds of non-attenders that cannot. Bloom's argument is not limited to educational research alone.

One way academics can stay appraised of practitioners' needs and practitioners can be kept informed of academic developments is through partnership in research enterprises. This can occur at a number of levels such as linking research elements of professional training programmes to commissions from local service providers such as local authorities and voluntary bodies; the purchase of research and consultancy expertise; and jointly sponsored research programmes. All these are recipes for 'Real World Research' (Robson, 1993).

Matching methodologies to research questions

Research questions with implications for helping young people, families and schools need to be carefully constructed if they are to be useful. The philosophical bases of qualitative and quantitative research methodologies provide vexing questions for social scientists (Henwood and Nicolson, 1995) and I cannot do justice here to the tenets and implications of phenomenological versus Cartesian premises for research. Like many others I wish to propose a relatively pragmatic line that takes account of the issues under consideration and the stage in the research process (Hammersley, 1995). If we want to know about the efficacy of an approach to teaching reading or improving attendance then it is difficult to imagine a useful research strategy that did not involve some quantification of results. If we want to understand the feelings and reactions of refugee children then a scored test will give a sterile view of their predicament.

Clarity in defining the research question and choosing a methodology fit for the purpose generates findings of greater utility to practitioners.

Practitioners as researchers: action or problem centred research

One method that moves the research process into the heart of practice is 'Action Research'. It involves the staged planning, implementation and evaluation of a change designed to alleviate a perceived problem. It departs from the traditional method of having a detached and objective researcher by integrating the roles of researcher and practitioner. Table 1.1 gives a framework for conducting action research, though stages tend to be less easily distinguishable than might be assumed from the table. Action research is a form of problem solving and is usually undertaken by groups of colleagues (Chapter 2 of this book discusses the contribution of psychology to group problem solving in more detail). Action research has a number of advantages. It addresses issues and concerns of the moment. It can demonstrate whether specific methods are applicable and effective within an actual context (rather than relying on generalising from others). It is a good method for involving and giving people ownership of changes in their organisations. It embodies the notion of the reflective practitioner (Schon, 1983).

Action research has some disadvantages. In a complicated cocktail of factors it may be difficult to tell which are the potent ones responsible for the success or failure of an initiative. There can be problems of replicability; while the main features of a strategy can be reproduced, the way they interact with other aspects of the host organisation may not be. None the less through an accumulation of such projects key aspects tend to become apparent. Good examples of this literature are the many small-scale studies of parental involvement in reading, described in Wolfendale and Topping (1995). (A recommended further reading on action research is Chapter 7 of Banister *et al.*, 1994.)

Table 1.1 An example of an action research framework

	Stages	Steps
Clarification	1. Describe the current situation	Collect data on the current level of the problem. How would you know if it had improved?
	2. Analyse the problem	What factors contribute to the problem? What factors might ameliorate the problem? What is alterable?
Intervention	3. Agree a general plan	Formulate a strategy.
	4. Agree an action plan	Who? Does what? When?
	5. Monitoring	Is it happening? Does it need amending?
Evaluation	6. Review	What is the level of the problem now? Did the action plan make any difference? What has been learned?

Protocols describing effective practice

This is the most challenging of the strategies I wish to propose and it is one that, because of its roots in the economics of health care, many professionals working in different disciplines may recoil from. If someone had 'gallstones' you might expect them to have an operation and some hospital care but you would not expect them to have psychotherapy. This judgement is based upon some reasoned expectation about the nature and duration of treatments required for different ailments. For the purposes of evaluating claims and costs of medical treatments these expectations are made explicit in the form of protocols. Once a protocol is defined it is possible to amass data about the comparative outcomes of treatment using different treatment protocols, for example the use of ultrasound rather than surgery for the removal of gallstones. The protocol, in effect, defines current effective practice and facilitates further research of alternatives.

Protocols in the helping professions are unlikely to be as clear and prescriptive as those for medicine; there are too many additional and 'uncontrollable' variables, but in many cases research can give us some broad parameters to frame intervention. A speculative protocol for teaching children with reading difficulties shown in Table 1.2 aims to be broad enough to allow professional judgement but clear enough to embody sound research findings.

Wolkind has highlighted the advantages of protocols in child psychiatry in describing a study on mental health services for children and young people which he conducted on behalf of the Department of Health. Its remit included, 'Descriptions of services and trials of treatments will be critically evaluated in order to clarify what has been demonstrated to be effective for different types of problems' (Wolkind, 1994).

Table 1.2 A protocol for children with reading difficulties?

The following is a brief overview of evidence for use in the design of programmes of support for primary aged children with reading difficulties. The comments made are professional opinion based upon a review of published research.

Context for learning

'High' expectations:

The setting of challenging but achievable goals for children is a consistent finding in effective teaching and effective schooling research.

Positive feedback:

A high ratio of success to correction, sometimes estimated as 3:1.

Short frequent teaching sessions:

There is a long-standing finding that frequency of rehearsal is more important than the absolute amount of time. Teaching of new skills should involve teaching/practice taking place 3 to 5 times per week.

Components of an intervention

Shared reading:

There is overwhelming evidence that reading with a sympathetic adult on a regular basis assists children with reading difficulties.

The main characteristics of this are:

sessions of about 15 minutes; as near to daily sessions as possible; ideally reading to the child's parent, but if not a familiar and sympathetic adult; sessions geared to fluent reading, perhaps through special techniques such as synchronous paired reading (which seeks to minimise errors) or speedy problem solving on unknown words (e.g. 'Pause, Prompt, Praise'); encouraging 'sensible' guessing at unfamiliar words; a general emphasis on praise and encouragement.

There is some evidence that similar benefits may occur where the child is matched with another child for reading under the same type of conditions.

Systematic and regular instruction on sound–letter(s) correspondence:

Regular and systematic instruction on sound–letter correspondence is a feature of a number of effective interventions.

The main characteristics of this are:

gearing instruction to the production of the sound on presentation of a word or letter(s) (rather than, for instance, asking the child to match a written letter to a picture); working towards small targets for the student; ensuring a relatively high level of skill on a step before moving on to new work; practice at using the skill in actual reading of texts.

Variety in literacy skills and context in teaching sessions:

An emphasis on variety of use of literacy skills and applications within sessions.

The main characteristics of this are:

the child undertaking some writing and reading of their own work; discussing alternative methods for reading and spelling unfamiliar words; reading familiar books; discussing both the stories and the conventions of texts and books; work on sound–letter(s) correspondence.

Multi-sensory learning experiences:

There is some evidence that children's memory for visual and sound aspects of letters may be enhanced where the child can learn an additional association with touch or kinaesthetic feedback. It may be that linkages between reading, writing, spelling and sounds within sessions (see above) provide equivalent experiences.

Could (*or should?*) there be protocols for the adoption of children, helping children who have been the victims of sexual abuse or for any field where there are significant numbers of clients with similar types of experiences and problems? Protocols seem to have enormous potential not only for guiding professionals in their day-to-day work but also in focusing debate on the practical interpretation and future foci of research.

Some concluding comments

The chapter began by stressing the need for soundly based practice in the helping professions if these are to justify the influence they have over people's lives. A number of reasons for an apparent dysjunction between research and practice have been discussed. Four strategies for establishing more satisfactory links have been described: the improvement of dialogue between researchers and practitioners, making better matches between research questions and methodologies, and the use of action research methods by practitioners. In my view the development of protocols that describe effective practice for different client difficulties has the *most* potential for securing effective practice for young people, families and schools, and for stimulating and focusing research efforts that can develop future practice.

References

Banister, P., Burman, E., Taylor, M. and Tindall, C. (1994) *Qualitative Methods in Psychology, A Research Guide*. Buckingham: Open University Press

Barr, R. (1986) 'Studying classroom reading instruction', *Reading Research Quarterly*, **21(3)**, 231–36.

Becker, W. (1977) 'Teaching reading and language to the disadvantaged – What have we learned from field research?' *Harvard Educational Review*, **47**, 518–45.

Bloom, B. (1980) *Better Learning In The Schools: A Primer for Parents, Teachers and Other Educators*. New York: McGraw-Hill.

Bryman, A. (1988) *Quantity and Quality in Social Research*. London: Unwin Hyman.

Hammersley, M. (1995) 'Opening up the quantitative–qualitative divide', *Education Section Review (British Psychological Society)*, **19(1)**, 2–9.

Henwood, K. and Nicolson, P. (1995) 'Qualitative research', *The Psychologist*, **March**, 109–110.

Lazar, I., Darlington, R.B., Murray, H.W. and Snipper, A.S. (1982) *Lasting Effects of Early Education: A Report from the consortium for longitudinal studies. Monograph for Research in Child Development*, **47**, (195, serial number 2–3).

Reason, P. and Rowan, J. (eds) (1981) *Human Inquiry: A Sourcebook of New Paradigm Research*. London: Wiley.

Reynolds, D. (1994) *Key note address to the annual course of the Association of Educational Psychologists*, Liverpool (UK), October.

Robson, C. (1993) *Real World Research: A Resource for Social Scientists and Practitioner-Researchers*, Oxford: Blackwell.

Schon, D. (1983) *The Reflective Practitioner*. New York: Basic Books.

Slee, R. (ed.) (1993) *Is There a Desk with my Name on it? The Politics of Integration*. Lewes: The Falmer Press.

Smith, F. (1988) *Understanding Reading: A Psycholinguistic Analysis of Reading and Learning to Read*, (4th edn.), Hillsdale, N.J.: Erlbaum.

Wolfendale, S. and Topping, K. (1995) (eds) *Family Involvement in Literacy: Effective Partnerships in Education*, London: Cassell.

Wolkind, S. (1994) 'Mental health services for children and young people: a national review', *Educational and Child Psychology*, **11(3)**, 84.

Woodhead, M. (1988) 'When psychology informs public policy: the case of early childhood intervention', *American Psychologist*, **43(6)**, 443–54.

Chapter Two

Using psychology to bring people together to solve problems

Allan Sigston

People have immense potential to solve their own problems and do so every day of their lives, yet there are times when all of us find ourselves stuck and seek the advice of family, friends or colleagues. Sometimes it is necessary to contact someone with expert knowledge to make progress: it would be foolhardy not to consult a doctor if you had chest pains but, more often than not, the nature of problems fall within the expertise of the people who are experiencing them. This is equally true in professional contexts: teachers who want to improve the reading progress of a particular child, parents worried about their children's friendships, care workers dealing with the conflictual behaviour of one of their charges and so on. Their difficulty is not that they do not have the skills and opportunities to resolve or mitigate the problems they face but that they have become stuck on their journey towards a solution. For the most part, therefore, problem solving is not about telling people how they should behave but rather how they can identify and apply their own knowledge and expertise.

This chapter examines some of the reasons people become stuck in problem solving and what psychology can offer us to help galvanise and motivate people toward implementing solutions for themselves.

Three reasons why people find it difficult to solve problems

Alan and Andrée Rushton (Chapter 11) discuss the importance of supporting fostering and adopting parents in their chapter. Picture a scenario where a 4-year-old newly-fostered child has been unsettled in her new home for several weeks. The foster mother's main worry is the child's reluctance to eat. The foster father is most concerned about the child's destructiveness toward toys and other household items. The supporting social worker is anxious about the foster parents' feelings of competence in dealing with a problematical child that might lead to a breakdown in the placement. Clearly, each has a different idea of what success would look like:

● for the foster mother success might be the child eating the meals she has cooked;
● for the foster father success might be the child playing constructively with toys;
● for the social worker success might be statements about confidence and coping made by the foster parents.

The example typifies the beginning of most problem-solving situations. The goals of any interventions are unclear and unshared and, as a consequence, so are the tasks that would need to be undertaken to achieve them.

Most of us have had friends turn to us for advice about everyday quandaries, such as changing their job or whether to move house or difficult relationships, where the solution seems to us to be extremely straightforward. We tend to see people who cannot take our advice as irrational. However, if we take a cool look at human behaviour in general, how rational is it? How many of us take enough exercise or desist from health threatening behaviours like smoking and drinking alcohol?

George Kelly (1955) proposed that everybody is a behavioural scientist trying to make sense of what is happening around them. Through developing a set of important beliefs, known as personal constructs, we are able to make sense of others' behaviour and guide our own. The argument is that we always act rationally but that our actions differ because our behaviour is based on different assumptions. If a parent's theory is that children behave well because of fear of punishment then he or she will use threats to obtain the children's compliance. Another parent's theory may be that children are inherently moral and therefore they would tend to use ethical reasoning to prevail upon his or her child. If you were to give advice to either of these parents that was disconsonant with their theories of child behaviour they would find it very difficult to act upon it.

An example of the complex way in which beliefs dictate our behaviour is the difficulty in persuading people to use condoms to prevent the spread of HIV. Despite the simplicity of avoiding risk, research suggests that intentions tend not to translate into action in high-risk circumstances. An influential factor is the meanings and interpretations that surround condom use. Using condoms, or asking sexual partners to use condoms, can be interpreted as meaning that you believe they are promiscuous or unfaithful. If this is the case then either the use of a condom or the insistence on use of a condom, may be seen as an implicit insult to the partner. The 'high-risk' behaviour has a rationality which is not apparent until you have appreciated the participants' perspectives.

When we bring people together to solve problems we can assume that they have differing personal theories to account for the malaise in which they find themselves and blinker them to ways in which they may be able to make progress.

A third impediment to problem solving is to do with the social support we receive to help us maintain our efforts in changing our behaviour.

Our daily meals result from a complex web of interactions that span shops, work routines, compromises between people's preferences and more. People who try to change their diet unilaterally tend to find this very difficult because the systems we are part of are very good at maintaining our previous behaviour.*

To illustrate the way social systems counter planned changes in our behaviour consider the example of an aspiring vegetarian teenage boy. His family erode the son's resolve at a number of conscious and unconscious levels. Firstly, there is an absence of support for the new behaviour through praise, encouragement or recognition of effort devoted to keeping to this new self-imposed discipline – as opposed to approbation for training hard for sports or doing homework well. Secondly, there is undermining through insinuations that this is a fashion, fad or a passing phase. Thirdly, at a more practical level, unappealing food is purchased on weekly shopping expeditions so that the son is faced with a contrast of hastily prepared, unappetising dishes presented alongside cherished old favourites.

The example illustrates the difficulty of modifying behaviour in ways that might solve a problem without having the social and practical support of the people around us.

The dimensions of Group Problem Solving

The preceding analysis suggests that helping people to work on a problem may require work on three fronts: clarifying goals and tasks, shifting thoughts and beliefs associated with the presenting problems and ensuring social support for the people who will need to act differently. Group problem solving is a promising way of meeting these needs.

The framework that follows has relevance for clinical work with groups of clients such as traumatised refugee children (see Chapter 5 by Randa Price and Joyce Iszatt), victims of sexual abuse (see Chapter 9 by Anna Harskamp) and fostering or adopting parents (see Chapter 11), as well as to professional work groups such as described by Michael Hymans and Trevor Bryans in Chapter 15.

---

*The ability of systems to control and maintain individual's behaviour has been of interest to many psychologists (e.g. reciprocal determinism; Bandura, 1986) and 'systems' approaches to understanding how families operate are discussed in more detail in Chapter 7.

A way of conceiving of group problem solving is to think of it operating along three distinct dimensions:

1. *A task dimension* – where the group stands in relation to planning goals and action to achieve them.

2. *A group dimension* – how the group as an entity is operating.

3. *A cognitive dimension* – individuals' beliefs and thoughts about the problems and solutions.

Imagine being an observer of a meeting of a problem solving group and calling a 'time out' – as happens in a basketball game. It would be possible to take stock of the progress of the group along each of these dimensions. If it is a successful problem solving group it will be proceeding simultaneously along all three. If the group has rushed ahead on the task aspect it may have some elaborate plans articulated but individuals will be confused about the underlying reasoning, and the group will be fragmented with members feeling unsupported or disengaged. Where a group has moved mainly along the group dimension communication may be easy but agreement about action that will follow the meeting will not be evident. Groups that have not taken account of the cognitive dimension will find that there are members who are unconvinced that an agreed strategy will work.

There are interactions between the different dimensions which are hinted at above. Most of us have had the experience of being hurried through an agenda (the task dimension) and being forced into making premature decisions and feeling alienated from other members of the group and uncommitted to the agreement. The prize is to be won where the group manages and co-ordinates its progress along all three dimensions creating a 'golden triangle' for problem solving that is depicted in Figure 2.1.

Figure 2.1 The relationship between group, cognitive and task dimensions of the problem-solving group

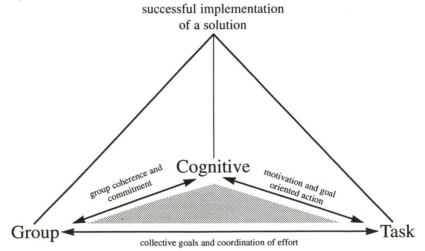

Many groups we will have come across muddle their way through tolerably well. A group whose members have enjoyed prior positive relationships, are like minded in their approach and are addressing an unthreatening problem, need only concern itself with the task itself. Unfortunately this is rarely the case when trying to resolve problems for young people or families. The process has become stuck for the reasons described earlier and the chances are more remote that they will negotiate their way to a solution without some more active guidance through the process.

It is worth considering the most appropriate membership of problem solving groups. Three criteria are applicable and I suggest that at least two should apply to each group member with all three represented across the group as a whole:

1. The person is concerned about the problem (otherwise they may not be motivated to do something to change it).
2. The person has direct experience of dealing with the problem (as they have information that would help to clarify it).
3. The person is likely to have opportunities to influence variables that affect the problem (otherwise action is likely to be thwarted).

Where the problems centre on the needs of young people I have argued that such groups have in-built safeguards for children in ensuring that there is 'triangulation' on the child's needs from different viewpoints (Sigston, 1992). They also provide a practical vehicle for the inclusion of young people themselves, which is an increasing legal obligation under the Children Act 1989 (in the UK) and the United Nations Convention on the Rights of the Child, as well as a moral and practical imperative.

Consultancy and problem solving

It was proposed earlier that the skills people need to solve most problems successfully are probably already within the repertoire of the members of a problem solving group. Mobilising them depends upon identifying them as relevant, linking them to specific goals and supporting the group members in their subsequent use. This work is done in meetings in which the group makes its transition from problem to potential solution.

This section will consider how a helping professional might aid such a group. The term consultant is used for this role because it conveys the idea of the group using a relative outsider (in respect of the presenting problem) to find a way forward. It is not a role confined to psychologists though, hopefully, it is informed by psychology.

In considering the role of the consultant I shall first consider the pervasive question of the nature of the relationship between the consultant and the group before looking more specifically at the way the consultant attempts to manage the task, group and cognitive dimensions of problem solving.

The relationship between the consultant and the problem solving group

Research on therapies and consultancy has consistently shown that the quality of the relationship between helper and helped is critical. Truax and Carkhuff's (1967) seminal review of counselling and psychotherapy came to the view that it was not so much the type of therapeutic approach that counsellors adopted but the personal qualities that they brought to the relationship with the client that accounted for success. They highlighted three characteristics of more effective counsellors that are summarised below:

- *Genuineness* – Being open, spontaneous and honest.
- *Non-possessive warmth* – A positive caring attitude to the client apparent through friendliness, encouragement and a non-critical manner.
- *Accurate empathy* – Being able to convey to the client a sense that his or her feelings and predicaments are understood.

For these qualities to aid the relationship they must be detected by the others involved. They are not transferred mysteriously through the ether but rely on the observation and interpretation of the consultant's behaviour. Mehrabian (1971) conducted a number of studies into the way people judged whether they were liked or not. He and his co-workers found that the facial expression of the speaker was relied on the most followed by voice cues (e.g. stress and inflexion). The choice of words used contributed only 7% toward the feeling of being liked or disliked by the listener. Perhaps this is not so surprising, if we think of the difference in impact between sophisticated and naive actors reading lines from the same play. It is apparent that non-verbal aspects of the consultant's behaviour are vital in conveying the qualities above and thereby developing the high quality of relationship conducive to effective problem solving.

Egan (1990) describes a number of skills and behaviours for the 'skilled helper' which are a useful practical guide for the problem-solving consultant. He uses the acronym S-O-L-E-R to describe a set of behaviours congruent with the characteristics described within a North American culture, which is probably quite similar to Western European culture and derivative societies. These are briefly described below:

- **S** – sitting **squarely**, turning the body toward the person when communicating to signal a personal involvement with the client.
- **O** – adopting an **open** posture with arms and legs relaxed and uncrossed to signal openness and accessibility to the client.
- **L** – refers to **leaning** forward to signal interest and involvement
- **E** – maintaining good (i.e. lengthy) **eye** contact showing attention and listening
- **R** – being **relaxed** and showing comfort with the message that the client is passing to the therapist.

The acronym is a very useful guide for the consultant with the caveat that these aspects of behaviour may be interpreted differently within other cultures. Those working with people from other cultures would be wise to be especially attentive to the reactions of their consultees.

It is relatively easy to see the ways in which the S-O-L-E-R behaviours contribute to the qualities of genuineness, warmth and empathy, but it is impossible to envisage a situation in which these qualities were attributed unless the consultee believed that consultant had listened carefully to what he or she had been told. The S-O-L-E-R behaviours would be strong signs to most of us that a person was attending to our words. Good, or active, listening must also focus on content which leads us to one of the most important skills for the consultant.

Paraphrasing is a means by which a therapist or consultant can demonstrate his or her understanding of the consultee's feelings, descriptions, proposals and reactions. It is an especially powerful tool in problem-solving groups because it serves a variety of purposes:

- it serves to cement the relationship between the individual group member and the consultant, in the ways described above;
- the re-wording of a message in a paraphrase is part of a process of reviewing and reformulating ideas that is vital if change is to take place;
- it helps the consultant to empower reluctant or intimidated participants through sharing the burden of communication;
- the re-presentation of contributions doubles the opportunities to appreciate and clarify the differing perspectives of group members.

As will become apparent later a paraphrase is an essential component part of a number of the other techniques a consultant might use with a problem-solving group.

It is difficult to use paraphrasing well if you do not have feelings of empathy for the people you are working with at the time. It is a skill that requires a lot of practice for it is not a part of most people's natural conversational style. To exemplify the use of the paraphrase a sample of dialogue is shown in Table 2.1. The mother of 8-year-old Ben thinks of him as boisterous but manageable at home. She has been asked to attend a meeting in school with the class teacher, headteacher and an educational psychologist about repeated misdemeanours in his classroom. Teachers in school have tended toward the view that Ben's mother is unsupportive in matters of school discipline. In this instance the paraphrases (shown in italics) indicate to the parent that her contribution is valued, past parental behaviour that was seen as unsupportive is open to a more constructive interpretation by the headteacher and class teacher, and a possible area of collaboration (the giving of school-related praise at home) has been identified.

Table 2.1 An example of the use of paraphrasing

Ben's mother: When I spoke to his teacher I was asked to punish him at home if he had had a bad day. But it seemed so unfair to be telling him off when he had not done anything to upset me.
Educational psychologist: *You are obviously uncomfortable in situations where you have to give out the consequences for someone else.* Would you feel the same way about praising and giving rewards for good behaviour in school?
Ben's mother: No, that's different it wouldn't spoil the time we have together.... I don't want to have to moan at him all the time.
Educational psychologist: *It sounds as if you are worried that your good relationship with Ben will be spoiled if you tell him off for things you have not seen him do, but that sharing good news about school might help it.*
Ben's mother: Yes I'd like to tell him he'd done well.

Managing the task, group and cognitive dimensions

It was argued earlier that the problem-solving group can be thought about along three dimensions, but a problem-solving group is of little use if it does not arrive at solutions. Facilitating the group and cognitive processes is only useful in so far as it makes for improved decisions and plans.

This section describes the stages we would expect a problem-solving group and its individual members move through highlighting some of the psychological insights, approaches and techniques that are useful.

The task dimension

There are three steps that the group must accomplish before they can implement a planned solution. They can be summarised in three questions to which the group must supply answers, though usually they will be embedded within a longer agenda tailored to the meeting and concerns of the group members.

In the first step the group must respond to the question 'Where do we want to get to?' which concludes with one or more collective goals that describe how things would be if the problem was solved. In reaching this watershed the group will have gone through some of the most important stages in group development that are discussed in more detail in the next section.

The question guiding the second step is 'How do we get there?' The group must construct a co-ordinated plan of action geared to the goals it has identified.

Belbin (1993) has described eight key roles with associated functions for effective work teams. It is unlikely that there will be eight members of a problem-solving group of the type discussed in this chapter. After taking account of the consultant's contribution these eight roles can be distilled into four key functions:

1. *Generating and exploring creative possibilities* – via brainstorming, helping people to generalise from previous experience etc. There are a number of

novel techniques for use at this stage (Hutchings, 1985; Lovejoy, 1988; Nolan, 1987).

2. *Shaping them into realistic options* – making the abstract concrete, e.g. 'What would this actually involve?'

3. *Evaluating options* – teasing out the implications, e.g. 'Is it possible to...'.

4. *Attending to necessary practical detail* – documenting the agreed plan, agreeing responsibilities, checking for hitches, e.g. 'What would happen if...'.

The third question the group must answer is 'How do we know that we are succeeding?' Over what period and how frequently should goals be achieved for the group to feel assured that progress has been made? Would there be other problems that warranted the attention of the group at a later date? The group's agreed goals are the basis for a review but a time is needed when the group can share perceptions of progress. The combination of clarity over agreed group members' contributions with the setting of a review date is a powerful means of, voluntarily, putting group pressure on individuals to conform to their part of an action plan (Asch, 1956).

A number of skills and techniques are helpful in mediating the group through the Task dimension. I want to draw special attention to agenda management, consensus testing and goal setting.

A natural and frequent response to joining a new group is uncertainty about the purposes of and contributions to the group (this is discussed again later). The negotiation and agreement of an agenda not only maps out the tasks of the group but also allays some of these personal concerns. There is a tendency amongst many helping professionals not to use agendas in an attempt to make meetings as informal as possible, but having no agenda makes it exceedingly difficult to keep track of where the group has reached. Most modern counselling approaches are based on helping clients to problem solve to which an agenda is implicit (e.g. Beck, 1985; Egan, 1990).

Consensus testing is a vital part of agenda management; it is the means by which agreements and decisions are reached. It involves closing part of the discussion with a summary and seeking endorsement of it as collective view. It is a skill, somewhat akin to paraphrasing, that needs practice both in succinctly capturing the key issues or decisions but also in reading the verbal and non-verbal responses of group members, for if the group is not prepared to go with the summary then later dialogue will be flawed.

The need for clear goals for the practical purposes of designing action plans and evaluating success has been emphasised already. Mager (1975) argues that useful objectives are couched in simple language that describe what you would see or hear if the objective was achieved. For example 'John will sit at his seat for 5 minutes during story time' would be preferred to 'John will to learn behave nicely at school.'

Tubbs (1986) reviewed a large number of studies carried out with work teams and groups in laboratory studies that showed clearly that the setting of clear and achievable goals also led to improved performance. This is also a tenet of solution focused therapy (see Chapter 3). West (1994) found goal clarity predicted the innovativeness of work teams. Goal setting has creative, practical and motivational benefits.

One of the difficulties people have in focusing on a goal is in unlocking themselves from the present problematical scenario, a key is to give them a fresh perspective. Fantasy techniques invoking miracles, fairy godmothers, visitors from outer space and so forth are often a useful tool for this purpose.

The group dimension

The group dimension concerns the way the group gels into a social unit that aids or impedes the tasks it has to perform. There have been many studies of group and team working in occupational settings. Of particular interest has been the observation that it is difficult to predict the effectiveness of a group from previous knowledge of the individual members. Belbin (1981, 1993) conducted a study where a high-ability group of managers, called the 'Apollo team', were pitched against a number of other teams composed of 'less able' individuals: the Apollo team came last! Some readers may remember the 'Supergroup' era in late 1970s rock music when famed musicians left the bands in which they had established their reputations to join 'all star' line-ups that never met the expectations of their fans.

Working groups lead a dual life. On the one hand they exist to carry out certain tasks while on the other they are a social unit comprising the complex interplay between group members. These two aspects interact: a friendly and supportive group is likely to arrive at consensus decisions more easily than an argumentative one and a group that experiences success and prestige through its work will probably develop stronger and deeper relationships between its members. Group cohesion and task performance reciprocally benefit each other (Mullen and Copper, 1994).

Evidence suggests that groups find it difficult to settle to their tasks without first dealing with some social and interpersonal issues. Gersick (1988) studied eight project groups and found that they tended to spend about half their time in 'inertia' before making rapid progress. Sundstrom *et al.* (1990) noted that American Navy gunnery teams tended to go through a 'teamwork' phase in which they learned inter-group co-ordination before what they termed 'taskwork' could begin.

What is it that is happening in groups during this 'teamwork' phase? Tuckman (1965) has described four stages of team development that seem to have stood the test of time (Margerison and McCann, 1991). It applies to work teams and contrived groups used in laboratory experiments (Moreland and Levine, 1988). Tuckman's model is outlined below.

During the 'forming' stage members have differing individual views about the tasks to be undertaken and attempt to establish appropriate ways of behaving in the group. They will look around the group for leadership and guidance from an authoritative figure.

The 'storming' stage emerges as the differences in individual needs and understanding of the task become apparent. Group members' views become polarised by the stress placed on their own views and there is resistance to control. Part of the difficulty the group will have at this stage will surround differing interpretation of the language used in the discussion.

Within the 'norming' stage co-operation and group cohesion grows. There is a shared understanding about rules of conduct, communication and decision making which are adopted by the group. The emphasis is on the avoidance of conflict. Cohesion will become apparent through verbal and non-verbal behaviour. A common vocabulary will emerge for the issues under discussion.

In the 'performing' stage goals and action begin to emerge. Interpersonal relationships serve to channel effort into the group's work tasks. Members of the group assume co-ordinated roles toward achieving the group's objectives.

Schein (1988) suggests that upon entering a new group there are understandable anxieties about identity, control and influence, compatibility of needs and goals, and acceptance and intimacy. During the 'storming' phase we can anticipate that some of the group will feel confused and perhaps frustrated because they are unclear about the rules of conduct and the vocabulary used to describe the problems being addressed. Individuals will move at their own pace through this stage but it is vital that the consultant is alert to signs of group member's discomfort, or more likely their wariness, shown through their non-verbal behaviour. Once observed the consultant should acknowledge the discomfort and attempt to clarify and resolve its cause.

There are overlaps between stages, in particular norming and forming will begin at the issuing of invitations for the first meeting, and be influenced by welcomes and introductions and the physical layout of the meeting room.

Readers are asked to put themselves in the position of a parent summoned to school by a formal letter from the headteacher, who on arrival is allocated a low chair on the opposite side of the headteacher's desk. You notice that the other attenders (some of whom are strangers) appear to be finishing off cups of coffee. It would be an unusual parent who did not surmise that they were being regarded as of lower status and that their contribution will probably not be highly valued. If the other participants felt no twinges of discomfort they would have begun to accept a set of norms governing communication and decision making. Any suspicions that this is a less than ideal beginning will be reinforced by Michael Argyle's (1969) observations:

> Members will be drawn towards the group if they are valued, popular and prestigeful in the group – those who are lowest in these respects are the most likely to leave it. Certain kinds of group behaviour are more satisfying and produce cohesion – democratic leadership, and co-operation rather than competition.

Leadership, in the sense to which it is referred to here, will fall to the consultant; his or her influence in both managing the agenda and as a model for other people's behaviour is of profound importance.

In summarising this section we can draw a number of inferences. Firstly, that any group is going to need some time to come together before it can very productively focus on its task, perhaps as much as half the available time will be taken to get to the 'performing' stage. Consultants should beware of pressing ahead too fast with the agenda (be it one meeting or a series of them). Secondly, democratic norms and leadership are likely to be most helpful in group development, these are signalled even before the first meeting takes place and will be influenced by the behaviour of the consultant (e.g. via S-O-L-E-R behaviours and the use of paraphrasing). Thirdly, that the group will find it difficult to commit itself to shared goals until there are signs of cohesiveness in the group and the emergence of a shared vocabulary that indicate that the group is entering the 'performing' stage.

The cognitive dimension

It was proposed early in this chapter that each of us has a set of assumptions and theories about why people behave in the ways that they do and we use these to guide our actions. If we conceive of problems in certain ways then we can make it harder to find a way forward. For example, if we take the view that Bernice is not learning to read because she is not very bright then we have set ourselves the difficult task of making Bernice 'brighter'. However, if we believe that Bernice is not learning because she does not get enough practice then some practical possibilities spring to mind. Whether these will have the desired effect is another question, but at least some routes into the problem have been found.

An area of psychology known as attribution theory can help us classify different types of beliefs group members may have about the difficulties being encountered and offer clues about how they can be adapted. Heider (1958) proposed that people infer a cause of behaviour (or attribution) as either to do with the characteristics of the person or the situation in which the behaviour occurs. Broadly speaking, these causes can be classified as relatively constant (stable) or changeable (unstable). This is summarised and exemplified in Table 2.2.

For our purposes external and unstable attributions are likely to be the most promising source of solutions for these assume both the capacity for change and situational causes that are likely to be within the control of the group members. Unfortunately Heider noted that people seem to have a preference for internal and stable causes of behaviour, the least helpful starting point for problem solving. He called this the 'fundamental attributional error', therefore the consultant can assume that some, possibly all, the members of that group start from such beliefs.

Kelley (1973) developed a model he called 'the co-variation principle' to explain the way people attribute behaviour to internal or external causes. He suggested that three criteria are used: consistency, distinctiveness and consensus. If a

Table2.2 Beliefs about the causes of people's behaviour illustrated by a child having difficulties in learning to read (After Heider, 1958.)

	Internal causes	External causes
Stable causes	Relatively unchangeable traits or qualities of the person (least helpful for problem-solving) *'Bernice is a slow learning child.'*	Relatively unchangeable aspects of the situation e.g, poverty, family background *'Bernice's family do not value books and reading.'*
Unstable causes	Relatively changeable or fluctuating characteristics of the person e.g. moods, tiredness, ideas *'Bernice sees school as a place to play rather than to learn.'*	Relatively changeable or fluctuating aspects of the situation e.g. opportunity, practice (most helpful for problem solving) *'Bernice does not get enough practice at reading.'*

person's behaviour is consistent across situations, not distinctively related to a particular situation and few people would react to this situation in this way (the consensus criterion) then the behaviour is more likely to be seen as internally caused. The converse set of judgements would lead the person toward an attribution of external causes.

The co-variation principle can be used by the consultant to a problem solving group, to challenge and modify attributions. In the example of Bernice, drawing the following points out in discussion would help to move toward external attributions:

- that Bernice's competence with reading depends on the type of reading material she is given (the consistency criterion);
- that Bernice's has talents in other areas (the distinctiveness criterion);
- that other children are also having difficulty with similar aspects of reading (the consensus criterion).

An advantage of group problem solving is that individuals are almost certain to be exposed to alternative attributional beliefs. There are a range of other techniques developed in counselling and family therapy such as reframing, externalisation (see Chapter 7) and using analogies/metaphors that have the same aim of shifting attributional beliefs.

An overview of the consultant's role in helping problem solving groups

The three dimensions of group problem solving are very interrelated. Change in one affects the others, all three develop over time. Table 2.3 cross-relates stages across the three dimensions.

Table 2.3 Summary of stages in group problem solving along the task, group and cognitive dimensions

Task dimension	Group dimension			Cognitive dimension
	Group stages	*Group issues*	*Emotional reactions*	
Where do we want to get to? (sharing perspectives and goal setting)	Forming	Cohesion and membership	Anxiety and uncertainty Confusion and frustration	Internal and stable attributional beliefs
	Storming			
	Norming	Rules of conduct Communication and decision making Co-operation		
			Confidence	
How do we get there? Who will do what? (action planning)	Performing	Roles	Commitment	External and unstable attributional beliefs
How do we know if it worked? (means of reviewing)		Internal and external accountability		

An effective consultant is someone who is sensitive to signals that progress along the three dimensions and have become out of step and intervenes accordingly. It is a complex role, rather like the juggler who must distribute his or her attention between three spinning plates to keep them all aloft.

It is probably a craft rather than a science and like most crafts is best learned by being able to watch others and reflecting on your work, as in family therapy where it is common to use co-consultants and video recordings to provide feedback.

Some conclusions

This chapter began by reviewing three crucial reasons why people get stuck in solving problems: lack of clarity about their goals, thoughts and beliefs that limit the perceived scope for action and lack of social and practical support to maintain changes in their behaviour.

Problem-solving groups have the potential for bringing people together in ways that can counter these difficulties, but to do so they need skilful assistance. In describing the role of a consultant to a problem-solving group, attention has been focused on the qualities of genuineness, non-possessive warmth and accurate empathy, drawn from counselling psychology.

I have proposed that the progress of groups can be plotted along three dimensions related to the task itself, stages of group development and participants' cognitions and that these need to be kept in tune with one another if the benefits of group problem solving are to be reaped. A selected set of skills and techniques consultants could use have been reviewed.

References

Argyle, M. (1969) *Social Interaction*. London: Methuen.

Asch, S. (1956) 'Studies in independence and submission to group pressure: A minority of one against a unanimous majority', *Psychological Monographs*, **70(9)**.

Bandura, A. (1986) *Social Foundations of Thought and Action: A Social Cognitive Theory*. Englewood Cliffs, NJ: Prentice-Hall.

Beck, A. (1985) 'Cognitive therapy'. In Kaplan, H.I. and Sandock, J. (eds) *Comprehensive Textbook of Psychiatry* (4th edn.) Baltimore: Williams and Wilkins.

Belbin, R.M. (1981) *Management Teams*. London: Heinemann Educational Books.

Belbin, R.M. (1993) *Team Roles at Work*. Oxford: Butterworth-Heinemann.

Egan, G. (1990) *The Skilled Helper* (4th edn.) Monterey, CA: Brooks-Cole.

Gersick, C. J. G. (1988) 'Time and transition in work teams: toward a new model of group development', *Academy of Management Journal*, **31**, 9–41.

Heider, F. (1958) *The Psychology of Interpersonal Relations*. New York: Wiley.

Hutchings, D. (1985) *Quality Circles Handbook*. London: Pitman.

Kelly, G. (1955) *The Psychology of Personal Constructs*. New York: W. W. Norton.

Kelley, H. H. (1973) 'The processes of causal attribution', *American Psychologist*, **8**, 107–28.

Lovejoy, S. (1988) 'How to zap your problems: synectics – a problem solving technique for psychologists and teachers', *Educational Psychology in Practice*, **3(4)**, 44–46.

Mager, R.F. (1975) *Preparing Instructional Objectives*. Belmont, CA: Fearon.

Margerison, C.J. and McCann, D. (1991) *Team Management: Practical Approaches*. London: Mercury Books.

Mehrabian, A. (1971) *Silent Messages*. Belmont, CA: Wadsworth.

Mullen, B. and Copper, C. (1994) 'The relation between group cohesiveness and performance: an integration', *Psychological Bulletin*, **115(2)**, 210–227.

Moreland, R.L. and Levine, J.M. (1988) 'Group dynamics over time: development and socialization in small groups'. In McGrath, J.E. (ed.) *The Social Psychology of Time*. Beverley Hills, CA: Sage.

Nolan, V. (1987) *The Innovators' Handbook: Skills of Innovation Management*. London: Sphere Books.

Schein, E. H. (1988) *Process Consultation* (vol. I). Reading, MA: Addison-Wesley.

Sigston, A. (1992) 'Making a difference for children: the educational psychologist as an empowerer of problem solving alliances'. In Wolfendale, S. *et al.* (eds). *The Profession and Practice of Educational Psychology: Future Directions*. London: Cassell Educational.

Sundstrom, E., De Meuse, K. and Futrell, D. (1990) 'Work teams: Applications and effectiveness', *American Psychologist*, **45(2)**, 120–133.

Truax, C. and Carkhuff, R. (1967) *Toward Effective Counselling and Psychotherapy*. Chicago: Aldine.

Tubbs, M.E. (1986) 'Goal setting: a meta-analytic examination of the empirical evidence', *Journal of Applied Psychology*, **71(3)**, 474–83.

Tuckman, B.W. (1965) 'Development sequence in small groups', *Psychological Bulletin*, **63**, 384–99.

West, M. A. (1994) *Effective Teamwork*. London: British Psychological Society and Routledge.

PART TWO: Young People

Chapter Three

Solution focused brief therapy: Working with young people

Chris Iveson

Introduction: some different rules

The school thought James H. was becoming 'psychotic', his doctor thought he needed psychiatric treatment, his father thought it was just a phase, his mother wasn't so sure and James himself did not offer an opinion. Brought to the attention of the educational psychologist and then referred specifically for 'brief therapy' as part of an informal collaboration between the psychologist and the brief therapy team at a local NHS family consultation service, James, who was 15, refused to attend. His mother, somewhat reluctantly, came alone. For the brief therapist this made no difference: the client is always right! This is in fact one of the most simple and fundamental principles of the brief therapy developed by Steve de Shazer and the team at the Brief Family Therapy Centre in Milwaukee (Berg, 1991; de Shazer, 1985, 1988, 1991a, 1994; Kral, 1987; Molnar and Lindqüist, 1989), Bill O'Hanlon in Nebraska (O'Hanlon and Hudson, 1995; O'Hanlon and Weiner-Davis, 1988; O'Hanlon and Wilks, 1987) and by the Brief Therapy Practice in London (George, Iveson and Ratner, 1990; Lethem, 1994). Brief therapy is characterised by a number of such apparently simple rules. Assuming that the client is always right (provided they are acting within the law and not limiting the rights of others) is a simple rule but one which leads the therapist into many untrodden paths and the probable breach of a number of other rules. In the case of the H family their 'decision' that Sue, James's mother, should attend was seen by most professionals as an indicator of 'resistance' and a precursor of failure. To the brief therapist, who sees resistance as the client's 'unique way of co-operating' (de Shazer, 1984), who comes and how they behave is the client's business. The business of the therapist is to find a way to co-operate with the client's way of doing things so that the client in return co-operates by answering some unusual questions. If the therapist is to be guided to this extent by the client, he or she must also have a means of knowing where they are: a framework within which to do the business of therapy. The most clear definition of such a framework is de Shazer's (1988) in which he lays down the essential principles of 'solution focused' brief therapy.

This framework has its roots in the work of Milton Erickson (de Shazer, 1975, 1985; Dolan, 1991; O'Hanlon and Martin, 1992) and the Brief Therapy Centre at the Mental Research Institute (MRI), Palo Alto (Watzlawick *et al.*, 1974; Fisch *et al.*, 1982). Erickson's emphasis on 'utilising' (de Shazer, 1991b) whatever the client comes with was the obvious forerunner (at least within the context of therapy!) of the notion that the customer is always right and the MRI's interest in 'pattern' led firstly to a study of *problem* pattern (de Shazer, 1982) and then to the study of *solution* patterns (Gingerich *et al.*, 1988). Added to these and other antecedents perhaps the most influential factor in the development of solution focused brief therapy was the Milwaukee team's interest in research (Nunnally *et al.*, 1986). In an attempt to discover what made therapy brief they undertook a study (de Shazer, 1988) of clients' behaviour during therapy to determine what clients themselves responded to most constructively. Surprisingly they found clients most responsive not during discussions about the problem but at times when either their futures or their achievements were the focus of attention.

Exceptions: when the problem rule is broken

One of de Shazer's greatest contributions to therapy came from his interest in pattern and in what clients were already doing well in their lives. Following Weakland and the MRI team (Watzlawick *et al.*, 1974) de Shazer began to see problem cycles as rules of life: 'I'm never on time therefore I'm likely to be late'. His creative leap was to become interested in *exceptions*. If problems were rules then there must always be exceptions because it is 'the exception that proves the rule'. de Shazer (1985, 1988) has developed the idea that because we, as human beings, are incapable of doing *anything* all the time we cannot 'do' our problems all the time: there must always be occasions when we do something different. It is in these *exceptions* to the problem pattern that de Shazer turns for clues to the client's own and *already existing* means to resolve the problem.

The study of exceptions led de Shazer to look for the client's achievements not just in the obvious places but right in the heart of the problem itself. With the notable exception of some 'psychotic' behaviours (de Shazer, 1988; Iveson, 1993), the exception rule always applies: no one can do their problem all the time, there will always be exceptions. The difficulty is that no one notices them or when they do they are not recognised for what they are: 'He did as he was told today – he must be coming down with something!'; 'She said "please", I wonder what she's after!'. Part of the skill of brief therapy is not so much finding exceptions but in getting client, referrer and other interested parties interested in exploring them because in the middle of the problem they sound like irrelevancies (Durrant, 1995; Rhodes and Ajmal, 1995).

Mundane miracles: defining possible futures

The notion of exceptions took the interest in clients' achievements and resources from a general level to one much more specific: to an interest in what the client is *already* doing which might help resolve the problem. de Shazer's 'miracle question' gives a similarly targeted focus to the client's interest in the future. Adapted from Erickson's 'crystal ball technique' (de Shazer, 1985) and based on the idea that to get somewhere by the shortest route it is necessary to know where you are going, the miracle question begins a process through which client and therapist discover a *possible* future in which the problem has no part:

> Suppose that tonight after you go to sleep a miracle happens and the problems that brought you to therapy are solved immediately. But since you were sleeping at the time you cannot know that this miracle has happened. Once you wake up tomorrow morning, how will you discover that a miracle has happened?
> (de Shazer, 1994)

The client's interest in the future is combined with the brief therapist's interest in goals (Cade and O'Hanlon, 1993) to create a picture of what life might look like if the problem was to be resolved. Here the skill is in asking questions about this possible future which keep it within the realms of reality without taking it out of the client's hands. To paraphrase Jerome Bruner's book title (Bruner, 1986) *actual* words can create *possible* worlds. Bruner illustrates the *creative* as well as the descriptive power of words: how they can be used not only to describe what exists already but how they can also create experiences which can then be lived. It is not surprising that de Shazer (1994) has a similar interest in language. If a client describes in realistic detail an imaginary life without the problem in sufficient detail and within the context of their everyday life and relationships that imaginary life can begin to be experienced as possible. When clients are stuck because they can see no possibility other than the continuation of the problem pattern the creation of other possibilities can be the first step towards change.

   The essential elements of solution focused brief therapy are thus set out: firstly to find out where the client is trying to get to or what is the client's preferred future and, secondly, to find out what the client is already doing or has done in the past which might help this future come about.

Elements of brief therapy

The 'miracle question' and exception finding are two of many possible ways these two aims can be pursued. A further group of questions, scaling questions, can be used to identify the client's progress towards his or her goal. 'How did you get to where you are now on the scale?' is an invitation to describe what the client has already done which will contribute in some way towards the resolution of the problem. 'How will you know when you have reached one point further up the scale?' begins a process of defining the next small steps. A session usually concludes with feedback to the client about anything he or she is doing which appears to represent a step towards the resolution of the problem. Problematic behaviour is usually not commented upon unless the 'therapist' has a responsibility and the legitimate authority to specify unacceptable behaviour (e.g. a teacher might need to point out that certain behaviours are forbidden and have consequences as well as compliment a pupil on constructive behaviours).

A typical first meeting with a client will involve four stages:

1. Identifying the goal of the work together in terms of clear, concrete and do-able behaviour, the 'miracle question' being one route to this description.

2. Exploring those occasions when the problem doesn't happen or happens less and amplifying the significance of these times by obtaining detailed accounts of them.

3. Locating the client's proximity to the goal by using scaling questions which also serve to identify further exceptions to the problem pattern and provide a vehicle for identifying the next small steps towards the goal.

4. Giving constructive feedback about anything the client is doing thinking or feeling which might contribute to a resolution of the problem.

Subsequent meetings will explore progress towards the goal, the ways in which the client deals successfully with any setbacks, the ways the client copes with and survives disappointment and further definition of the next small steps towards the goal.

Assumptions by the wayside

With the success of brief therapy many assumptions about problems and problem solving have fallen by the wayside. This does not mean the therapies based on such assumptions are wrong or misguided – if they work then they are worth having – but they can no longer so easily claim their premises as truths.

Assessment and diagnosis

Brief therapy offers no framework for the assessment, diagnosis and classification of problems and information about problems gives the therapist no useful guidance about how to act in a meeting with a client. This is the most radical of all the shifts and needs examining in the light of the importance of educational assessments. As such assessments lie outside the remit of psychotherapy, brief therapy principles and practices need some adaptation to accommodate them.

Client as expert

Another difference, at least from some therapies, is that the client remains the expert in their own and their family's lives. The therapist takes no view about what ought or needs to happen to resolve the problem assuming that only the client can know the uniquely 'right' way for him or herself. Even when the giving of advice is 'demanded' by the client such advice is carefully constructed from information the client has provided about what works. If the therapist is to be an expert at anything it is in co-operating and in asking questions which reveal the extent of the client's own expertise.

The 'unconscious'

The therapeutic content of a brief therapy session lies largely in what the client says which he or she did not know they knew. The therapist's task is to ask questions which do not lend themselves to 'scripted' answers: clients then find themselves responding with ideas and information which appears to be new but which only the clients themselves could 'know'. It is this 'new' information which begins to create possibilities other than the feared future which has brought the client to therapy in the first place. It could be said that this is therefore a process whereby the unconscious is brought into the conscious or at least becomes more accessible for the client's everyday use. Within brief therapy such unconscious processes are assumed and implicit and do not form a part of the therapist's operational repertoire. If unconscious processes are at work, as they undoubtedly are, they are left·to work in whatever way they do and no attempt is made within the therapy to analyse or deliberately influence them.

Past experience

The past plays a part in brief therapy not to understand current behaviour but to trace the history of exceptions in order to bring to light accounts of the past which are more likely to promote and endorse the client's preferred future. A growing assumption about problem histories is that they hide oppressive experiences (White and Epston, 1991). Just as history at a societal level is recorded by the more powerful groups in society leaving the less powerful either marginalised or even without a voice at all so are many accounts of individual lives also 'written' by dominant and oppressive others. The common experience of small children, raped by their fathers or other 'trusted' men, of feeling guilty for this abuse and that guilt then becoming a dominant influence in their teenage and adult lives is an obvious example of a 'false' account being perpetrated by the oppressive party in an abusive relationship. Ways to challenge such accounts without challenging the integrity of the client form an important part of any effective therapeutic approach. A brief therapist will 'challenge' by helping the client trace back the history of his or her 'exceptions' and so begin to construct alternative and more fitting accounts of the client's past.

James: who 'grew out of it'

Session one (part one): where are we trying to get to?

Sue came to the session because she was sufficiently worried about James's education to try anything but she did not really hold with therapy and was far from convinced that it would be in any way helpful. She was very clear that whatever his behaviour at home she could handle it and was only attending because she did not want her son to be excluded from school.

Therapist	Imagine that tonight a miracle happens and all the problems you're experiencing with James are sorted out. What is the first difference you'll notice tomorrow that begins to tell you a miracle has happened?
Sue	He'd actually be getting up out of bed.
Therapist	What time would this be – after the miracle?
Sue	About quarter-to-eight usually because I like them out by twenty-five past at the latest.
Therapist	After the miracle would he get himself up or would you wake him?
Sue	Well, usually I wake him. First of all I wake him up and then I get the other one up.
Therapist	Who's the other one?
Sue	Jo – Joanne, she's a year younger.
Therapist	So tomorrow morning, this miracle has happened (*laughter*) but you don't know about it so . . .
Sue	It'd be nice if it did!
Therapist	. . . so you'd wake James up – and how would he respond?
Sue	He'd go under the covers.
Therapist	And after the miracle?
Sue	After the miracle?
Therapist	Mmm.
Sue	Get up, get out of bed get washed and dressed without having to be shouted at!
Therapist	Okay, so you'd wake him up and instead of going under the covers he comes out of the covers. How would you react to that? Would it be a surprise?
Sue	I don't think I'd actually realise until he'd got out of bed and had a wash and then . . . (*pause*)

Therapist	And where would you be when this happens?
Sue	Usually just going down the stairs.
Therapist	So will you know that he's actually getting up and getting washed or will you only find out when he's done it?
Sue	Usually when he's finished.
Therapist	So what time would you see him coming down all washed and dressed?
Sue	If the miracle had happened?
Therapist	Yes.
Sue	About eight o'clock – not so much dressed but washed.
Therapist	Would you be surprised then or would you take it in your stride?
Sue	I suppose I'd just let it carry on and I suppose for it to actually hit me it would have to carry on for a few days.
Therapist	If this was just the first day of the miracle would you be surprised to see him or does he sometimes come down washed already?
Sue	I suppose once out of two weeks he actually does do it.
Therapist	So you wouldn't know whether this was just the once out of two weeks or the actual miracle?
Sue	Yeah, that's what I'm saying. After a couple of weeks I'd think to myself, "Oh, what's going on? He's been getting up!"
Therapist	Are you pleased to see him when he does turn up washed?
Sue	Yes, I suppose so. You see I'm in a rush too – rushing round trying to get myself ready – Jo's trying to get herself ready, ironing or sorting out the dogs.
Therapist	So James would come down at about eight o'clock. What difference would it make to you to see him at eight o'clock?
Sue	Make a change not having to shout!
Therapist	How will he know that you are pleased with that?
Sue	Suppose one of us, Jo or me, will turn around and actually say to him "Oh, you're down then!" you know but apart from that . . .
Therapist	So he'd know you were quite pleased?
Sue	I don't know to tell you the truth. Sometimes you know – it sounds horrible when you say it but sometimes you don't realise at the time – not until after a couple of days and you turn round and say to yourself "It's been a couple of days now" you know . . . *(pause)* . . . He'd know if I'm annoyed because if he's been mucking about and he comes down he knows then!
Therapist	And if you're pleased, how does he know then – what does he see?
Sue	I think we'd be more laughing and joking and messing about, you know.
Therapist	So if you found yourself making a joke in the morning it would be likely to be one of those mornings when James gets up and washed by eight?
Sue	Yes.
Therapist	So it's eight o'clock and he's come down stairs washed. It's no big deal because he sometimes does it anyway. What would be the next thing you noticed which started to tell you that this miracle was continuing?
Sue	Well' he's got a shirt on that's ironed!
Therapist	Would he come down with that on?
Sue	No, he'd put it on after he'd come down but he'd have ironed it the night before . . . *(pause)* . . . which he sometimes does.

Therapist	So that bit of the miracle might have happened the night before?
Sue	Mmm.
Therapist	So he's got his shirt on and it's ironed. Would that be something you'd particularly notice or does that happen often enough for it to be just one of those days?
Sue	I suppose with the shirt it usually happens about once a week.
Therapist	So again you wouldn't necessarily know it was a miracle because it already happens once a week. And the next thing? what would be the next thing that told you the miracle was continuing?
Sue	He'd brush his hair and that would be when he'd got everything else ready. Got his coat on and everything.
Therapist	Okay. You've woken him up at about quarter to eight and he's got straight up. You've got on with your own things and at eight o'clock he's appeared downstairs washed. You see him putting on an ironed shirt. You have a bit of a joke and a laugh. He's got himself ready and brushed his hair and goes out of the door. You say goodbye. What will you notice then?
Sue	I won't have a headache!
Therapist	You won't have a headache. And if the miracle continues all day and he really does get down to some work at school, but you don't know that because you're not there, what difference will you notice when you see him after school? What will be the first thing you notice which begins to tell you that he's had a good day at school?
Sue	He'd be excited, pleased with himself, you know.
Therapist	And how would that show – what does he do when he's pleased with himself?
Sue	Acts stupid or gets silly and aggressive – that's why you can't tell him!
Therapist	After the miracle how will he show that he's pleased?
Sue	What, doing it my way?
Therapist	Yes, how will he show that he's pleased in the way you would like him to show it?
Sue	Well, not so stupid. Like more calm and to talk about it, sort of more mature if you know what I mean.

Session one (part two): not very helpful

And so the session continued. Drawing out a painstakingly mundane description of what life would be like when the problem has gone. By locating the description in actual times and places and with actual people responding as they would normally do but to the changed circumstances the 'miracle' is kept well within realistic bounds – so much so that the relevance of such everyday detail can seem difficult to fathom. But after a description as ordinary and doable as this it would be difficult for Sue to avoid, in Bruner's words, stepping into the possible world she has created with her actual words. Not that Sue herself is aware of this!

At the end of the session the therapist as is normal gave Sue some 'constructive feedback': feedback about anything which she and her family were doing, thinking or feeling which might contribute towards the resolution of the problem. But when asked if she would like to come back Sue said she didn't know because this session had done nothing for her. She wanted to know what would happen if she came back. The therapist responded:

Therapist	You've said a lot today which would suggest that you are a very considerate, thoughtful and flexible woman . . .
Sue	Sometimes! . . .
Therapist	. . . and like all parents you can also be tough and inflexible when necessary. You're also someone with a history of getting on and sorting things out so I suppose my view is that you are a 'doer' rather than a talker – that you prefer to get on and get things done rather than talk about them. You've got that determination which says that you're not going to let this behaviour beat you down even when you can't yet think how to deal with it and you are also prepared to experiment like coming here.

Now all these qualities are helpful to me and are good news though of course they won't be news to you.

So if you come again I'd be really interested in seeing how these qualities can be used to sort out this problem which is worrying you so much. And given the nature of your strengths I'd think there was a good chance of finding a way to sort things out.

The feedback highlights what Sue appears to be doing which might contribute to a resolution of the problem and maps out the next stage of the work so that she knows what she is deciding about when asked if she would like a further meeting.

Therapist	So would you like to come back?
Sue	I'm not sure really. This hasn't been much use, has it?

Sue's response is somewhat unnerving but it is also probably more honest than many people's! The therapist also knows that the fact that she has still answered all the questions fully and with thought is likely to have an impact even if the changes are not associated with the therapy.

Second session: a loquacious James

Sue decided to come again and 3 weeks later came with James even though he had previously been adamant that he would have nothing to do with me or the clinic. Sue reported little change while James sat looking disinterested. With children and young people it is usually a good idea to check if they are prepared to answer questions. If not then the therapist needs to find someone else to talk to – a parent or teacher or someone who wants the situation to be different. James gave the most minimal of indications that he would answer questions but however minimal the agreement has to be taken seriously and serious questions asked.

Therapist	If tonight there was a miracle and life started going as you would like it to go, but because you're asleep you miss the miracle. Tomorrow morning how

	would you know the miracle had happened. What would be the very first thing you noticed?
James	(*long pause*) Dunno.
Therapist	What time do you think it would be when you woke up?
James	(*long pause*) I dunno.
Therapist	After the miracle what would be a good time for you to wake up?
James	(*long pause*) About quarter past eight.
Sue	(*half-muttered*) You have to leave by quarter past eight!
Therapist	(*an aside to Sue*) This is only a miracle. (*To James*) So at quarter-past-eight you'd wake up and what would be the very first sign you'd notice which began to tell you something was different?
James	(*pause*) No moaning.
Therapist	And if there was no moaning what would there be instead?
James	(*long pause*) Silence.
Therapist	So you'd wake up and there would be silence. And what would you do next?
James	Get up, get washed – get dressed.
Therapist	How long would that take you?
James	(*pause*) Dunno.
Therapist	So after the miracle how long do you think it would take you so it was how you'd like it to be?
James	(*pause*) About quarter of an hour.
Therapist	Okay. So after the miracle you'd wake up at quarter-past-eight, hear silence, get up, washed and dressed, come down at about half-past-eight. What next – after this miracle?
James	I'd get my stuff, get some money and go?

The interview proceeds at this very slow pace and like his mother's miracle James's is also kept at a very mundane level. After trying not very successfully to elicit more detail about his sister's, mother's and father's responses to his 'miracle', and after some description of the journey to school and James's post-miracle wish to be on time for things the therapist becomes interested in how this miracle will look at school. Once again attention is focused on times, places and people, in this instance on registration by his form tutor at five-past-nine.

Therapist	So what will be the first thing Mr Jones notices which begins to tell him this miracle has happened and things are going exactly as you would want them to go at school?
James	(*pause*) Dunno.
Therapist	What time is registration?
James	About five-past-nine.
Therapist	And do you always have it in the same room?
James	Yes.
Therapist	And do you all have to sit down or can you stand around?
James	We all sit down.
Therapist	So at five-past-nine you come into the room: what will Mr Jones see you do that tells him there is something different happening?
James	I'd sit down.

Therapist You'd sit down – would Mr Jones be pleased with that?
James   Dunno.
Therapist What do you think?
James   (*pause*) Probably.
Therapist And when he saw you sitting down what else would he see?

The importance of the concrete detail becomes especially apparent when working with reluctant teenagers who are likely to conserve as much conversational energy as possible. 'Dunno' is often not a sign of resistance but simply a way of telling the therapist that the question is not specific enough. As the interview proceeds it remains at this decidedly unmiraculous level. At one point the therapist becomes worried that Sue will be finding this second interview as big a waste of time as the first but she turns out to be gripped by it: she hasn't seen James so loquacious for months!

Third session: noticing the difference

Three weeks later they return for a third session. At first there seems to be little different: James is still slow in the mornings, the shouting and moaning continue and James and his sister are still fighting. But then Sue says there is a 'sort of difference'. Though he's still doing all these things he's doing them like a 'normal teenager' and though it's still annoying it doesn't really worry her any more. She says he has 'sort of grown up'. When asked what other signs there are of this growing up Sue catalogues a number of significant changes. He had started to attend the youth club again, was back on his football team at weekends, his friends were once again calling for him on the way to school, he was going out in the evenings and was looking after himself better – even brushing his hair! It was only as Sue ran through this list that the magnitude of James's changes began to sink in.

Because he was still doing most of the things she had complained about she was still seeing him from within the framework of a 'problem focus'. These other changes, though noticed in one way had not been noticed enough to judge their potential significance. Sue and James both visibly lightened as the session went on and the repercussions of these changes were amplified. To Sue it showed the whole thing had been a storm in a teacup and that 'his dad was right all along – he said he'd grow out of it and he was right!'

Checking back with the school similar changes had occurred. During the past year James had isolated and alienated himself so much from staff and pupils that he was being shunned and made fun of in return. He appeared to be sinking week by week into a fantasy world of his own and was beginning to lose control of reality. The referral had been precipitated by James behaving as if one of his fantasy experiences was real. All this disturbing behaviour had come to an end, he was not the most hard-working young person in the school but he was there, paying attention most of the time and back in with his friends. Some curiosity remained about what the whole thing had been about but as the family saw it as 'just a phase' they were not interested in further exploration.

Does it work: maybe

For

Unique as the interviews with James and Sue were they also followed a similar route to most other brief therapy interviews in that their central elements were the descriptions of life without the problem and the exploration of occasions when aspects of that problem-free life were already happening. Whether it was the 'therapy' which made the difference or simply that James grew out of it or both it was impossible to say. But for Sue, as for anyone else, there would be an 80% chance of the problem being significantly improved after coming for therapy for an average of four to five sessions.

The claim is based on a number of follow-up studies conducted by de Shazer's team in Milwaukee (de Shazer, 1988, 1991a; Iveson, 1991; Macdonald, 1994; Parsloe, 1993) in which clients have been asked whether the problem they went to therapy for is better, the same or worse than when they started. The Milwaukee studies are the most comprehensive and involve periodic follow-up over several years. Eight out of ten clients report significant improvement and most of these have no experience of 'symptom substitution'. In fact two-thirds of those reporting improvement also report improvement in other areas of their life not discussed in therapy. Iveson (1992) found similar outcomes in a pilot follow-up of 25 clients with a variety of problem presentations. Parsloe's smaller sample of outpatients of a community mental health service also showed an 80% improvement. Macdonald's (1994) follow-up showed 70% of clients of a psychiatric in-patient unit reporting improvement.

So far no common factors between those 20% of clients not reporting improvement have been found. Iveson screened for age, gender, race, type and chronicity of problem and like the Milwaukee research found no predictive features. Who was seen – individual, couple, family, or part of family, or whether the 'person with the problem' or a person complaining about the 'person with the problem' – also seemed to have no bearing on outcome. Even more interestingly for therapists with 'involuntary clients', there was no difference between those who wanted to come and those who were 'sent'. With this information all that can be said to any client is that there is an 80% chance that there will be some significant improvement after therapy.

Against

However, dramatic as this sounds it is a very limited finding. Miller (1994) quoting a variety of research findings argues that there is no proof that brief therapy is either briefer or more effective than any other therapy: what is different is that it *intends* to be brief and has made a virtue of asking the client about outcome. Miller suggests that the very act of asking the client will colour the results and this would be achieved whatever the therapeutic model used. There is no 'objective' indication that brief therapy has any effect on clients' lives and Sue's assertion that James just grew out of his problem might be as true as anything else.

The future

Further research is called for but how to do it is a matter of some debate. The intellectual and philosophical framework within which solution focused brief therapy has grown is humanistic rather than scientific: we attempt to understand human behaviour not by explanation and definition but by exploring its possibilities. Bruner (1986) in his account of 'narrative' thought argues that the process of scientific analysis can do as much to limit our understanding of ourselves as it can to expand our knowledge. White and Epston (1991) apply these ideas to therapy and see this as essentially a creative process in which assessment and diagnoses have a limited part to play. Solution focused brief therapy goes even further and argues that the problem has no bearing on outcome and that diagnosis is entirely irrelevant. As most *scientific* research is problem-focused then it is philosophically and methodologically at odds with the subject of its study.

As yet there is no answer to these questions which are by no means confined to the issue of brief therapy but represent a much wider debate in the academic world at large. de Shazer (personal communication) is currently interested in conducting outcome research not on problem-resolution but on goal achievement, and at a recent meeting of the European Brief Therapy Association (London, 1995) the question was raised that if asking clients directly has an effect on their perception of outcome then such 'therapeutic' research should perhaps be encouraged!

The debate will continue and whether brief therapy proves to be any more effective or not it is likely to continue to attract therapists interested in an approach which has no means of pathologising clients, which is led by the client's idea of where they want to get to and which more than most approaches takes the trouble to ask clients how they are getting on after it is all over!

References

Berg, I. K. (1991). *Family Preservation: A Brief Therapy Workbook*. London: BT Press.
Bruner, J. (1986) *Actual Minds, Possible Worlds*. Cambridge, Mass.: Harvard University Press.
Cade, B. and O'Hanlon, B. (1993) *A Brief Guide to Brief Therapy*. New York: Norton.
de Shazer, S. (1975) 'Confusion technique', *Family Therapy*, **2(1)**, 23–30.
de Shazer, S. (1982) *Patterns of Brief Family Therapy*. New York: Guilford.
de Shazer, S. (1984) 'The death of resistance', *Family Process*, **23**, 11–17.
de Shazer, S. (1985) *Keys to Solution in Brief Therapy*. New York: Norton.
de Shazer, S. (1988) *Clues: Investigating Solutions in Brief Therapy*. New York: Norton.
de Shazer, S. (1991a) *Putting Difference to Work*. New York: Norton.
de Shazer, S. (1991b). 'Utilisation: The foundation of solution', In Zeig, J. and Lankton, S. (eds) *Developing Ericksonian Therapy: State of the Art*. New York: Brunner/Mazel, pp.112–24.
de Shazer, S. (1994) *Words Were Originally Magic*. New York: Norton.
Dolan, Y. (1991) *Resolving Sexual Abuse*. New York: Norton.
Durrant, M. (1995) *Creative Strategies for School Problems*. New York: Norton (in press).

Fisch, R., Weakland, J.H. and Segal, L. (1982) *The Tactics of Change: Doing Therapy Briefly*. San Francisco: Jossey-Bass.

George, E., Iveson, C. and Ratner, H. (1990) *Problem to Solution: Brief Therapy with Individuals and Families*. London: BT Press.

Gingerich, W.J., de Shazer, S. and Weiner-Davis, M. (1988) 'Constructing change: a research view of interviewing'. In Lipchick, E. (ed.) *Interviewing*. Rockville, Md.: Aspen, pp.21–32.

Iveson, D. (1991) *Outcome Research: What is it and Who for?* MSc dissertation, Birbeck College, University of London.

Iveson, C. (1993) 'Hell's bells', *Community Psychiatric Nursing Journal,* **June**, 12–16.

Kral, R. (1987) *Strategies That Work: Techniques for Solution in the Schools*. Milwaukee: BFTC.

Lethem, J. (1994) *Moved to Tears, Moved to Action: Brief Therapy with Women and Children*. London: BT Press.

Macdonald, A. (1994) 'Brief therapy in adult psychiatry', *Journal of Family Therapy*, **16**, 415–26.

Miller, S. D. (1994). 'The solution conspiracy: A mystery in three installments', *Journal of Systemic Therapies*, **13(1)**, 18–37.

Molnar, A. and Lindquist, B. (1989) *Changing Problem Behaviour in the Schools*. San Francisco: Jossey-Bass.

Nunnally, E., de Shazer, S., Lipchik, E. and Berg, I. K. (1986). 'A study of change: Therapeutic theory in process'. In Efron, D. (ed.) *Journeys: Expansion of the Strategic–Systemic Therapies*. New York: Norton, pp.77–96.

O'Hanlon, B. and Weiner-Davis, M. (1988) *In Search of Solutions: A New Direction in Psychotherapy*. New York: Norton.

O'Hanlon, B. and Wilks, J. (1987) *Shifting Contexts: The Generation of Effective Psychotherapy*. New York: Guildford.

O'Hanlon, W.H. and Martin, M. (1992) *Solution-oriented Hypnosis: An Eriksonian Approach*. New York: Norton.

O'Hanlon, W.H. and Hudson, P. (1995) *Love is a Verb*. New York: Norton.

Parsloe, S. (1993) *On a Scale of 1 to 10: A Different Way of Evaluating Solution Focused Brief Therapy*. MSc dissertation, Birbeck College, University of London.

Rhodes, J. and Ajmal, Y. (1995) *Solution Focused Thinking in Schools*. London: BT Press.

Watzlawick, P., Waekland, J.H. and Fisch, R. (1974) *Change: Principles of Problem Formation and Problem Resolution*. New York: Norton.

White, M. and Epston, D. (1991) *Narrative Means to Therapeutic Ends*. New York: Norton.

Chapter Four

Understanding health risk in adolescence

Debi Roker

This chapter looks at key areas of health risk during the adolescent years. There are many risks to young people's health, including accidents and abuse, depression and suicide, abuse of alcohol and illicit drugs, and HIV infection. Concepts of risk in many of these areas are, however, open to debate. Some risk behaviours, such as a young person who is having unprotected sex, are clear. Other potential risk behaviours are less clear – for example is a 13-year-old boy at risk when he tries his first cigarette, or a 14-year-old girl who has intercourse for the first time?

I will not be able to explore all areas of health risk in adolescence in this chapter. I will therefore focus on risks relating to substances and sexual behaviour, specifically smoking, alcohol, illegal drugs, sexual behaviour, teenage pregnancy, sexually transmitted diseases (STDs) and HIV/AIDS. The chapter is divided into three sections. Part one identifies what we know about adolescents' behaviour in each of these areas, identifying recent trends and summarising research findings. Part two suggests five main aims of practice in working with young people in these areas. Part three explores current models of effective practice in helping young people to reduce risk in relation to substances and sexual behaviour.

First, however, it would be useful to consider briefly the concept of risk and its relationship to adolescent development in general. Whilst few researchers now see the period as one characterised primarily by 'storm and stress', most do see the period as characterised by exploration and experimentation, and the trying out of different roles, identities, and behaviours (see for example Coleman and

Hendry, 1990; Springhall, 1983). As such, most young people will begin to undertake adult activities during these years, such as drinking alcohol and commencing sexual relationships. In all of these areas of development and experimentation there are potential risks, including using a dangerous drug, drinking to excess, or having unprotected sex.

As has already been suggested, however, risk is not a unitary, one-dimensional concept. Nor is it something which applies only to young people. Many adults engage in risk-taking behaviour every day, whether in sporting activities or on the road. This chapter, therefore, will focus on *understanding* risk in the areas concerned, and on strategies to help young people to recognise and *reduce* potential harm.

Current research suggests that whilst most young people are not exposed to serious risk during adolescence (Plant and Plant, 1992) there is evidence that risk behaviours amongst young people are increasing. A recent Department of Health (DoH) report concluded that:

> Young people are adopting patterns of risk at an earlier age, and in choosing such lifestyles may appear heedless of the health consequences of, for example, cigarette smoking, alcohol, or sexual activity.

(DoH, 1994:74)

We will start, first, by looking at research and current trends in each of these areas: what do we know about young people's smoking behaviour, alcohol consumption, use of illegal drugs, sexual behaviour, and sexual health risks?

Adolescent health risk: research findings

Smoking

A report by the Royal College of Physicians (RCOP) (1992) presents some key facts about adolescent smoking. The report shows that:

- 450 children and young people start smoking every day in the UK.
- One-fifth of school leavers smoke regularly, with smoking most common amongst girls.
- Most adult smokers started to smoke regularly before the age of 18.

In addition, they show that the uptake of smoking amongst teenagers hasn't changed for over a decade, and that once a young person starts to smoke regularly, most continue to do so into adulthood. The report continues with a lengthy analysis of the effects of smoking on adolescents, concluding that 'Tobacco smoking is addictive and does far greater harm than any other addictive drug' (p.vii).

Children and young people are now experiencing their first cigarette at a younger age than in previous generations. Recent research shows that one-third of children who had experimented with cigarettes had done so before the age of 11 (Thomas *et al.*, 1993). The RCOP report gives age for first experimentation as 9–12 for boys and 10–13 for girls (RCOP, 1992). Many of these young people go on to become regular smokers, representing approximately 10% of girls and 9% of boys in secondary education. By the fifth year of secondary schooling, one fifth of young people smoke (Thomas *et al.*, 1993).

Goddard (1992) identifies five main factors in starting to smoke:

- being female;
- having siblings or parents who smoke;
- living with a lone parent;
- having less negative views about smoking;
- not intending to stay on in full-time education after age 16.

Personal factors said to be associated with starting smoking include rebelliousness, poor self-esteem, lower academic attainment, and poor refusal skills (RCOP, 1992). Young people are five times more likely to smoke if their parents do. Parental attitudes to smoking are also important – young people are seven times less likely to smoke if they perceive strong parental disapproval of smoking (RCOP, 1992).

Alcohol

In a review of the British research into adolescence and alcohol, Sharp and Lowe (1989) demonstrate that alcohol has now become a normal part of growing up. They also point out, however, that drink-related problems amongst young people are on the increase, including cirrhosis of the liver. Heavy binge drinking is also being reported at a younger age, with convictions for drunkenness amongst teenagers doubling between 1964 and 1984. Plant *et al.* (1990a) similarly conclude that '. . . alcohol misuse amongst young people has reached unprecedented or at least epidemic proportions' (p.685).

Research shows that most young people will be using alcohol regularly by the age of 16. A study of alcohol use amongst a representative sample of over 6,000 14–16 year-olds showed that 75% of the sample drank for the first time between age 9 and 14 (Plant *et al.*, 1990a). Ten per cent of the sample were classified as heavy drinkers, who on their last drinking occasion had drunk 11 units or more for males, and more than 8 units for females. There is also evidence that the age at which young people first drink is declining. Sharpe and Lowe's review concludes that 95% of young people have had a 'proper drink' by age 16, with many studies reporting first drink by age 10.

A number of studies have explored where and how adolescents start to drink. British studies show that most young people start drinking in the family home, often on a special occasion (Aitken, 1978; Sharp *et al.*, 1988). Later in the teenage years, alcohol consumption is most likely to take place outside of the home (Sharpe and Lowe, 1989). Consumption of alcohol in adolescence is generally associated with peer pressure to drink, although some researchers have identified other factors as important, including curiosity, and to have a good time (Plant *et al.*, 1990a). A gender difference is also apparent in teenage drinking, with boys drinking more, and more often (Marsh *et al.*, 1986).

Many risks are associated with excessive alcohol consumption by young people. The increase in rates of liver cirrhosis have already been mentioned. Researchers have identified many other risks. First, one study showed that a fifth of a sample of adolescents had travelled in vehicles driven by someone who had been drinking (Plant *et al.*, 1990a). Second, young heavy drinkers are more exposed to acute risks such as accidents (Plant *et al.*, 1990b). Third, there is evidence that alcohol affects a young person's ability to negotiate and use contraception when having sexual intercourse (see for example McEwan *et al.*, 1992; World Health Organisation, 1993).

Illegal drugs

All the research evidence available suggests that adolescents today are more likely to be offered illegal drugs, to try them, and to be using them regularly. Reflecting this, one group of researchers have concluded that '. . . a process of normalisation is underway in respect of adolescent recreational drug use' (Parker and Measham, 1994:5).

A major study of adolescents' drug awareness has surveyed 14–15 year-olds at the same school every 5 years since 1969 (Wright and Pearl, 1995). Throughout this period, the number of young people who knew someone taking drugs increased from 15% in 1969 to 65% in 1994. Those being offered drugs increased from 5% to 45% in the same period.

A survey of drug use amongst 752 15–16 year-olds in north-west England also found widespread familiarity with illicit drugs (Parker and Measham, 1994). Of this group, 71% had been offered drugs – most often cannabis, followed by LSD; 41% had used cannabis, and 25% LSD, at least once. These authors note a change from their earlier research, in that young women were equally as likely to have been offered and to have tried illegal drugs as young men, and that few social class differences were evident in patterns of drug use. Previously working-class males had been viewed as the main users of illegal drugs. Research also demonstrates that the numbers of young people using hard drugs (heroin and cocaine in particular) remains small (Davies and Coggans, 1991). The drug young people are overwhelmingly likely to be offered, and to use, is cannabis (Bean *et al.*, 1988; Balding, 1995). Overall, the available research supports the view of Wright and Pearl (1995) that:

. . . an increasing proportion of young people are in contact with illicit drugs from their early teens . . . a greater variety of drugs are more widely available socially and geographically, and young people expect to enjoy the pleasurable effects with minimal harm.

(Wright and Pearl, 1995:24)

Studies of adolescent drug-taking frequently report a link between use of illegal drugs, use of alcohol, and cigarette smoking. Bean *et al.* (1988) show that the heaviest drinkers in their sample of 15 year-olds had the greatest knowledge of drugs, and were more likely to have been offered drugs. They concluded that '. . . using large quantities of alcohol places the child in a drug-taking milieu' (p.81). Many other research studies have identified a link between adolescents' use of alcohol, smoking, and illegal drugs (Newcombe *et al.*, 1995; Rundall and Bruvold, 1988).

Sexual behaviour and risk

The area of young people's sexual behaviour and lifestyles is a complicated and broad-ranging area. Consequently, only a brief summary of the current situation and research findings is possible here, and will focus on sexual behaviour and contraceptive use, teenage pregnancy, sexually transmitted diseases (STDs) and HIV/AIDS. (For a broader review of adolescent sexuality see Meyrick and Harris, 1994; Moore and Rosenthal, 1993.)

There have been many changes in young people's sexual attitudes, behaviours and lifestyles in recent decades. It is important to start with the fact that young people are now maturing physically at a younger age, approximately 4 months earlier each decade this century; as an indication of this researchers have shown that one in ten primary school girls have now begun menstruating (Prendergast, 1992). A crucial development in young people's sexual behaviour is the lower age at which young people are now having their first sexual experience. A recent large-scale study of sexual lifestyles and behaviours found that the average age of first sexual intercourse is now 17 (Wellings *et al.*, 1994); one in five of the under 16s in this survey were also sexually active. Overall, the evidence is that most teenagers will have experienced sexual intercourse by age 18 (Abraham and Sheeran, 1994; Kruss, 1992).

Despite these changes in sexual behaviour, and the greater prevalence of sex and sexuality in our society, research shows that many young people remain ignorant and uninformed about their bodies and developing sexuality. A qualitative study of young people in Norfolk concluded that young people are generally ignorant about sex and sexuality (Walker, 1994), but that many found it difficult to admit to this. Similarly, a study of sex education classes with 465 13–14 year-olds found that a 'significantly large' proportion of this group had wrong and inaccurate information about puberty and sexuality (Phelps *et al.*, 1992). A review of research by the Sex Education Forum concluded that:

> While young people may be more familiar with certain sexual words and phrases than their parents, for many there is a real lack of understanding of their own bodies and of sexual issues.
>
> (Sex Education Forum, 1994)

Agreeing with this, Phelps *et al.* (1992) comment that ignorance has serious implications for young people's health:

> If knowledge is power, then most young people lack the power to communicate effectively about their own sexuality and to make informed decisions . . .
>
> (p.31)

These changes in sexual behaviour and lifestyles, combined with lack of knowledge, have considerable implications for young people's sexual health and well-being. Recent research findings for contraceptive use, rates of teenage pregnancy, and STDs (including HIV/AIDS) demonstrate this well. These will be explored in turn.

Contraceptive use and non-use amongst young people

Despite the risks of pregnancy and HIV infection, a low level of contraceptive use has been found amongst young people. One study of 16-year-olds in the south-east of England found that 50% of those who were sexually active had not used any contraception the first time they had intercourse (Ford, 1991); other studies report rates of 30–50% not doing so (Kruss, 1992; Meyrick and Harris, 1994). Failure to use contraception is undoubtedly related to lack of knowledge amongst some young people. However, other personal and situational factors are also involved. Kruss (1992) shows that of 220 sexually active young people, 75% failed to use any contraception at their first experience of intercourse. The most common reasons given included that they had no contraception, had not expected to 'go all the way', and were too embarrassed to get any. Overall, many research studies into young people's contraceptive use and non-use confirm the view of Heaven (1994:132) that:

> Many adolescents seem to be apathetic and irresponsible about condom use and the risks associated with unsafe sex.

The implications of non-use of contraception, and strategies to combat it, are discussed later in the chapter.

Teenage pregnancy

Britain's rate of unplanned pregnancy is the highest in Europe. About 8,000 under-16s become pregnant every year in the UK (OPCS, 1993), with two-thirds of this group going on to have terminations. Many of these pregnancies are caused not only by non-use of contraception, but also by ignorance of the need to use any. One study of 80 young women who became pregnant at age 16 and under found that 60% were unaware of the facts of conception and fertility that could have prevented their pregnancy (Clark and Coleman, 1992). Thus health education strategies need to tackle both motivation to use contraception and knowledge of its importance.

STDs and HIV/AIDS

Rates of infection of many STDs, including HIV, have increased amongst young people during the 1980s and 1990s. The cervical abnormalities that are associated with these STDs have also increased amongst this age group (Donovan, 1990; Elliot, 1989). Yet many young people demonstrate a poor understanding of the risks of STDs and HIV. Phelps *et al.* (1992) report that their sample of young people believed that HIV was the most common sexual infection, and that in addition HIV was not a risk for them personally. They conclude that this finding '. . . may explain why we are looking at an epidemic rise in warts and genital herpes' (p.30).

Infection with the HIV virus is a risk for young people, in particular because of the failure of many young people to use contraception (see above). Studies of young people's knowledge of HIV transmission and risk of HIV infection give contradictory results. Some researchers suggest that, although many do not act in a safe manner, young people's knowledge about HIV/AIDS is high (Woodcock *et al.*, 1992). However, many young people perceive themselves to be invulnerable, and often deny that risks of infection apply to them.

Other research suggests that many young people do not have even the most basic knowledge about these topics. White *et al.* (1988) looked at 14–15 year-olds perceptions of HIV/AIDS. Most knew that AIDS was incurable, and that condom use and limiting number of partners reduces the risk of infection. However, White *et al.*, also found that this group '. . . saw themselves as more knowledgeable than they really were about preventive measures' (p.117). They suggest that educational strategies need to tackle not only the failure of many young people to acknowledge their personal risk of HIV infection, but also their over-confidence about knowledge of preventive strategies. The consequences of this are addressed later in the chapter.

Promoting healthy behaviour amongst adolescents: Frameworks for practice

This section will focus on the aims of working with young people, in terms of their use of substances and sexual behaviour. Five main aims of effective practice are presented, which can be applied to all the areas of health risk discussed so far – smoking, alcohol, illegal drugs, and sexual behaviour.

Increasing young people's knowledge

The first part of the chapter highlighted young people's lack of knowledge in many areas of potential health risk. It is clear, for example, that many young people are unaware of key facts about fertility, conception and contraception (Clark and Coleman, 1992; Phelps *et al.*, 1992; Sex Education Forum, 1994), and about alcohol (Plant *et al.*, 1990a). In recent years, however, knowledge has become an unfashionable concept within research and health education; the emphasis has been, rather, on the development of adolescents' interpersonal skills and communication abilities. Yet knowledge is a crucial factor in helping young people to reduce their exposure to risk. For example, it is a prerequisite for safe sexual behaviour – a young person who is not aware of the facts about fertility and contraception will be unable to act safely (see Winn *et al.*, (1995) for a discussion). Increasing young people's knowledge, and tackling both misunderstanding and ignorance, must therefore be a key aim of health education in these areas. How this might be achieved is discussed in the following section.

Developing interpersonal skills

The first part of the chapter showed that for young people to reduce the risks to which they are exposed, a number of key interpersonal skills are needed. Skills relating to smoking and illegal drug use are good examples: young smokers are claimed to have poor refusal skills (RCOP, 1992), and peer influence has been identified as a key factor in adolescents' consumption of alcohol and use of illegal drugs (Plant and Plant, 1992; Wright and Pearl, 1995). Thus a key aim of health education with adolescents must be to develop effective interpersonal skills – for example to feel (and be) able to say no to sex, or to resist pressure from friends to try cigarettes. These skills include being clear about what you want, assertiveness, and knowing how to convey messages.

Promoting harm reduction

A key aim of practice in these areas must be harm reduction. Rather than aiming to stop young people from drinking alcohol, or promoting sexual abstinence, the emphasis of much health education is now on harm reduction. Thus if a young person decides to have sexual intercourse or to use illegal drugs, then the aim is to encourage that person to use contraception during intercourse, or to use the safest drugs in the safest ways.

Increasing perceptions of personal risk

It has already been demonstrated that a common characteristic of adolescence is a sense of personal invulnerability, of risks applying only to other people. Clearly, young people will not undertake safe behaviour or harm reduction if they believe that they personally are not at risk. Thus a key aim of working with young people must be to present them with, and convince them of, the realities of risk - that their health can be damaged by using particular drugs, or that they can become pregnant or infected with the HIV virus from just one incident of unprotected sex. It is of note that many of the models of health behaviour traditionally used in health promotion contexts (such as the health belief model, and the theory of planned behaviour) emerged from social cognition models which depend on young people perceiving themselves to be at risk (see Abraham and Sheeran, 1993). Clearly, however, many young people do not see themselves as at risk, and so such strategies have been of limited effectiveness.

Targeting multiple risk takers

There is evidence that a small group of young people are exposing themselves to multiple risks (Plant and Plant, 1992; WHO, 1993). These young people often drink heavily, smoke, and use illegal drugs. Many have also been shown to be characterised by personal characteristics such as impulsiveness (Clift *et al.*, 1993). Targeting these young people must be an aim of health education, as they are at particular risk from ill health (Bagnall and Plant, 1987).

Approaches to reducing risk in adolescence

There are many strategies currently underway to help young people to reduce risk in their use of tobacco, alcohol and illegal drugs, and in their sexual behaviour. This section reviews some of the health education approaches, methods and issues, particularly as they relate to the five main aims of practice listed above – i.e. increasing knowledge, developing interpersonal skills, promoting harm reduction, increasing perceptions of personal risk, and targeting multi-risk takers.

Smoking

It was demonstrated in section one that, despite the fact that smoking is now less socially acceptable, about one-fifth of adolescents become regular smokers. Further, smoking education programmes have been largely unsuccessful in reducing the numbers of young people who take up smoking (RCOP, 1992; Rundall and Bruvold, 1988). What is clear is that the *least* effective method of educating adolescents about smoking is to highlight the long-term health risks. Adolescents live essentially for the 'here and now', and are particularly resistant to messages which focus on what may happen to their bodies or health in 40 years time (see for example Morgan and Grube, 1991).

A number of features have been identified, however, which show some effectiveness in preventing young people from taking up smoking. These include same-age peer education (Morgan and Grube, 1991) and the development of refusal skills (see for example Presti *et al.*, 1992). Developing a young person's refusal skills are particularly important in light of research showing that young occasional smokers are 26 times more likely to be offered a cigarette than a non-smoker (Ary and Biglan, 1988). These young people may have particularly poor refusal skills and thus need particular help.

Understanding the nature of peer pressure at different ages is crucial for smoking education. It is known that peer conformity increases from childhood to adolescence, and then declines in later adolescence. One implication of this is that:

> While teaching resistance to peer pressure may be effective in early adolescence, the usefulness of such techniques may be smaller in late adolescence.
>
> (Morgan and Grube, 1989:188)

Following on from this, Morgan and Grube add that if social skills and resistance training are effective in early adolescence, then a useful strategy may be to focus with older adolescents on the effects of smoking on physical appearance and personal attractiveness.

Some particularly important work on young people's refusal skills has been undertaken in the USA. Reardon *et al.* (1989) report that people respond to different offers in different circumstances and in different ways. Yet this concept is rarely applied to developing young people's interpersonal skills. Thus:

> Interventions have been developed on the basis of what researchers believe adolescents should be able to say, rather than on the basis of what adolescents report they would say.
>
> (Reardon *et al.*, 1989:310)

These authors demonstrate that there are many ways of saying no – making an excuse, changing the subject, being assertive or aggressive. They therefore propose that we need a better understanding of what adolescents feel most comfortable in saying when pressurised to smoke, or when first offered a cigarette. Thus, skills training must explore both the circumstances of the offer and the nature of the relationship. For example if a relationship is not very important to a young person, they may feel able to respond by walking away. If a relationship is important, they will want a repertoire of responses which are less likely to threaten their relationship, such as giving excuses or being assertive.

Further, some health educators have stressed the need to attend to adolescents' wider environments, and to the broader role of smoking within adolescent identity development (Leventhal *et al.*, 1991). Thus the RCOP (1992) emphasise the need to involve families and parents in re-enforcing the message, and to implement no-smoking policies where young people congregate. They demonstrate, for example, that schools with teachers who smoke (and particularly a headteacher who does) have more pupils who do. Leventhal and colleagues also point out that smoking education starts from the premise that young people want to resist the pressure to smoke; helping young people explore the role of smoking in teenage lifestyles and identity is an important place to start. This view is confirmed by research studies showing that many young people say they smoke not because of 'weakness' or 'peer pressure' (as is commonly supposed) but because they enjoy smoking and the image associated with it (Warburton *et al.*, 1991).

Alcohol consumption

Traditional approaches to alcohol education – in terms of providing facts and information – have been largely ineffective (May, 1991). This approach is based on the premise that young people are unaware of the long-term health consequences of alcohol use, and that becoming aware of the risks will lead young people to modify their behaviour. Some have also criticised this as an over-individualised approach to alcohol education, saying that:

> . . . doubt has been raised about the validity of emphasizing individual choice and responsibility in health-related behaviour, at the expense of socio-economic factors beyond the control of the individual.
>
> (Bagnall, 1987:162)

Thus, like Leventhal *et al.*, in relation to smoking, Bagnall suggests that alcohol education materials must aim to increase young people's perceptions of the social factors influencing alcohol consumption, and to develop the skills that young people can use to resist pressure from peers.

A number of features have been shown to increase the effectiveness of alcohol education with young people. These include student participation, particularly in the form of discussion, group work, and role play (Bagnall, 1987; May, 1991). Involving those with alcohol problems also appears to be effective (Dennison, 1977). Again, the most successful programmes appear to be those which place alcohol education within a social context, and focus on exploring drinking behaviour and skill development in a number of different contexts, including the peer group, the family, and social events.

Illegal drug use

In the first part of this chapter, it was demonstrated that most young people today are likely to be offered drugs, and many will try and/or use them; this applies particularly to cannabis. Yet, as one research study concluded, this is in spite of the fact that this generation

> . . . has been systematically exposed to primary drug education. Clearly, the 'say no to drugs' message has been rejected or at least neutralised by other processes and pressures.
>
> (Parker and Measham, 1994:13)

Much drug education, particularly school-based drug education, has been of the primary prevention type. Davies and Coggans (1991) describe this as education which aims to prevent young people from ever using illegal drugs. This approach uses two methods:

1. *Fear arousal* – focusing on the dangerous and unpleasant effects of drug-taking.

2. *Information giving* – providing young people with information that convinces them not to use drugs.

Davies and Coggans conclude that the first method has been ineffective, and the second counter-productive. Indeed, they suggest that there is evidence that these methods may have increased experimentation. This is because the risks presented (such as those in the 'heroin screws you up' campaign) are not seen by young people as things that would happen to them; also the message that drugs kill or are addictive is contrary to the popular image that some illegal drugs, particularly cannabis, can be used occasionally without these dangerous effects. Davies and Coggans suggest that these methods may therefore actually stimulate interest in drug use (see also Plant *et al.*, 1985).

As a result of this many organisations are now promoting a harm-reduction approach to young people's use of illegal drugs, which focuses on safe, occasional use. As with smoking and alcohol use, a life-skills and skills training approach is generally used, to help young people to make safe, sensible and personally chosen decisions about drug use. Thus the development of assertion and refusal skills are the focus, so that young people can say no when they want to. If they don't want to, then these skills help them to understand the risks and to use drugs safely. Indeed, Davies and Coggans propose that such an approach should be integrated into a broader health education programme:

> It seems intuitively obvious that telling young people that they should always reject the offer of drugs . . . is less subtle than a program which informs in a less directive manner about the consequences, good and bad, of drug use in the context of an integrated and wide-ranging positive health choice curriculum.
>
> (Davies and Coggans, 1991:56)

Sexual behaviour

It has been suggested by some researchers that sexual behaviour may be qualitatively different (in terms of young people's risk and health behaviour) to the other areas discussed here, such as smoking and drug use. Abraham and Sheeran (1994), for example, demonstrate that traditional models of health behaviour fail to predict young people's condom use. They conclude (1994:175) that '. . . sexual behaviour may be inherently different from other health behaviours', primarily because of its interactive nature and high emotional and arousal content. They therefore suggest that social skills, and in particular interpersonal negotiation, are particularly important aspects of sex education with young people. These authors add that psychological models used to predict health behaviour must include one additional feature in relation to young people's sexual behaviour – perceived self-efficacy. This is the extent to which an individual believes they are capable of carrying out a particular action, such as buying a condom. Many programmes of skill development in settings such as schools and youth clubs are therefore now being directed at such skills and actions – participatory sessions encouraging young people to explore what they need to do to reduce risk, and how can they overcome any problems encountered.

One method which has been identified as particularly effective in promoting healthy sexual behaviour is peer education. Its effectiveness is related to the belief that people their own age have the best understanding of young people's needs and views (see for example Walker, 1994). Peer education is probably particularly effective in helping young people to acknowledge their personal risk of pregnancy and HIV infection.

The widespread perception of invulnerability amongst young people has already been demonstrated. Woodcock *et al.* (1992) have shown that many young people do not have a good grasp of issues such as risk and probability. Yet models of young people's health behaviours are generally based on their being able to understand the concept of risk. Woodcock *et al.* suggest that there are clear implications of this for sexual and HIV education:

> Ideally, young people should be allowed to explore their beliefs about risks in an environment which enables them to see for themselves the inconsistencies between their knowledge about HIV transmission and their perceptions of personal risk of infection, as well as the influence of emotions and trust within relationships upon rational judgements of risk.
>
> (Woodcock *et al.*, 1992:246)

Group discussions, using same-age peers as facilitators, are likely to be a good way of facilitating this. Peer facilitation and education are likely to be particularly effective with multiple risk-takers, for whom a teacher or nurse may seem particularly distant from their own experiences. Similarly, White *et al.* (1988) propose that young people's ignorance about methods of reducing HIV infection can be tackled using small group and individual meetings.

Overall, it is clear that young people need a combined approach focusing on knowledge, discussion of emotions and feelings, and skills-based training. They also need help to anticipate potential risk situations, such as the effects of alcohol on decision-making and negotiation in sexual encounters. As Abraham and Sheeran (1993) conclude, education about sexuality needs to shift from a focus on biology to social psychology, and from information-giving to participation (see also Bunton *et al.* (1991) and Tappe (1992) for a discussion of these issues).

This chapter has focused on some of the main areas of health risk in adolescence – smoking, use of alcohol and illegal drugs, unprotected sex, teenage pregnancy, and HIV/AIDS. In the introduction to the chapter it was suggested that some forms of experimentation and risk-taking are a natural part of adolescent development. Some of the risks described here, however, are life-threatening, or have very serious implications for the well-being of the young person. The chapter has aimed at identifying ways in which a better understanding of adolescent development – and of the nature of young people's relationships with peers, teachers, parents and professionals – may help those working with adolescents to reduce their exposure to serious health risk.

References

Abraham, C. and Sheeran, P. (1993) 'In search of a psychology of safer-sex promotion: Beyond beliefs and texts', *Health Education Research*, **8(2)**, 245–54.

Abraham, C. and Sheeran, P. (1994) 'Modelling and modifying heterosexuals' HIV-preventive behaviour: A review of theories, findings and educational implications', *Patient Education and Counselling*, **23**, 173–86.

Aitken, P. (1978) *Ten to Fourteen Year-Olds and Alcohol: A Developmental Study in the Central Region of Scotland.* London: HMSO.

Ary, D. V. and Biglan, A, (1988) 'Longitudinal changes in adolescent smoking behaviour: Onset and cessation', *Journal of Behavioural Medicine*, **11(4)**, 361–82.

Bagnall, G. (1987) 'Alcohol education and its evaluation – some key issues', *Health Education Journal*, **46(4)**, 162–65.

Bagnall, G. and Plant, M. A. (1987) 'Education on drugs and alcohol: Past disappointments and future challenges', *Health Education Research*, **2(4)**, 417–22.

Balding, J. (1995) *Young People and Illegal Drugs, 1989-1995.* Exeter: Schools Health Education Unit.

Bean, P. T., Wilkinson, C. K., Whynes, D. K, and Giggs, J. A. (1988) 'Knowledge about drugs and consumption of alcohol amongst Nottingham 15 year-olds', *Health Education Journal*, **47**, 79–81.

Bunton, R., Murphy, S. and Bennett, P. (1991) 'Theories of behavioural change and their use in health promotion: Some neglected areas', *Health Education Research*, **6(2)**, 153–62.

Clark, E. and Coleman, J. C. (1992) *Growing Up Fast.* London: St Michaels Fellowship.

Clift, S. M., Wilkins, J. C. and Davidson, E. A. F. (1993) 'Impulsiveness, venturesomeness and sexual risk-taking among heterosexual GUM clinic attenders', *Personality and Individual Differences*, **15(4)**, 403–10.

Coleman, J. C. and Hendry, L. (1990) *The Nature of Adolescence.* London: Routledge.

Davies, J. and Coggans, N. (1991) *The Facts About Adolescent Drug Abuse.* London: Cassell.

Dennison, D. (1977) 'Effects of selected field experiences upon the drinking behaviour of university students', *Journal of School Health*, **47**, 38–41.

Department of Health (1994) *On the State of the Public Health.* London: HMSO.

Donovan, C. (1990) 'Adolescent sexuality', *British Medical Journal*, **63**, 935–41.

Elliot, P. M. (1989) 'Changing character of cervical cancer in young women', *British Medical Journal*, **298**, 288–90.

Ford, N. (1991) *The Socio-sexual Lifestyles of Young People in South-west England.* South-West Regional Health Authority.

Goddard, E. (1992) 'Why children start smoking', *British Journal of Addiction*, **87**, 17–25.

Heaven, P. C. L. (1994) *Contemporary Adolescence: A Social Psychological Approach.* Melbourne: Macmillan.

Kruss, G. (1992) *Young People and Health.* Belfast: Whiterock.

Leventhal, H., Keeshan, P., Baker, T. and Wetter, D. (1991) 'Smoking prevention: Towards a process approach', *British Journal of Addiction*, **86**, 583–87.

McEwan, R., McCallum, A., Bhopal, R. and Madnok, R. (1992) 'Sex and risk of HIV infection: The role of alcohol', *British Journal of Addiction*, **87**, 577–84.

Marsh, A., Dobbs, J. and White, A. (1986) *Adolescent Drinking.* London: HMSO.

May, C. (1991) 'Research on alcohol education for young people: A critical review of the literature', *Health Education Journal*, **50(4)**, 195–99.

Meyrick, J. and Harris, R. (1994) 'Adolescent sexual behaviour, contraceptive use and pregnancy: A review', *ACPP Review and Newsletter*, **16(5)**, 245–51.

Moore, S. and Rosenthal, D. (1993) *Sexuality in Adolescence.* London: Routledge.

Morgan, M. and Grube, J. W. (1989) 'Adolescent cigarette smoking: A developmental analysis of influences', *British Journal of Developmental Psychology*, **7**, 179–89.

Morgan, M. and Grube, J. W. (1991) 'Closeness and peer group influence', *British Journal of Social Psychology*, **30**, 159–69.

Newcombe, R., Measham, F., and Parker, H. (1995) 'A survey of drinking and deviant behaviour among 14/15 year-olds in north-west England', *Addiction Research*, **2(4)**, 319–41.

OPCS (1993) *Population Trends.* London: HMSO.

Parker, H. and Measham, F. (1994) 'Pick 'n' mix: Changing patterns of illicit drug use amongst 1990s adolescents', *Drugs: Education, Prevention and Policy*, **1(1)**, 5–13.

Phelps, F., Mellanby, A. and Tripp, J. (1992) 'So you think you really understand sex?' *Education and Health*, **10(2)**, 27–31.

Plant, M. and Plant, M. (1992) *Risk-Takers: Alcohol, Drugs, Sex and Youth.* London: Routledge.

Plant, M., Peck, D. and Samuel, E. (1985) *Alcohol, Drugs and School Leavers*. London: Tavistock.

Plant, M., Bagnall, G., Foster, J. and Sales, J. (1990a) 'Young people and drinking: Results of an English national survey', *Alcohol and Alcoholism*, **25(6)**, 685–90.

Plant, M., Bagnall, G. and Foster, J. (1990b) 'Teenage heavy drinkers: Alcohol related knowledge, beliefs, experiences, motivation and the social context of drinking', *Alcohol and Alcoholism*, **25(6)**, 691–98.

Prendergast, S. (1992) *This is the time to grow up: Girls experiences of menstruation in schools*. London: Health Promotion Research Trust.

Presti, D. E., Ary, D. V. and Lichtenstein (1992) 'Context of smoking initiation and maintenance: Findings from interviews with youths', *Journal of Substance Abuse*, **4**, 35–45.

Reardon, K. K., Sussman, S. and Flay, B. R. (1989) 'Are we marketing the right message: Can kids "just say no" to smoking?' *Communication Monographs*, **56**, 307–24.

Royal College of Physicians (1992) *Smoking and the Young: A Report of a Working Party of the Royal College of Physicians*. London: RCOP.

Rundall, T. G. and Bruvold, W. H. (1988) 'A meta-analysis of school-based smoking and alcohol use prevention programs', *Health Education Quarterly*, **15(3)**, 317–34.

Sex Education Forum (1994) *Highlight No. 128: Sex Education*. London: National Children's Bureau.

Sharp, D. J. and Lowe, G. (1989) 'Adolescents and alcohol – A review of the recent British research', *Journal of Adolescence*, **12**, 295–307.

Sharp, D. J., Greer, J. and Lowe, G. (1988) *The 'normalisation' of under age drinking*. Paper presented at the Annual Conference of the British Psychological Society, April 1988.

Springhall, J. (1983) 'The origins of adolescence', *Youth and Policy*, **2**, 20–35.

Tappe, M. K. (1992) 'The model of personal investment: A theoretical approach for explaining and predicting adolescent health behaviour', *Health Education Research*, **7(2)**, 277–300.

Thomas, M., Holroyd, S. and Goddard, E. (1993) *Smoking Among Secondary School Children in 1992*. London: HMSO.

Walker, B. (1994) *No-one to talk with: Norfolk young people's conversations about sex - a basis for peer education*. Unpublished paper, University of East Anglia.

Warburton, D.M., Revell, A.D. and Thompson, D.H. (1991) 'Smokers of the future', *British Journal of Addiction*, **86**, 621–25.

Wellings, K., Field, J., Johnson, A. M. and Wadsworth, J. (1994) *National Survey of Sexual Attitudes and Lifestyles*. London: Penguin.

White, D. G., Phillips, K. C., Pitts, M., Clifford, B. R., Elliot, J. R., Davies, M. M. (1988) 'Adolescents' perceptions of AIDS', *Health Education Journal*, **47(4)**, 117–19.

Winn, S., Roker, D. and Coleman, J. C. (1995) 'Knowledge about puberty and sexual development in 11–16 year-olds: Implications for health and sex education in schools', *Educational Studies*, **21(2)**, 187–201.

WHO (1993) *Alcohol and HIV/AIDS*. Denmark: WHO Regional Office for Europe.

Woodcock, A. J., Stenner, K. and Ingham, R. (1992) 'Young people talking about HIV and AIDS: Interpretations of personal risk of infection', *Health Education Research*, **7(2)**, 229–47.

Wright, J. D. and Pearl, L. (1995) 'Knowledge and experience of young people regarding drug misuse, 1969-1994', *British Medical Journal*, **310**, 20–24.

Chapter Five

Meeting the needs of refugee children, their families and schools

Randa Price and Joyce Iszatt

When the time came to begin the task of writing this chapter, it was difficult to know how to start. Despite having read a wealth of material, and being practising educational psychologists, we experienced a pervading sense of still not knowing enough. This was later overtaken by concerns that the subject area was too broad and too complex.

These feelings of being both deskilled and overwhelmed are common to practitioners who work with refugees. Even very experienced teachers express a sense of hopelessness and uselessness when they approach us for support.

Recognition of these powerful dynamics help to re-establish professionalism. This highlighted for us the need to raise some of the particular difficulties and contradictions as well as the challenges and opportunities associated with this work from the outset.

When confronted with acute distress and pain, there is a tendency to protect ourselves through denial. This can lead to a frozen state of inactivity or propel us into inappropriate action which may be based on untested assumptions. The intense sense of dislocation and uncertainty which surrounds the refugee experience reverberates into professional networks and those involved can lose the capacity to think.

Professionals in Britain are faced with the very real problem that there is no proven theoretical base from which to apply their skills and little evidence about the impact of psychological practice in this area. However, work carried out with refugees by psychologists in other countries has enriched and expanded both understanding and practice.

A multi-cultural perspective, acknowledging and making difference explicit, and being able to tolerate 'not knowing' are intrinsic to work in this area. It highlights the need for reflective practice and working in partnership. In this chapter we will explore whether there are universal principles of good psychological practice or whether our practice needs to change in specific ways to meet the needs of children and their families from refugee communities.

We begin by looking at who refugees are. We then provide an overview of theoretical frameworks. An ecological model is described through which some aspects of child and adolescent development are applied to our understanding of the refugee experience. We outline implications for psychologists working in the field and an example of good practice is described. Finally, the unique role of the Educational Psychologist is explored using two case studies.

Who are refugees?

Movements in population have always taken place and are an integral part of human experience. Throughout history, each migrant group has made significant contributions to the host community. The term 'refugee' has been used in recent times to describe particular categories of migrants.

Definitions are social constructs and as such they are open to different interpretations. The United Nations' Convention defines a refugee as:

> a person who has fled from his or her own country, or is unable to return to it, owing to a well founded fear of being persecuted for reasons of race, religion, nationality, membership of a particular social group or particular political opinion.
>
> (UNHCR, 1993)

An 'asylum seeker is a refugee who has crossed an international border in search of safety' (Rutter, 1991). Although these definitions have been accepted by all the United Nations members, they are open to interpretation by each member state, and outcomes will depend on the host country's perception at any given time (Jones, 1993).

International borders following the world wars, the post-colonial era and more recently the collapse of the Eastern Bloc have both sharpened and altered perceptions of migration. Wars and armed conflict have increased over recent decades and evidence suggests that strategies aimed at terrorising and deliberately de-stabilising civilian populations have become more prevalent (Widgren, 1988; Vernez, 1991).

In 1993 the United Nations High Commission estimated that there are 18 million refugees worldwide and half are thought to be children. The majority, over 80%, seek refuge in neighbouring states. Comparatively very few reach Europe and the Americas (UNHCR, 1993).

Refugees in Britain

In 1994 the Refugee Council estimated that there are 23,500 refugee children living in Britain. 200–500 unaccompanied children are thought to enter the UK each year and approximately half will live in children's homes (Rutter, 1994).

Refugees do not form a homogeneous group and although the term is often equated with vulnerable and helpless victims, it is important to remember that refugees will have been very resourceful to have overcome the many obstacles, to have survived and reached the country of exile.

Refugee children in Britain come from a wide range of ethnic backgrounds with diverse cultural values and varying religious and ideological beliefs. Recent arrivals include Kurds from Iran and Turkey, Sri Lankan Tamils, Somalis and asylum seekers from former Yugoslavian states (Rutter, 1994).

Each child is an individual, and prior to arrival will have experienced different levels and forms of stress associated with the conflict and displacement. These will include dislocation and most likely multiple losses. Children arriving in Britain will have left behind friends, members of their family, their school, homes and personal possessions. They will be bereft of all the familiar ways of communicating and are likely to have lost a sense of belonging or purpose. One or more of the child's parents may be killed or missing. Some children may have been abused or tortured, or witnessed torture being carried out on loved ones. Others may have lived in a war zone and been subject to regular bombing. Some children may not have been in direct physical danger themselves but live in perpetual fear that their family or friends might be harmed (Flood, 1994).

The journey to the country of exile is likely to have been long and frightening. Refugees continue to experience difficulties throughout their stay in the host countries. The reception on arrival can be very traumatic. Families can be interrogated and detained for long periods and live through months or years of uncertainty about their legal status. Recent changes in the law have reduced entitlements and access to services. This means that families suffer practical problems such as lack of money, insecure housing and possibly difficulties obtaining medical services. Children and families will all suffer stresses associated with cultural transition and have to adjust to an essentially racist society. Unaccompanied children are particularly vulnerable (Ressler *et al.*, 1988).

Despite these numerous hurdles, there are protective factors. Many refugee children manage very well and do not come to the attention of Educational Psychologists, working in schools in Britain.

Research

There are a number of factors that need to be taken into account when interpreting relevant research findings. These involve both theoretical considerations and practical difficulties inherent in the work.

As stated in the previous section, the very term 'Refugee' is a social construct. Researchers from different traditions within the social sciences will be asking different questions and seeking to answer them in different ways.

Our practice as psychologists is rooted in a Eurocentric discipline and the application of psychology to different cultures needs to be viewed with caution. The comparison of studies informed by different research traditions and assessments across cultures is not always valid.

Carrying out studies in areas of conflict is problematic for a range of practical reasons. Population groups are unstable and there can be difficulties finding control groups. Absence of trust is likely to be a key obstacle to data collection. Refugees who have experienced considerable difficulties with authorities in both home and host countries may not feel comfortable about giving information about themselves to researchers, especially when the value of the work is not always apparent.

Richman (1993a) has drawn attention to a basic difficulty over some of the terms in current use. There is confusion in the literature about the meaning of 'trauma' and 'stress'. Both are used to describe the cause as well as the manifestation of the psychological affect. This suggests that stressors inevitably cause a traumatic reaction and ignores the active role played by refugees and their communities in rebuilding their lives.

Despite the many difficulties outlined above, there is a growing body of literature emanating from refugee communities actively engaged in rehabilitation, which can contribute to our understanding (Boothby, 1994; Frederick *et al.*,1991).

The studies referred to in this chapter should be viewed as explorations in an area of work where consensus does not yet exist because of the vastness of the field, the number of variables, the differences among the populations under study and the lack of cross-cultural measurements.

In the next section we describe theoretical frameworks which have informed research.

Theoretical frameworks

Initially the predominant theories put forward by front line professionals working with refugees were one dimensional and intrapsychic. The Post Traumatic Stress Disorder (PTSD) framework adopted by the American Psychiatric Association (1987) is an example of this approach.

Although some aspects of the PTSD paradigm can be useful, its narrow perspective provides an over-simplified view of the refugee experience (Richman, 1993b).

Recently a number of practitioners have incorporated key themes arising from their clinical practice into a broader theoretical framework. This involves respecting different world views, acknowledging the role politics plays in regulating the lives of citizens and professional practice and draws upon expertise that exists within the refugee community networks (Woodcock, 1995).

A multi-dimensional perspective relocates refugee experience within the universal continuum. Refugees share similar needs to all other groups, and they also encounter many of the difficulties experienced by previous migrant populations, e.g. urban blacks.

There have been attempts to generalise professional understanding informed by cross-cultural debates to psychological work with refugees. Korkin (1991) suggests that cross-cultural literature on child abuse and neglect can help us understand the extreme distress suffered by refugee children. Berry (1991) used a cross-cultural perspective to argue that the needs of refugee children could be better served through understanding the general phenomena of acculturation and psychological adaption.

However, it is important to acknowledge the unique factors associated with being a refugee: enforced dislocation, disconnection with previous life, fragmentation of communities and often incomprehensibly brutal experiences.

Child and adolescent development in the context of an ecological model

Research shows that the context in which children find themselves before and after a traumatic experience will influence the extent to which they can understand and integrate their life events (Ajdukovic and Ajdukovic, 1993; Aronowitz, 1984).

Models of child and adolescent psychology which embed children's emotional and social development within the interactive framework of the family, school, community and culture, can be useful in helping to explain some of the commonalities and wide differences in children's responses to stressors (Hicks *et al.*, 1993). Elbedour *et al.* (1993) has extended this multi-dimensional framework and developed an ecological model adapted from earlier research on child abuse.

This comprehensive and dynamic model serves as a useful theoretical base in which to locate the different levels of psychological interventions outlined in this chapter. Aspects of the interacting dimensions described by Elbedour are discussed below.

Developmental factors

A number of studies have investigated the impact of age and gender on a child's ability to adjust to difficult situations (Eisenbruch, 1988; Flood, 1994).

Studies focusing on age as a variable have drawn different conclusions, (Bowlby, 1969; Eth and Pynoos, 1985; Gleser *et al.*, 1981; Kinston and Rosser,

1974). However, it has been shown that pre-school children have a greater understanding of war and conflict than adults realise (Miljevic-Ridjicki and Lugomer-Armano, 1994). There is also some evidence to suggest that children cope better if they are given clear explanations of events that have occurred (Montgomery *et al.*, 1992).

Research comparing the effects of gender in coping skills suggests that girls demonstrate less vulnerability to stresses than boys (Elbedour *et al.*, 1993). However studies in this are too limited to draw definitive conclusions (Flood, 1994).

Factors within the family system

Attachment theory alongside other theories of child development places the child within the context of dynamic relationships (Bowlby, 1969; Erikson, 1950; Winnicott, 1960). Research in Croatia by Ajdukovic and Ajdukovic (1993), supports this approach and these studies corroborate findings from World War II where parents' ability to cope was found to have a powerful impact on the way children manage (Freud and Burlingham, 1942).

Mothers can act as a protective shield against the stresses of conflict and displacement (Hunter, 1988). Conversely, parents' fears can permeate through to their children in threatening situations (Bowlby, 1973).

Rohner's (1975) cross-cultural studies emphasise the universal importance of early secure attachments on the child's development. Where a child loses her ideal parent through death or separation, or because the parents themselves are distressed, the support provided through the extended family and community is even more crucial.

Factors within the community including the extended family and social support networks

For children and young adults settling into an essentially racist society, identification with role models from within the community provides important opportunities for the young person to practise future adult roles and achieve a positive identity. Where the family may be described as 'the first ring of security', the community acts as the 'outer ring of security' (Ressler *et al.*, 1988). Boothby (1994) argues that 'for uprooted children, strengthening and re-establishing primary relationships with parents, families, communities and, in some cases, their larger ethnic group . . . is a priority'.

Rutter (1994) outlines the breadth of work carried out by the refugee community organisations in Britain to enable refugees to regain control of their disrupted lives. The range of this long-term support is impressive given their limited resources. Supplementary schools and mother-tongue classes, play groups, cultural events which serve a healing function, advice sessions and newsletters are all part of a rich network of services offered by different organisations.

Research in kibbutz communities in Israel illustrates how community ethos helps the children to cope better (Ziv and Israeli, 1973). Such a proactive approach might be compared with that advocated by professionals involved in other areas of trauma work (Hodgekinson and Stewart, 1991).

The school context

Nurseries and schools play an important role in supporting refugee children (Rutter, 1994) and teachers are developing new and creative ways of working to meet refugee pupils' learning needs (Demetriades, 1995; Lodge, 1995).

Schools can offer pupils a normalising experience and sense of hope and purpose. They are helped to feel more secure through following the established routines maintained by understanding and sympathetic adults who respect the child's own culture and integrate their experiences into the curriculum.

When a group of Eritrean refugee children in Sweden were asked what they found helpful in school, they identified the following (Melzac and Warner, 1992):

1. Teachers who have made some adjustment to their teaching methods to accommodate the child's past experiences in a more formal education system.

2. Teachers who have clear and high expectations. (This probably reflects the children's past experience of how good teachers behave.)

3. Teachers who ask them about themselves.

4. Teachers who made an effort to include refugee children's experiences into the curriculum.

5. Teachers who take racism seriously.

6. Teachers who invite members of their community to school.

7. Teachers who attend special cultural events held by refugee communities.

Cultural and ideological factors

Studies carried out in Israeli and Palestinian occupied territories underline the importance of taking into account culture, ideology and religion as protective factors (Gibson, 1989; Punamaki, 1988). Gibson (1989) argues that the professionals working with refugees need to understand the political nature of the conflict. Said (1995) suggests that national identity and the strong belief that the struggle is just, is an essential part of the Palestinian refugee experience. Roberson (1992) discusses how women and girls of the West bank have been empowered by participating in the Palestinian uprisings, which has transformed their identities from victims to survivors.

Intensity and duration of war

Studies from Israel and Northern Ireland suggest that children can become habituated to conflicts that are low intensity and ongoing (Elbedour *et al.*, 1993). Some children can learn how to accept and cope with situations that may predispose others to stress and trauma. In some instances apparent 'denial' of danger may be perceived as protective. In other circumstances it may be perceived as pathological. In situations where children are supported by adults who share protective ideological beliefs, stressors can be understood and dealt with more effectively.

Risk factors and emotional responses

As outlined above, there is a wealth of research which supports the notion that refugee family and community networks find creative and effective ways of coping, often drawing on their religious and ideological belief system to help them and their children make sense of their experiences. Indeed, when asked at a conference in 1994, refugee participants associated the terms 'hope', 'resourcefulness', 'achievement' and 'strength', with the refugee experience, alongside their feelings of pain and sorrow. However, there are some particular risk factors which can affect children and young people. These include loss of parents or key family members, separation from family, loss of physical capacity and direct exposure to violence (Melzak, 1994).

All refugees will have suffered enormous losses and will need opportunities to mourn and grieve. This is an important part of the natural healing process, enabling the child to come to terms with and integrate difficult and distressing experiences. It involves feeling and expressing a range of emotions, including sadness, guilt and fear. The first stage of this process involves acceptance which can be very hard to achieve if surrounded by uncertainty, as in the case where a child does not know a parent's whereabouts or whether or not she or he is dead. Children who have lost their ideal reliable adult or whose parents have changed in some way because of their own experiences, may become prematurely independent or regress. They are likely to feel angry and abandoned and may blame themselves.

Typically, young children who are very egocentric will think that they are responsible for the hurt and damage. They can become very frightened of the power they suppose that they wield and feel guilty (Melzak, 1992). Adolescents who are in the process of developing their own identities may suffer particular difficulties (Jupp and Luckey, 1989). Dislocation and disorientation related to cultural transition, and bullying and racism, may be even more traumatic than the young person's war experience (UNHCR, 1993).

Children who witness killings and atrocities are often profoundly traumatised, especially if that person is a loved one, as are those who are directly exposed to violence, abused or tortured themselves (Richman, 1993b). These children lose their innocence and belief in the world as a safe place. They may feel blamed, intensely guilty and ashamed. It is extremely hard to integrate painful and distressing experiences such as these. Some children will try to block them out. They may withdraw and have problems concentrating.

Some children may be agitated and suffer mood swings. Other behaviours that may be expressed include depression, sleeping difficulties, enuresis, eating disorders, somatic problems, or they may act out their distress and exhibit aggressive or violent behaviour. Some children show symptoms of Post Traumatic Stress Disorder which may include intrusive thoughts, flashbacks, panic attacks and nightmares.

Children in distress need opportunities to express themselves but will find this difficult in an unfamiliar language and setting. Some children may find drawing or painting a helpful way to communicate their thoughts. Although the school will need to establish links with child and adolescent health services, referral to clinics may not be practical or appropriate. Teachers are not and should not be therapists but they will have a special role in helping children assimilate their experiences. What children tell us, however, depends largely upon what we are prepared to hear (Garbarino and Stott, 1989). For teachers and other professionals it is often very difficult to hear, listen to or even acknowledge distress. The pain and despair of children who have lost a great deal can awaken pain and despair within adults. To support their pupils, teachers will require support themselves.

Sometimes a child's difficulties may pre-date the refugee experience and it will take longer to disentangle the various factors. Some children may be malnourished, have health problems or learning difficulties.

Unaccompanied children

Unaccompanied children are especially vulnerable. If the child or young person does not know the whereabouts of their parents they will be extremely anxious and need to be kept informed about whether or not their parents or family are safe. Research findings indicate that the impact on the child will depend on the family's separation from the child's perception, and the child's developmental stage (Ressler, 1988).

The younger the child the more quickly the loss is experienced as permanent and the more readily new and important attachments can be made with other significant adults. Placements within the extended family or community networks are preferable and access to their cultural milieu is important.

Although younger children may be placed successfully in a new family, studies suggest that adolescents may manage better if placed together in a group. In any event, the young person should be consulted and participate in the decision making (Melzak, 1994).

Where children have established new relationships with other significant adults and later returned to estranged families, follow-up work has been recommended.

Implications for psychologists' practice

The findings outlined in the previous sections have implications for psychologists engaged in understanding the needs of children from refugee communities and planning interventions. The following points need to be considered:

1. The importance of supporting the family and engaging them in our work.

2. The development of whole school approaches.

3. Using the community as a resource.

4. Taking into account the beliefs of the family and community in intervention programmes.

5. Multi-agency co-operation.

6. The importance of identifying support systems for workers in the area.

The following section cites an example of good practice which incorporates the above.

An example of good practice

This example demonstrates how innovative psychological practice applied in the context of partnership with other professionals and agencies can contribute to a whole-school approach. Not only does this style of work enable refugee pupils to be supported at a range of levels throughout a school system, but it has also provided the impetus for the development of new models of multi-professional and multi-agency work.

Hampstead School is an inner-city comprehensive. Over 60% of the children are bilingual and 87 languages are spoken. A multi-cultural approach which celebrates diversity has been developed over the years.

Five years ago a refugee pupil collapsed in the school playground. She was hospitalised, but soon discharged as there was nothing wrong medically. She continued to have black-outs. Staff were at loss about what to do and eventually she dropped out of school. This incident highlighted the inadequacy of the various support systems. It brought to a head the teachers' anxieties about how to meet refugee pupils' needs in school and prompted them into action.

M. Fox, Consultant Child Psychologist at the Tavistock Clinic, responded to a request for support from school by setting up a series of awareness raising sessions with groups of teachers and offered regular consultations to key members of staff. This intervention enabled staff to draw on their professional expertise to think and plan constructively. Following on from this, teachers requested in-service training. This involved all the staff, the governors, school inspector and members of the LEA and the Borough's refugee co-ordinator. Other agencies included the Tavistock Clinic, the Institute of Education and the Refugee Council. Members of the local communities were invited and a professional from the Somalian community addressed the audience. Guidelines and a range of strategies were formulated and whole-school approaches were implemented to support the school's 139 refugee pupils. This included actively encouraging parental involvement.

An induction programme was established and a refugee co-ordinator appointed. A group of sixth formers and staff jointly organised a support network in school which is ongoing. Out of this initiative and led by pupils' enthusiasm, the charity 'Children of the Storm' evolved, which focuses on providing practical support to refugee children and young people (Children of the Storm, 1994). Staff and pupils have shared their experiences with other schools and at conferences to raise the profile of the needs of refugees and to encourage more initiatives.

From the outset, Hampstead School has emphasised the importance of working in partnership. By establishing links within the community networks and Borough support agencies, a co-ordinated approach has gradually developed which benefits all pupils. Developments have included new ways of liaising between agencies and Borough-wide initiatives have evolved in tandem.

A 2-year project funded by section 11 money has enabled the LEA refugee service to employ specialist teachers with community links and an Educational Social Worker. Part of the whole-school approach has been to examine the ways in which English as a Second Language support can be targeted effectively to meet the needs of all bilingual learners (Jennings and Kerslake, 1994).

Alongside these developments, core members of staff have received support through regular consultations from the Tavistock Clinic (Fox, 1995). Pupils who are experiencing particular difficulties are offered individual or group support, either in school or at the Clinic, as appropriate.

As work has progressed it has become increasingly apparent that those working with refugee pupils, no matter how experienced, need to have their own support systems. In being available to refugee pupils who have been traumatised, the worker is also exposed to the pain and trauma the pupil has been through. Workers need their own opportunities to think, reflect on its impact and to give it meaning so that they can help the pupil do the same.

The professionals from the Tavistock include child psychologists, psychiatrists and psychotherapists. All attend a regular workshop, which provides mutual support and offers opportunities to consider critically the work carried out. The close links between the Clinic, school and other agencies means that this support is delivered in the context of a multi-professional and co-ordinated framework through which new models of work can be developed.

The unique role of the educational psychologist

The ecological model described earlier on in the chapter would seem to advocate that professionals approach their work in a holistic way. Educational psychologists who work at the interface of home and school and in partnership with other agencies are ideally placed to do this. The following case studies are examples of multi-level psychological interventions.

Case study 1: Work with home and school to support an individual child

The Educational Psychologist (EP) in this example draws on clinical practice within the context of a joint school and family systems approach (Dowling and Pound, 1994). This case also exemplifies the crucial role of professional support in this work.

Patrice, an Angolan boy of 8 years, recently arrived from Zaire to rejoin his family in London. He had been left behind in his uncle's care while his mother and two older sisters escaped to Britain. His father had been killed in combat. Patrice was referred to the EP because of aggressive behaviour towards other children. He seemed cut off and repeatedly drew pictures of violent scenes. His teachers felt frustrated with his mother who did not seem to understand their concerns.

Patrice was a fluent French speaker and although the EP talked with him in French during the assessment, he said nothing. However he did communicate his distress to her though frightening pictures of people getting hurt.

When the EP met with Patrice's mother she explained that Patrice and his uncle had been tortured in Zaire. Although Patrice had wanted to talk about this she found it too painful to listen. Her daughters felt this was too much for her and the family decided that Patrice needed to put the past behind him and prepare himself for a new life in England.

The EP met Patrice weekly in school for 8 weeks. Very gradually he began to find words to explain his pictures and share some of the 'unspeakable' events that had happened to him.

During this time the EP visited the family at home. Patrice's mother told her about her extreme, deep sense of guilt and shame about having left Patrice behind in Zaire, unprotected. The EP consulted to Patrice's teachers who were able to express their own overwhelming sense of outrage and hopelessness.

After several months, at the EP's suggestion, Patrice's family decided that they would like to meet his teachers to think together how to help him and monthly reviews were set up.

By the end of a year, Patrice was able to tell his story to his teachers and family who were now able to bear to hear his account in a supportive and accepting way.

By bearing testimony to Patrice's pain and suffering, his extreme experiences were validated. At the same time seeing his teacher and family working together, helped him begin the long journey of regaining some trust in the adult world.

To enable the EP to manage the powerful feelings evoked and maintain her professional stance, regular support from colleagues was essential, throughout the intervention.

Case Study 2: Working in Partnership

This case study highlights how good EP practice in relation to an individual child can bring about change at a whole-school level and contribute to the development of new methods of service delivery.

Mia, a 15-year-old girl from Sri Lanka was temporarily housed with her disabled parents in an outer London Borough. Other members of her family were either left in Sri Lanka or had fled to Canada.

Mia was profoundly deaf and had never used hearing aids. She had not attended any school prior to her arrival in England 1 year ago.

Because of the unique nature of Mia's special educational needs and the difficulties in finding an appropriate school willing to work with her at this stage of her school career, she was placed in a school for students with severe learning difficulties. It was acknowledged by all the professionals, including her EP, that this was inappropriate.

When the EP became aware that Mia and her family were being transferred into a neighbouring borough, he contacted the Educational Psychology Service to alert them of her arrival. Both the current EP and the prospective EP visited the family home together with an interpreter. This helped the family establish a link between their current and future experience of the education system, at a time of great upheaval. Communication in the family's home language also enhanced their sense of connectedness.

Assessment within the home context, with parental contributions enabled the EPs to gain an understanding both of Mia's experience, her abilities and potential. This clarified that her learning difficulties were secondary to her social and communication needs and transfer to a school for the hearing impaired was recommended.

The newly allocated EP was able to request adjustments to specialist provision, proactively. In consultation with the specialist EP for the hearing impaired, she provided consultations to the school prior to Mia's entry, which helped the teachers overcome their initial reservations and to draw on their own expertise. Monthly consultations continued after Mia joined the school which have supported staff in their development of innovative practice which later became incorporated into a whole-school approach. Liaison with the interpreter who was linked into the Tamil community helped the family to receive practical support.

Conclusion

Working with children and families from refugee communities offers psychologists a unique opportunity to examine their practice and to question established beliefs about the nature of psychological work.

Throughout the chapter, we have attempted to outline some of the implications for EPs engaged in understanding the needs of children from refugee communities and planning suitable interventions. The following points deserve careful consideration:

- Good practice can be time consuming.
- Psychologists need to be proactive.
- The importance of early interventions.
- The need for integrated psychological/educational approaches.
- The networking role of an EP.
- The importance of developing and integrating current good practice, e.g. bilingual and anti-racist work, good home/school liaison, establishing links with community organisations and working with professionals based in the refugee communities.
- EPs need to identify their professional development needs to help them expand facets of their work, e.g. clinical practice and work at a systems level.
- The need to provide ongoing forums for professional support.

These are universal features of good practice.

References

Ajdukovic, M. and Ajdukovic, D. (1993) 'Psychological well-being of refugee children', *Child Abuse and Neglect*, **17(6)**, 843–54.

American Psychiatric Association (APA) (1987) *Diagnostic and Statistical Manual of Mental Disorders* (3rd edn.) Washington, DC: American Psychiatric Association.

Aronowitz, M. (1984) 'The social and emotional adjustment of immigrant children: A review of the literature', *International Migration Review*, **18(2)**, 237–57.

Berry, J. W. (1991) 'Refugee adaptation in settlement countries: an overview with an emphasis on primary prevention'. In Frederick, L., Ahearn, Jr. and Jean, L. (eds). *Theory, Research and Services. The John Hopkins Series in Contemporary Medicine and Public Health.* Baltimore MD: John Hopkins University Press.

Boothby, N. (1994) 'Trauma and violence among refugee children'. In Marsella, J., Bornemann, T., Edblad, S. and Orley, J. (eds) *Amidst Peril and Pain: The Mental Health and Well-being of the World's Refugees.* Washington DC: American Psychological Association.

Bowlby, J. (1969) *Attachment and Loss* (Vols 1 and 2). New York: Basic Books.

Bowlby, J. (1973) *Separation Anxiety and Anger* (Vol.3). New York: Basic Books.

Children of the Storm (1994) *Children of the Storm* (charity launch paper). London.

Demetriades, A. (1995) 'Working with refugee children in schools', *Young Minds Newsletter*, **20**, 11.

Dowling, J. and Pound, A. (1994) 'Joint interventions with teachers, children and parents in the school setting', In Dowling, E. and Osborne, E. (eds) *The Family and the School: A Joint Systems Approach to Problems With Children.* (2nd edn.) London: Routledge.

Eisenbruch, M. (1988) 'The mental health of refugee children and their cultural development', *Migration Reviews*, **22(2)**, 282–300.

Elbedour, S., ten Besel, R. and Bastien, D. (1993) 'Ecological integrated model of children of war: Individual and Social Psychology'. In *Child Abuse and Neglect*, Vol. 17 *The Family and the School: A Joint Systems Approach to Problems.* Oxford: Pergamon Press, pp.805–19.

Erikson, E. (1950) *Childhood and Society.* New York: Norton.

Eth, S. and Pynoos, R. (eds) (1985) *Post-traumatic Stress Disorder in Children.* Washington, DC: American Psychiatric Press.

Flood, S. (1994) *War and Refugee Children: The Effect of War on Child Mental Health.* Young Minds Report, October.

Fox, M. (1995) 'Working with refugee children in school'. In Trowell, J. and Bower, M. (eds). *Emotional Needs of Young Children and Their Families.* London: Routledge. (in press).

Frederick, L., Ahearn, Jr. and Jean, L. (eds) (1991) *Refugee Children: Theory, Research and Services.* The Johns Hopkins series on contemporary medicine and public health. Baltimore, MD: Johns Hopkins University Press.

Freud, A. and Burlingham, D. (1942) *Young Children in Wartime.* London: Allen & Unwin.

Garbarino, J. and Stott, F. (1989) *What Children Can Tell us.* San Francisco: Jossey-Bass.

Gibson, K. (1989) 'Children in political violence', *Social Science and Medicine*, **28**, 659–67.

Gleser, G., Green, B. and Wright, C. (1981) *Prolonged Psychological Effects of Disaster.* Toronto, Canada: Academic Press.

Hicks, R., Lalonde, R. and Pepler, D. (1993) 'Psychological considerations in the mental health of immigrant and refugee children special issue: Cultural diversity: Voice, access and involvement', *Canadian Journal of Community Mental Health*, **12(2)**, 71–78.

Hodgekinson, P.E. and Stewart, M. (eds) (1991) *Coping with Catastrophe – A Handbook of Disaster Management.* London: Routledge.

Hunter, E.J. (1988) 'Long term effects of parental wartime captivity on children: Children of PoW. and MIA servicemen', *Journal of Contemporary Psychotherapy*, **18(4)**, 312–28.

Jennings, C. and Kerslake, H. (1994) 'Children in transition: Work with bilingual learners many of whom are refugees – shaping the learning environment', *Educational Psychology in Practice*, **10(3)**, 164–73.

Jones, C. (1993) 'Refugee children in English urban school', *European Journal of Intercultural Studies*, **3(2/3)**, 29–39.

Jupp, J. J. and Luckey, J. (1989) 'Educational experiences in Australia of Indo-Chinese adolescent refugees', *International Journal of Mental Health*, **18(4)**, 78–91.

Kinston, S. and Rosser, R. (1974) 'Disaster: Effects on mental and physical state', *Journal of Psychosomatic Research*, **18**, 437–56.

Korkin, J.E. (1991) 'Child maltreatment and the study of child refugees'. In Frederick, L., Ahearn, Jr. and Jean, L. (eds) *Theory, Research and Services.* The Johns Hopkins series in contemporary medicine and public health. Baltimore, MD: Johns Hopkins University Press.

Lodge, C. (1995) 'Working with refugee children in schools', *Young Minds Newsletter*, **20**, 11.

Melzak, S. (1994) *You Can't See Your Reflection When The Water is Always Full of Soap Suds.* London: Medical Foundation for the care of Victims of Torture.

Melzak, S. and Warner, R. (1992) *Integrating Refugee Children into Schools.* Minority Rights Group.

Miljevic-Ridjicki, R. and Lugomer-Armano, G. (1994) 'Children's comprehension of war', *Child Abuse Review*, **3(2)**, 134–44.

Montgomery, E., Krogh, Y., Jacobson, A. and Luckman, B. (1992) 'Children of torture victims: Reactions and coping', *Child Abuse and Neglect*, **16(6)**, 797–805.

Punamaki, R. (1988) 'Historical, political and individualistic determinants of coping models and fears among Palestinian children', *International Journal of Psychology*, **23(6)**, 721–39.

Ressler, M., Boothby, N. and Steinbock, D. (1988) *Unaccompanied Children: Care and Protection in Wars, Natural Disasters and Main Population Movements.* New York: Oxford University Press.

Richman, N. (1993a) 'Children in situations of political violence', *Journal of Child Psychology and Psychiatry*, **34(8)**, 1286–1302.

Richman, N. (1993b) *Communicating With Children.* London: Save the Children.

Roberson, M.K. (1992) 'Birth, transformation and the death of a refugee identity. Women and girls of the

Interfada', *Women and Therapy Special Issue: Refugee Women and their mental health: Shattered Societies, Shattered Lives*, **13(1–2)**, 35–52.

Rohner, R. (1975) *They Love Me, They Love Me Not: A World-Wide Study of the Affects of Parental Acceptance and Rejection*. New Haven, CT: HRAF Press.

Rutter, J. (1991) *Refugees: We Left Because we Had to*. London: The Refugee Council.

Rutter, J. (1994) *Refugee Children in the Classroom*. Stoke-on-Trent: Trentham Books.

Said, E. (1995) *Culture and Identity*. Talk presented to the American University in Beirut Alumini, London.

UNHCR (United Nations High Commission on Refugees) (1993) *The State of the World's Refugees*. Harmondsworth: Penguin.

Vernez, G. (1991) 'Current global refugee situations and international public policy', *American Psychologist*, **46**, 631–32.

Widgren, J. (1988) 'The uprooted within a global context'. In Miserez, D. (ed.) *Refugees: The Trauma of Exile*. Dordrecht: Martinus Nijhoff.

Winnicott, D. W. (1960) 'The theory of the parent/infant relationship', *International Journal of Psychoanalysis*, **41**, 585–95.

Woodcock, J. (1995) 'Family therapy with refugees and political exiles'. In Gorrell Barnes, G. (ed.) *Context: Ethnicity, Culture, Race and Family Therapy*. Canterbury: AFT Publishing, pp.25–28.

Ziv, A. and Israeli, R. (1973) 'Effects of bombardment on the manifest anxiety level of children living in Kibbutzim', *Journal of Consulting and Clinical Psychology*, **40**, 28–91.

Chapter Six

Media influences and young people

Alan Labram

Introduction and Rationale

Violence and the media are big business not only for those directly involved but for a whole coterie of professionals and lay people. There has been intense public debate within the UK and beyond concerning the amount of media violence to which individuals are exposed. Naturally enough, much concern has been expressed about the issue of children and young people and their reactions to these images. The debate has been fuelled by a number factors. Within the UK a number of crimes of violence, with children as the perpetrators, including murder, have had a high public profile. In some of these cases there has been the suggestion that those responsible for the crimes were influenced by what they had seen on the screen.

The increasing availability of screen images via satellite, cable, video, computer games and over the Internet have enabled these media to take their place alongside the existing TV and cinema outlets. While these last two have been subject to regulation and censorship, such devices may be inappropriate, unworkable and indeed impossible when it comes to the more recent technologies.

Two questions are crucial. The first is whether exposure to violent images influences the rate of actual violence. The second is, does it matter? These fundamental questions raise others, not the least of which is whether there is a thing that can be identified as 'violence in the media'. Perhaps the second of these two main questions, whether the issue is important, is easier to answer. The British Crime Survey of 1992 shows that there were half a million significant incidents of domestic violence during the year. Furthermore, 80% of the victims were women. If only a small percentage of such incidents where there is no obvious pecuniary motive, were exacerbated by exposure to screen violence, the issue would be a significant one and worthy of serious debate and research. Yet although the issue appears to be a crucial one, actual surveys of public opinion have produced equivocal results. Typically about 60% of adults interviewed agree that there is too much violence on TV (for example) but lack agreement about which actual programmes they are referring to (Cumberbatch, 1991).

Within this chapter the intention is to highlight some of the psychological hypotheses concerning the effects of the media, then to report some research, particularly that of recent origin. Finally an indication of any conclusions and recommendations for action will be considered.

Psychological theory

Within the psychological literature there have been several attempts to generate hypotheses to explain the research findings. Perhaps the best known of these is social learning theory based largely on the work of Bandura (1973). He investigated the influence of filmed models on the behaviour of children. In these experiments, children watched a film of a model acting violently towards a 'Bobo' doll which is a large plastic knockdown clown that bounces back up again due to its weighted base. Unsurprisingly, the children subsequently behaved in similar fashion towards the doll when observed through a one-way screen. One key feature of the experiment was that between watching the aggressive model on film and being led into the room containing the doll, the children were 'frustrated' by being shown some attractive toys with which they were not allowed to play.

While there has been little argument that children can and do learn by 'observational' or 'social' learning, the ecological validity of these laboratory studies has been called into question. As Cumberbatch comments:

> children do not typically imitate all that they see or even attempt to do so. There is a quite fundamental discrepancy between the high incidence of imitation in Bandura's results and what children typically do after watching television.
>
> (Cumberbatch, 1989:35)

Another obvious observation on the children's behaviour towards the doll is that there is little else that can be done with it apart from knock it down.

Another possible explanation for the effects of screen violence is that of arousal. If television programmes or video games are generally arousing, it could be that the non-specific but aroused emotional effect increases the likelihood of participants in the studies displaying those behaviours that were most recently observed or experienced. This explanation has its origins in the work of Schacter (1964) who found that people in a state of generalised arousal could be subsequently manipulated into a variety of emotional states dependent on surrounding contextual cues.

While much of the research reported later in this chapter shows positive correlations between on-screen portrayals of violence and subsequent behaviour, in every experiment there are individuals who are not adversely affected by the screen images. There appear to be some people who are influenced by what they see and others who are not. Although not an articulated theory as such, the idea that some individuals are more susceptible than others has face validity.

A recent commentary by Ryder (1993) suggests that violence portrayed in the media is a contributory factor to violence in real life but only as part of an overall culture of machismo. He argues that although it may seem surprising that violence could be attributed to culture, violent acts committed particularly by young people are often induced by the norms of their social group:

> In some delinquent subcultures members may feel compelled to conform to the orthodoxy that manhood can only be demonstrated by being anti-social, criminal or violent.
>
> (Ryder, 1993:712)

Despite these possible explanations, some psychological explanations of the effects of violence on behaviour have suggested that viewing such images may actually decrease the likelihood of subsequent aggression. This theory is rooted in psychoanalysis. It suggests that violence in screen images is cathartic. As such it allows people to assuage feelings of violence towards others via fantasy and provides a harmless release.

Early indicators of anti-social behaviour

The effects of environment on behaviour are well documented, e.g. Bronfenbrenner (1979). Variables that particularly affect the behaviour of children and young people including parenting styles, living conditions, and employment within the family are some of those that also affect social behaviour. Some of these environmental factors have been implicated in the development of anti-social and criminal behaviour in a number of research studies. Among recent and ongoing longitudinal studies that have attempted to chart the development of offending and anti-social behaviour, the Cambridge Study in Delinquent Development is one of the most comprehensive in the UK (Farrington, 1995). A sample of more than 400 males from London have been followed up over a period of some thirty plus years. A major aim of the survey is to measure as many factors as possible that are alleged to be causes or correlates of offending. Although a detailed analysis of the findings to date is beyond the scope of this chapter, a number of the key features will be summarised.

The original aim of the study was to describe the development of anti-social behaviour, including delinquency and criminal activity in a substantial group of males from an inner city area. By means of detailed recording of personal histories over time, it was hoped to be able to identify those factors that appeared to correlate with and possibly influence subsequent anti-social, delinquent and criminal behaviour. The study was not intended to test any particular theory of development. The sample population were aged at the outset (1961 and 1962) between 8 and 9 years of age. They all came from mainstream and special schools in south London. The boys were interviewed and tested at ages 8–9, 10–11, 14–15, and after leaving school at 16, 18, and 32 years. Sub-groups were interviewed at the ages of 21 and 25. Thus eight face-to-face interviews have been conducted with the sample over a period of 24 years, with a very low attrition rate. At the age of 32 years the sample consisted of 94% of the original.

Up to the age of 32, it was found that more than one third of the sample had been convicted of criminal offences. The prevalence of offending increased up to the age of 17 and then decreased. Delinquency, however, was shown to be only one element of a much larger assemblage of anti-social behaviour. At the ages of 8–9 years, the subsequent convicted delinquents could be differentiated from the non-delinquents in many respects. They were more likely to have been described as troublesome and dishonest in their primary schools. They tended to be from larger and poorer families. Their housing was often poor and they were more likely to have been physically neglected by their parents and known to the social agencies.

As a result of the findings of this longitudinal study, the authors have attempted to arrive at a set of indicators or predictors of later delinquency. They distinguish six categories of factors identifiable at ages 8–10 years that they argue are the most important predictors of later delinquency:

1. Troublesomeness at school including dishonesty and aggression. Boys who became delinquent also often attended secondary schools from the age of 11 years that had high rates of delinquency.

2. Hyperactivity – impulsivity – attention deficit.

3. Low measured intelligence and poor school attainment.

4. A history of criminality in the family.

5. Family poverty and poor housing.

6. Poor parental supervision and harsh, authoritarian discipline.

An important finding of the study was that there was significant continuity between childhood aggression and adult violence (Farrington, 1989, 1991). Boys who were aggressive in childhood or adolescence tended to be more deviant in adulthood, and committed more offences, including violence. It can be argued therefore that any factors in childhood and later adolescence that tend to increase the likelihood of violence and aggression may have long-lasting and profound effects for both individuals and society.

Evidence on the influence of television

Three key issues

As a means of mass communication TV is hard to better in terms of its intimacy, immediacy and availability in the home. For many decades there has been a great deal of both public and academic debate about the possible effects of exposure to TV programmes on the viewer. Professional groups such as social workers have also voiced concerns about possible influences on their client groups (Lazar, 1994). These worries appear to break down into three main areas, according to Gunter and Wober (1988).

The first is whether there is too much violence on TV. A rider to this concern is that there is a trend towards increasing violence (Cumberbatch, 1991). This clearly begs the question as to exactly what constitutes violence. As Gunter and Wober (1988) point out, hard data appears to vary according to the method of collection. Surveys have found that 60% of people agreed with statements such as 'There is too much violence in TV entertainment shows'. However, surveys without prompt type questions, asking respondents to name areas of concern on TV, show violence as much less of a concern. Furthermore, these authors showed that of those members of the UK public who reported being offended by something they had seen on TV, the percentage who cited violence remained steady over the years 1975 to 1987.

The definition of what constitutes violence and additionally what specifically might be a potential negative influence on the viewer is less than clear. Researchers have often taken the position of defining their terms at the outset of their research. This example comes from Wiegman *et al.* (1992):

> We define aggression as an act in which a person harms or injures another person (or persons) such that the actor knows beforehand that his/her behaviour will result in negative consequences for the other person(s).

Since the research has often looked at the converse of this behaviour, termed prosocial behaviour, a definition of this from the same authors may help:

> We define prosocial behaviour as an act in which a person supports or helps another person (or persons) such that the actor knows beforehand that his/her behaviour will result in positive consequences for the other person(s).

Much of the academic research has however eschewed the term 'violence' in favour of 'aggression'. Even this approach has had its limitations since studies have frequently used aggression to refer to physical behaviour only (Huesmann and Eron, 1986). Part of the difficulty has been the ethical problem of using violent material with subjects. This has not prevented a substantial amount of research using material commonly available on the TV screen, which has been judged violent for the purposes of the research. To quote from Gunter and Wober (1988):

We may all have some idea in our heads of what we mean by violence, but the truth of the matter is that what one person sees as violent may not be seen in the same way by someone else.

Furthermore, research evidence has emerged which shows that viewers' sensitivities to apparent violence may be highly discriminating (Gunter, 1985).

The second issue is whether TV violence causes or encourages actual social violence. Many newspaper and magazine articles convey the idea that this link is well established. A number of individual examples of fact following fiction appear to confirm this relationship. There also seems to be an element of common sense appeal to the notion that if TV influences the viewer (and if it does not why are advertisers wasting all that money?), then prolonged exposure to violence is not without its consequences.

The third issue is what do people, i.e. the public at large, think about TV violence?

The relationship between televised violence and young people's behaviour

Concerns have primarily centred on possible effects on children's and young people's behaviour by programmes showing violent and aggressive images. One of the earliest and most influential studies was that conducted by Eron *et al*. (1972). Theirs was a longitudinal study spanning 10 years. They had originally gathered information on a sample of children aged around 9 years. Two pieces of information constituted an aggression score based on peer ratings and a measure of preferences for violent TV, via an interview with the child's mother. Ten years later, a peer–rated aggression score and a 'preference for violent television' score were obtained, the latter via a face-to-face interview with the subjects. Their results showed a significant positive correlation between boys' preferences for violent TV programmes at age 8–9 years and their peer rated aggression 10 years later.

The authors concluded in unequivocal fashion:

> The above results indicate that television habits established by age 8–9 years influence boys' aggressive behaviour at that time and at least through late adolescence.
>
> (Eron *et al.*, 1972)

While much criticism was levelled at this research, principally because the authors had found a correlational relationship but asserted a causal one, they nevertheless persisted with their initial conclusion that early exposure to TV violence has a causal influence on aggression in males.

These authors became instrumental in initiating a cross-national study to investigate the effect of the viewing of violence of TV drama programmes. This longitudinal study over a period of 3 years reported equivocal results. In The Netherlands, for example, Wiegman *et al*. (1992) found a significant positive relationship between aggressive behaviour and viewing of violence on TV.

However, when the influence of the starting level of violence in subjects was statistically controlled for, their results gave no support for the hypothesis that viewing TV violence will in the long term contribute to a higher level of aggression in children.

Many studies have shown that after watching TV programmes containing aggressive and violent images, children's subsequent behaviour is affected. Sometimes this effect has apparently been to desensitise the subjects to subsequent violence. An experimental study by Molitor and Hirsch (1994) reported increased tolerance of aggression in others after watching an aggressive programme. Children were shown a condensed version of either a karate film or Olympic competition scenes. They were then asked to report on the behaviour of two other children via a TV monitor. The two children on the monitor subsequently became violent towards each other. Results confirmed those of an earlier study that the children who had watched the karate programme took significantly longer to summon help than did the group who had watched the sport. The authors explain the results in terms of the subjects becoming desensitised to real-life aggression, at least in the short term, by the violent images on the screen.

Research has also shown that for children the violent images that they watch do not have to be realistic to have an effect. Sanson and di Muccio (1993) investigated the effect of watching aggressive cartoons on the play of pre-school children as compared with those watching neutral cartoons. They found in their sample of children aged between 36 and 61 months that when playing with potentially aggressive toys those children who had watched the aggressive cartoon displayed significantly higher levels of aggression in their play than did the groups who had watched the neutral cartoon or none at all. They also found an opposite trend for pro-social behaviour.

Comstock and Srasburger (1990) examined the literature on possible effects of TV violence on teenage behaviour. The reviewed studies gave empirical support to the hypothesis that exposure to TV violence increases the likelihood of subsequent aggressive or anti-social behaviour in children and adolescents. They concluded that the evidence is overwhelmingly indicative of a link between TV violence and aggressive behaviour. Paik and Comstock (1994) conducted a meta-analysis of more than 200 studies relating to the effects of TV violence and aggressive behaviour. They separated studies by several factors including research design, treatment variables and subsequent behaviour and then analysed the effects. They found a positive and significant correlation between TV violence and aggressive behaviour although different studies showed this to different degrees. The authors also found that erotica emerged as a strong factor, even when not accompanied by portrayals of violence.

A recent UK survey of the viewing habits of children and young people was carried out as part of an enquiry by Hagell and Newburn (1994). Although the main thrust of their research was to investigate the viewing habits and preferences of young offenders, to make comparisons a sample of 538 schoolchildren was also surveyed. They were aged between 12 and 18 years at the time of the survey and came from 60 different schools. Data was gathered by means of an anonymous school questionnaire that was a short, self-administered booklet, designed to be completed by the subjects without additional instruction from teachers. Questions relating to TV viewing habits included items such as:

'How many television sets do you have in your house?'
'Do you have a television set in your bedroom?'
'Which channels can you get via cable/satellite?'

Other items examined the times of the day when the subjects usually watched and the average amount of time spent viewing during different days of the week. Some attempt was made to analyse the types of programmes watched by asking about favourite programmes, and people on TV.

Results of the survey confirmed the self-evident fact that TV is widely available to young people and they spend a great deal of time watching it. Only 3% of the schoolchildren reported having only one TV set in their household and nearly 50% reported having more than three. More than three-quarters (78%) of the school-children had a TV set in their bedroom. This figure shows an increase over the 48% reported in an earlier survey by Gunter *et al.* (1991) possibly due to a trend of increasing access or differences in the sample populations. Between 20% and 30% of the children had access to cable and satellite TV stations.

Schoolchildren were asked to estimate how many hours of TV they watched during an average weekday and on Saturdays and Sundays. Most of the children (52.5%) watched less than 4 hours per weekday although this left 47.5% who watched at least 4 hours. Only 1.5% of the children watched no TV during weekdays. These viewing figures increased dramatically for Saturdays (61% watching at least 4 hours) but reduced again on Sundays (45% watching 4 hours or more).

More detailed information was derived from questioning about specific times of the day when TV was watched. Many children watched TV after the 9 p.m. watershed, when programmes that are only suitable for adults are shown. On weekdays 59% watched programmes between 9 p.m. and 11 p.m., while 65% did so on Saturdays. As many as 27% of children reported watching programmes on Saturday night between 11 p.m. and 6.30 a.m.

The kinds of programmes that the children reported watching, reflected the viewing habits of the adult population. Thus, soap operas were by far the most popular programmes with *Home and Away* being the most popular programme for both boys and girls.

The offenders in the sample were selected on the basis of being charged or cautioned a minimum of three times within one calendar year. They were aged between 12 and 18 years with an average age of 15½ and were 71 in number. They had committed a broad range of offences, representative of juvenile crime as a whole. They were described by the authors as a fairly extreme group, having a history of many offences and substantial involvement with the criminal justice system. Data was gathered from this group via an individual interview.

The authors concluded that there was little consensus among the group of juvenile offenders regarding the TV programmes they watched. A subgroup of violent offenders showed a similar lack of agreement and both groups had comparable viewing habits to the group of schoolchildren.

The influence of films and video

Similar concerns have been voiced about violence in films and video to those about TV programmes. Films, however, when shown in a cinema have a rating certificate which should only allow certain age groups access. Thus films which (in the UK) the British Board of Film Classification have deemed unsuitable for children below a certain age are normally shown to adults only. Films on video go through a separate classification and indeed some films granted a certificate for cinema viewing are refused one for video release. This is because video shares some of the features of TV. It is accessible to children, and can be viewed repeatedly.

Much of the recent debate in the UK concerning video violence was initiated by the publication of a discussion paper written by Elizabeth Newson (1994) from the Child Development Research Unit at Nottingham University. The paper was written at the invitation of a Member of Parliament who cited it as evidence to support an amendment to the Criminal Justice Bill which was then going through Parliament. A unique feature of the paper was that it was publicly endorsed by a group of academics and professionals, principally psychologists, psychiatrists and paediatricians.

The paper makes it clear that the impetus for its publication was the conviction of two 10-year-old boys for the abduction and murder of James Bulger in February 1993. During his address to the Court following the conviction and sentence of the two boys the trial judge commented that he suspected that exposure to violent video films may have in part explained their behaviour. Newsom suggests that although it is unlikely that any single cause for the behaviour of the perpetrators can be identified, contributing factors such as physical abuse, severe emotional neglect, poverty and disturbed family relationships have been suggested. She comments, however:

> although neither Jon nor Robert could be said to have come from happy and nurturant homes, there was little evidence of the extremes of neglect and abuse that could be documented in any Social Services department. What, then, could be seen as the 'different' factor that has entered the lives of countless children and adolescents in recent years? This has to be the easy availability to children of gross images of violence on video.
>
> (Newson, 1994:273)

The paper by Newson offers no new evidence to inform the debate on screen violence and behaviour but it does draw attention to some of the research carried out over a number of years on the effects of violent screen images on children's behaviour and calls for further research, particularly the careful collection of both retrospective and prospective case history material. The paper also suggests that while it would be preferable to rely on the discretion and responsibility of parents to control their children's viewing and to give models of negative reaction to brutality, many parents cannot be relied on in this respect.

In a detailed account of the James Bulger case, Smith (1994:2) makes the point that while cases such as this are rare, they are by no means unknown: 'The sad truth is that similar cases have happened in Britain in recent times, in not so recent times, and long, long ago'. Smith points out that the fundamental precept in the Newsom paper, specifically that 'a willingness of two or more children or adolescents together to carry out brutally violent assaults likely to result in protracted suffering and death' (Newsom, 1994:273) as a recent phenomenon is mistaken. Smith documents a number of cases in the UK going back 250 years. Clearly such cases could not have been caused by the advent of screen violence. Furthermore, Smith goes on to comment that it is unclear why the trial judge had referred to violent videos, since there had been no mention in evidence of any videos in the Bulger case. Nevertheless, after the trial it was the judge's comments about videos that made headlines.

In their study of the viewing habits of juvenile offenders, Hagell and Newburn (1994) found no significant differences between the film and video habits and preferences of the offenders, both violent and non-violent when compared with a group of schoolchildren. They found that in terms of the frequency of viewing, the pattern of use of the two groups was in most respects very similar. Offenders tended to display a broader range of hiring videos with higher proportions hiring videos more than once per week compared with the non-offenders; but contrastingly, a greater proportion of offenders were infrequent users.

In terms of cinema visits, over half of the offenders never went to the cinema, compared with less than one-third of the schoolchildren. Preferences for cinema viewing were also investigated. To assess whether there was any difference in the extent to which the two groups had access to and viewed violent images, the titles were distinguished by film classification. It was found that the offenders mentioned 18 certificate films with almost identical frequency as the schoolchildren. The authors paid particular attention to the frequency with which a number of films attracting scrutiny because of their violent content were mentioned by the two groups. They found no evidence that those films were watched by anything more than a tiny minority of young people.

When the authors concentrated on violent offenders, they found a similar pattern of film viewing following the general trend for the rest of the offenders and schoolchildren. They concluded that there were no generalisable statements that could be made concerning the preferences of the 'violent' group when compared with the rest of the offenders or the schoolchildren.

Evidence on the influence of computer games

Incidence

What might be called the leisure arm of the computer industry has now been with us for more than 20 years. Innovations in hardware and software have proliferated within the mainstream of computer design and technology and these have been reflected in games and delivery systems of greater sophistication. Computer games can be available through arcade machines, home video consoles, personal computers and hand-held machines.

The popularity particularly of hand-held machines over the past few years has led to some press and public disquiet as to the effects these activities might be having, particularly on young people who seem to be the main consumers. There is no doubt of the popularity of these games. The Economist Intelligence Unit reported sales of hand-held games rising by 700% during 1991 and predicted that by 1995 one in four boys within the UK will own a hand-held game (Griffiths, 1993). In the USA, a 1982 Gallup poll found that more than 93% of the young people polled at least sometimes played video games (Dominick, 1984). In 1992, the US computer games industry grossed more than US$5.3 billion. Sega's *Sonic the Hedgehog II* game made more than US$28 million on its first day of release and has grossed more than any cinema film in history.

The trend towards games becoming more realistic will probably continue with the latest developments in CD–ROM technology. The animated cartoon characters and modest graphics found previously are giving way to high-resolution screen images more akin to film and TV. The next major developments using systems already available will surely be the availability of such images via the Internet and the utilisation of virtual reality technology, making viewer participation feasible.

There has been little research on the demographics of computer game playing. One study in the USA by Fling *et al.* (1992) surveyed 11–18 year olds. The survey questionnaire included items on demographic data, frequency and length of home and arcade play, favourite games and feelings after playing. They found that 83% of their sample owned or rented a home system and 41% went to an arcade at least once a week. In addition they found that the boys in their sample played video games significantly more than girls. This significant association between gender and frequency of electronic game playing replicates the findings of a number of other authors (e.g. Loftus and Loftus, 1983). Within the UK similar findings and a survey of fruit-machine playing are cited in Griffiths (1991).

Possible explanations for these differences have been put forward. Perhaps the most obvious is that they reflect the content of the video games themselves. Video games software is usually designed by males for males (Griffiths, 1991). Braun *et al.* (1986) reported that in 21 video games they examined, 12 contained exclusively masculine images, two contained both masculine and feminine, seven contained neither and none contained exclusively female images.

In a study that investigated the viewing habits and preferences of young offenders and compared these with a sample of schoolchildren, Hagell and Newburn (1994) found that there was little difference in the amount of time each group spent playing computer and video games. While 81% of the schoolchildren reported playing such games, 77% of the young offenders did so. There was a difference, however, in the location where the games were played. While similar proportions of the two groups played games in arcades, a far smaller proportion of the offenders played in their own or a friend's home. Hagell and Newburn suggest that the cost of the equipment may be the explanation for this. These researchers also found little difference in the amount of time the two groups reported spending playing the games. In addition, each group reported playing a large number of different games with the same games being popular in both.

Possible effects

Despite the singular lack of scientific evidence either way, there has been no shortage of public pronouncements about the harmful effects of video game playing. In the USA, as long ago as 1982 the Surgeon General warned that video games were producing 'aberrations in childhood behaviour' despite the lack of any supporting evidence (Selnow, 1984). More recently, in 1993 the US Senate held joint hearings as part of the Judiciary Subcommittee on Juvenile Justice and the Government Affairs Subcommittee on Regulation and Government Information on the issue of violence on video games. Concern was expressed about the increasingly graphic representations of violence that were being portrayed in many video games. Similar anxieties had been expressed in equivalent Australian hearings earlier that year. In the USA manufacturers of video games were required to produce a rating system describing the content of the games.

It is perhaps the portrayal of violence and its possible effects on children's behaviour that has been at the forefront of the public disquiet. This has been part of the larger debate about the possible effects of media violence in general on children and young people already addressed in this chapter. Obviously there are similarities between TV and film images and those in a computer game. However, as Provenzo (1994) points out, although parallels between images on the film or TV screen and those on the video game screen seem obvious, there are important distinctions. While film and TV are passive media, video games are active with the viewer having control over what goes on. This greater degree of involvement and participation, it can be argued, may result in the viewer becoming more influenced by the screen images. Furthermore, while film and TV allow attention to wander, video games require complete concentration. Most importantly, however, films and TV may show actual acts of aggression and violence, even death, while games show these acts more crudely. The fact is many computer games are violent in nature, featuring death and annihilation. Dominick (1984) found that the most popular video games at that time were violent in nature. A review of the literature on video games by Provenzo (1991) found that of the 47 *Nintendo* games analysed, only seven did not include violence. Characters populating the stories were typically robotic cops, fighters, terrorists with any women portrayed as 'victims' and any foreigners as 'baddies', observations that led Provenzo to conclude that such games encourage violence, sexism and racism. The mechanism proposed for this was conditioning. Nevertheless, in what may be a shift from the situation reported by Dominick in 1984, by no means are the most popular games in the nineties of a violent nature. As Griffiths (1993) reports, many of the most popular games such as *Super Mario* and *Sonic the Hedgehog* are not.

The evidence for actual effects

There has been little research conducted on the possible effects of video game playing on subsequent behaviour. Much of what has been done has been conducted in the USA, often using self-report. Anderson and Ford (1986) found hostile feelings in subjects after playing an aggressive arcade game. Many of the studies have been correlational. For example, Lin and Lepper (1987) found a positive relation between boys' use of arcade video games and teachers' ratings of aggressiveness and impulsiveness.

An experimental study by Silvern and Williamson (1987) examined the play behaviour of children aged 4–6 years after watching a violent cartoon and after watching or playing a violent video game. Relative to a baseline measure the researchers found that both the video and the cartoon raised levels of children's aggression in subsequent play activity. This was evident both when the children were passive watchers of the video game and active participants. A commensurate decrease in pro-social behaviour was also recorded. The authors additionally found that boys were significantly more aggressive than girls.

Evidence that children's subsequent behaviour can be influenced by video games has been found by Schutte *et al.* (1988). They exposed children aged between 5 and 7 years to either a violent or a non-violent video game and then observed subsequent play behaviour. They found that their play was significantly correlated with the type of video game to which they had been exposed. This applied not only for the violent game. Children who had seen a non-violent game subsequently played with the type of toys they had seen in their game. The authors concluded that playing a video game tends to lead to subsequent behaviour similar to that of the character the individual controlled while playing the game. This seems to suggest that video games, as well as having the power to induce aggressive behaviour, may also have the potential to impel that which is more positive and socially desirable.

Although experimental studies seem to have some advantages over self-report studies, one of the methodological difficulties associated with any of these pieces of research is the extent to which the results are specific to the particular video game being played. Furthermore, the degree to which the 'violent' video games are in fact violent and those described as 'non-violent' are in fact so is a matter of judgement on the part of the researchers.

Apart from the possible influential effects of computer and video games playing, there has also been a great deal of disquiet about the amount of time young people apparently spend playing the machines and that this may be because the activity is addictive. However, a consideration of these possible effects is beyond the scope of this chapter.

Summary and conclusions

Having looked at some of the psychological research, the question remains as to the direction this points us in. Those with responsibility for the welfare of children and young people will look for indications of how to act responsibly. Straightforward censorship seems to be an option. There are now available computer programs which can be loaded into a home computer to filter out material arriving over the Internet which might be offensive. Within the USA there is now legislation which requires the manufacturers of TV sets to incorporate so-called 'V' chips which can recognise and prevent access to programmes of an 'adult' nature.

However, a number of commentators regard censorship as either a lost cause or undesirable. The advent of news appearing on the TV screen as it happens has led to real images of war and violence in the home. To try and censor fictional images while non-fictional ones are available would appear to be illogical. The Director of the British Board of Film Classification, James Ferman has gone on record as endorsing the inclusion of media studies on the curriculum for school pupils. The education of young people so that they can make better choices and interpret what they see on their screens may be the only way forward and a fruitful area for further research.

What is clear from the research is that despite its now long history, there is still much to do. The existing research is flawed methodologically. Little attention has been paid to those individuals who appear unaffected by screen images of violence. The underlying psychological processes are also relatively un-researched.

Public anxiety typically rises with the introduction of any new mass medium of entertainment, especially with respect to young people. However, there is little evidence to support the view that society is currently significantly more violent than at any other time or that large numbers of individuals are adversely affected by what they see on their screens. Pictures appearing via the TV, video or computer cannot be considered in isolation from the social context of society and the real-life experience of those who live within it.

References

Anderson, C.A. and Ford, C.M. (1986) 'Affect of the game player: Short-term effects of highly and mildly aggressive video games', *Personality and Social Psychology Bulletin,* **12**, 390–402.

Bandura, A. (1973) *Aggression: A Social Learning Analysis.* Englewood Cliffs, NJ: Prentice–Hall.

Braun, C.M.J., Goupil, G., Giroux, J. and Chagnon, Y. (1986) 'Adolescents and Micro Computers – sex differences, proxemics, task and stimulus variables', *Journal of Psychology*, **120**, 529–42.

Bronfenbrenner, U. (1979) *The Ecology of Human Development*. Cambridge, MA: Harvard University Press.

Comstock, G. and Strasburger, V.C. (1990) 'Deceptive appearances:Television violence and aggressive behaviour', *Journal of Adolescent Health Care*, **11**, 31–44.

Cumberbatch, G. (1989) 'Violence and the mass media: the research evidence'. In Cumberbatch, G. and Howitt, D. (eds) *A Measure of Uncertainty: The Effects of the Mass Media*. London: John Libbey.

Cumberbatch, G. (1991) 'Is television violence harmful?' In Cochrane, R. and Carroll, D. (eds) *Psychology and Social Issues: A Tutorial Text*. Lewes: The Falmer Press.

Dominick, J.R. (1984) 'Videogames, television violence and aggression in teenagers', *Journal of Communication*, **34**, 134–47.

Eron, L.D., Huesmann, L.R., Lefkowitz, M.M. and Walder, L.O. (1972) 'Does television violence cause aggression?' *American Psychologist*, **27**, 253–63.

Farrington, D.P. (1989) 'Early predictors of adolescent aggression and adult violence', *Violence and victims*, **4**, 79–100.

Farrington, D.P. (1991) 'Childhood aggression and adult violence: early precursors and later life outcomes'. In Pepler, D.J. and Rubin, K.H. (eds) *The Development and Treatment of Childhood Aggression*. Hillsdale, NJ: Erlbaum.

Farrington, D.P. (1995) 'The development of offending and anti social behaviour from childhood: key findings from the Cambridge study in delinquent development', *Journal of Child Psychology and Psychiatry*, **360**, 929–64.

Fling, S., Smith, L., Rodriguez, T., Thornton, D., Atkins, E. and Nixon, K. (1992) 'Videogames, aggression, and self–esteem: a survey', *Social Behaviour and Personality*, **20**, 39–46.

Griffiths, M.D. (1991) 'Amusement machine playing in childhood and adolescence: A comparative analysis of video games and fruit machines', *Journal of Adolescence*, **14**, 53–73.

Griffiths, M.D. (1993) 'Are computer games bad for children?' *The Psychologist*, **6**, 401–407.

Gunter, B. (1985) *Dimensions of Television Violence*. Aldershot: Gower.

Gunter, B., and Wober, M. (1988). *Violence on Television: What the Viewers Think*. London: John Libbey.

Gunter, B., McAleer, J. and Clifford, B. (1991) *Children's Views About Television*. Aldershot: Avebury.

Hagell, A. and Newburn, T. (1994) *Young Offenders and the Media*. London: Policy Studies Institute.

Huesmann, L.R. and Eron, L.D. (eds) (1986) *Television and the Aggressive Child: a Cross-National Comparison*. Hillsdale, NJ: Erlbaum.

Lazar, B.A. (1994) 'Why social work should care: Television violence and children', *Child and Adolescent Social Work Journal*, **11**, 3–19.

Lin, S. and Lepper, M.R. (1987) 'Correlates of children's usage of videogames and computers', *Journal of Applied Social Psychology*, **17**, 72–93.

Loftus, G.A. and Loftus, E.F. (1983) *Mind at Play: The Psychology of Video Games*. New York: Basic Books.

Molitor, F. and Hirsch,. K.W. (1994) 'Children's toleration of real life aggression after exposure to media violence: a replication of the Drabman and Thomas study', *Child Study Journal*, **24**, 191–207.

Newson, E. (1994) 'Video violence and the protection of children', *The Psychologist*, **7**, 272–74.

Paik, H. and Comstock, G. (1994) The effects of television violence on anti-social behaviour – a meta analysis. *Communication Research*, **21**, 516–46.

Provenzo, E.F. (1991) *Video Kids: Making Sense of Nintendo*. Cambridge, MA: Harvard University Press.

Provenzo, E.F. (1994) 'The social and psychological meaning of video games for children', *Association of Child Psychology and Psychiatry Review and Newsletter*, **16**, 113–19.

Ryder, R. (1993) 'Violence and machismo', *Journal of the Royal Society of Arts*, **561**, 706–17.

Sanson, A. and di Muccio, C. (1993) 'The influence of aggressive and neutral cartoons and toys on the behaviour of preschool children', *Australian Psychologist*, **28**, 93–99.

Schacter, S., (1964) 'The interaction of cognitive and physiological determinants of emotional state'. In Berkowitz, L. (ed.) *Advances in Experimental Social Psychology* (Vol. 1). New York: Academic Press.

Schutte, N.S., Malouff, J.M., Post–Gorden, J.C. and Rodasta, A.L. (1988) 'Effects of playing videogames on children's aggressive and other behaviours', *Journal of Applied Social Psychology*, **18**, 454–60.

Selnow, G.W. (1984) 'Playing videogames: the electronic friend', *Journal of Communication*, **34**, 148–56.

Silvern, S. and Williamson, P.A. (1987) 'The effects of video game play on young children's aggression, fantasy and prosocial behaviour', *Journal of Applied Developmental Psychology*, **8**, 453–62.

Smith, D.J. (1994) *The Sleep of Reason*. London: Arrow.

Wiegman, O., Kuttschreuter, M. and Baarda, B. (1992) 'A longitudinal study of the effects of television viewing on aggressive and prosocial behaviours', *British Journal of Social Psychology*, **31**, 147–64.

PART THREE: Families

Chapter Seven

Family therapy: A review of current approaches

David Jones

Family therapy provides a method of intervention which is qualitatively different from individual therapy. Problems are seen as belonging to the whole family unit or system and distinctions between healthy and sick family members are avoided as far as possible. In this chapter the family is described as a system which passes through a life cycle and attention is drawn to the influence of general systems theory on the major models of family therapy. Brief reviews of the Structural, Strategic and Milan approaches provide a summary of the history of family therapy and give an introduction to many of the techniques used by family therapists. Further sections indicate the importance of communication patterns and give examples of the measurement of family style. The chapter concludes with a consideration of more recent developments in approaches to family therapy based on second-order cybernetics and social constructionism.

Definition of a family

It is surprisingly difficult to arrive at a universally acceptable definition of the term family. A rather restrictive approach is to limit the definition to those who are sharing a household unit at any given point in time. Such a family has been likened to a system passing through time (Carter and McGoldrick, 1989). However, it is a system which is constantly changing as the different members pass through the stages of their individual life cycles and vary in the contributions they make to the family and the demands they place on it.

Quite a number of children live in reconstituted families in which one or both parents have been married previously and may have children from these earlier relationships. Attempts to decide who should be regarded as belonging to a given family get complicated in such circumstances (Frude, 1991). The definition of family is not restricted to households containing children and encompasses adults of one or more generations living together in a committed long-term emotional relationship. Individual family members may feel they are part of a wider family which may be more special to them than the unit they live with.

Several writers have suggested that it is useful to evaluate the stage the family has reached in its life cycle (Carter and McGoldrick, 1989; Haley, 1976). Just as there are identifiable stages in the life cycle of the individual, there are often clear stages for the family. The new couple coming together following a period of courtship to marriage or a committed relationship can be regarded as the starting point for a new family unit. A new spouse sub-system has been formed and each of the families of origin has to some degree both lost a member and gained a new member.

The second stage is reached with the birth of children and requires the spouse couple to make many adjustments, not least in relationships with the new grandparents. There is a further transition to being a family with school-age children. Providing for children may involve the parental couple in considerable economic adjustments and for many women there may be difficult decisions related to childcare and career.

The stage of adjusting to having adolescents in the household is often a challenge to family life. The role of the parental sub-system has to undergo a transition or the maturation of the offspring will result in a period of exceptional stress for the whole family. The problem of adjustment may also reflect the difficulties adolescence presents as a stage in the life cycle of the individual (Erikson, 1959).

The stage of launching single young adults from the parental home is a period of change and emotional adjustment for both the young and for the parents. Part of the cycle is complete when the children have moved on from the parental home. Nevertheless the parental couple who remain behind may have to re-discover that they are a spousal couple and establishing a pattern of relationships with the newly formed couple is not always easy.

Families may encounter difficulty making satisfactory transitions across the major life cycle stages and seem vulnerable to external stresses in the period immediately following a transition. Working with the family to create a genogram or simple family tree during one of the early family therapy sessions is an effective method for gathering information and identifying transition points. This can be a good time for the therapist to note some of the important myths, scripts or legends which may be a feature of the particular family.

Family myths have been described as patterns of mutually agreed but distorted roles which family members adopt as a defensive position (Ferreira, 1963). For example, myths of harmony often paint a rosy picture of past and present family relationships which will not be congruent with an outsider's view of the family (Stierlin, 1973). Legends in families are seen as condensed history from both families of origin which supports family mythology and lays down rules. Family scripts provide more detail and are conceptualised as forming a blueprint for family behaviours and actions in specific contexts (Byng-Hall, 1985). Problems can arise when the parents bring with them very different scripts from their separate families. To take an example, corrective scripts would involve attempts by the parents to avoid what they see as the mistakes made by earlier generations, particularly their own parents. Scripts can cause difficulties when they lead to children being given labels and roles in the family which they find unacceptable.

Family systems theory

General systems theory (von Bertalanffy, 1968) defined a system as a complex of interacting elements with the whole having properties greater than the sum of the parts. Considering families as systems has provided family therapy with a powerful model for understanding the interactions between family members and for finding ways to induce change. A family is compared with an open system which is one which has some permeability in the boundaries between itself and the environment and wider social systems in which it exists. When the boundaries between a family system and the wider social systems are relatively impervious then the family may come close to behaving as a closed system. This may come about when families are in protracted stable states over time, e.g. the period of years when all of the children are at school and the employment pattern of the parents is constant. Permeability of boundaries refers to the passage of information (stresses, etc.) from outer systems such as schools, the workplace of one of the parents, the neighbours or the extended family systems to the family. The family will also communicate with (have an effect on) these wider systems.

Another implication from systems theory is that families as systems will be governed in their operation by general rules. A system has sub-systems – in a family the most obvious are the parental sub-system (which has different functions from the spouse sub-system) and the sub-system of children. Other possible sub-systems are all the males or all the females in the family, everyone in a job, the grandparents, etc. It is important for the therapist to understand the patterns of communication between the sub-systems and to be aware of atypical boundaries. The functioning of boundaries would be expected to change in response to developmental changes in the family life cycle. Problems may arise if the rigidity of boundaries, especially between sub-systems, hinders the transition between stages.

Homeostasis and stability

The concept of homeostasis in the functioning of a family has been influenced by cybernetics (Ashby, 1960; Bateson, 1972). Healthy individuals and healthy families can adjust to mild and even moderate life stresses and rapidly return to a state of equilibrium. Negative feedback can be corrective, as in the example of a thermostat in a heating system; as the temperature falls the boiler is turned on to generate heat and when the temperature rises the boiler is turned off. The function of the thermostat is to stabilise the room temperature near the set level. Such a corrective system resists change. An example of negative feedback in families is when family members on perceiving change in one of the family act to minimise the effects of that change.

Stresses which distort the system, e.g. death of a family member, call for major re-adjustments to allow a return to a new state of equilibrium (see Holmes and Rahe (1967) for a discussion of major life stresses). Families which are functioning at a relatively stable state which is far from equilibrium, for example coping with a chronically ill child, appear to be vulnerable to further stresses.

Positive feedback in a system can often be self-destructive – the run-away engine effect or the microphone picking up the output of the loudspeaker. An example in family functioning would be the hyperactive child who annoys the mother – she tries to exert control by restraining the child which results in even more active behaviour. Many interactive situations result in positive feedback, as in both members of a dyad getting more and more angry with each other. An example of positive feedback influencing the individual would be anxiety over the possibility of physical illness when the individual increases the self-monitoring of symptoms resulting in even greater anxiety. Bateson discussed the development of paranoia in similar terms – the individual is distrustful of others but by his or her behaviour triggers responses from them which result in even more distrust.

One of the major contributions from family therapy to our thinking about illness behaviour and the origins of symptoms is the move away from linear causality to circular causality. Individuals within the family interact with each other and only rarely is there a simple linear effect.

Family therapy often distinguishes between different kinds of change within individuals and within families. First-order change refers to producing more or less of a given behaviour. A first-order approach in therapy would involve direct attempts to reduce troublesome behaviour or increase desired behaviour. Second-order change involves modifying the behaviour at a different level or attributing an alternative meaning to it so that it is perceived as a different type of problem.

Family therapy settings

Typically family therapy is carried out by multidisciplinary teams in the context of Departments of Child and Adolescent Psychiatry or Child and Family Clinics. More recently many Social Services Departments have established Family Therapy Teams, some addressing a wide range of problems and others providing specific support to Child Protection Teams. There are also specialist Family Therapy Clinics in the Voluntary Sector.

Frequently the setting will include a therapy room with a viewing screen and/or videocamera so that members of the team can observe from outside the room. Some families find the idea of being watched difficult to accept and may need reassurance about what is happening. Mostly there is a team of at least two therapists, although it is possible for an individual therapist to work systemically with a family. The great majority of family therapists will have trained initially in child psychiatry, social work, clinical psychology or nursing. Generally family therapy training includes an introduction to the major models of therapy with an opportunity to specialise in the application of one or more models.

Structural model

The structural school of family therapy began in the 1960s with the work of Minuchin and his colleagues. The concepts of sub-systems and the quality of the boundaries between them are used to give a picture of the structure of the family. The term kaleidoscope is used since individuals may belong to more than one sub-system giving different impressions of the pattern of relationships (Minuchin, 1974, 1984). It may be helpful to consider the holon model described by Minuchin where the family is represented as a polygon but for each individual only certain segments of the self are included in the family organism. In these terms the functioning of the family may have a greater influence (and be more necessary) for some members than for others. The pattern may change over time or at different stages of individual and family development. The model also explains the different patterns of interaction between different family members at different times. Minuchin gives the example of a child who operates with helplessness to elicit nurturance when interacting with her over-involved mother, but in contrast is competitive when playing with her older brother. Other examples draw attention to the different roles played by individuals inside and outside the family. The structural therapist seeks to become aware of these different involvements and encourages the family to reveal interactional patterns in the here and now.

Enmeshment

Minuchin and others have developed the systems based interpretation of boundaries to explain the function of families with problems. Enmeshed families are characterised by a high degree of inter-dependence between individuals. Something which happens to one member of the family rapidly has an influence on other members. For example, a low mark on a school test for one of the children can quickly become a talking point and potential crisis for the whole family. Such families are at risk when they need to cope with stress. Minuchin suggested that enmeshed families 'resemble an error-activated system with high resonance between the parts'. There are also constraints on the development of individuals in such families in that attempts on the part of one member to change elicit resistance on the part of others.

Enmeshment is also considered to have the effect of weakening the boundaries that allow sub-systems to work and the boundary separating children from parents may be weak. Another feature is that boundaries between the nuclear family and families of origin tend not to be well maintained. There may be role confusion with particular problems around distinctions between the roles of spouse and parent. In enmeshed families important discussions between pairs of people (dyadic transactions) rarely occur and the interactions tend to be triadic or group. For example, the father may criticise the behaviour of one of the children but immediately the mother or one of the siblings joins in to protect the child. The original issue quickly becomes lost or diffused in a wider debate. In these conditions coalitions between family members do not remain stable for long.

Hoffman (1981) points out that whilst there are whole schools of family therapy devoted to improving communication within families, the techniques for working with enmeshed families may require attempts to block some communications. Enmeshment involving too many cross-connections between individuals can block attempts by the therapist to induce change. The therapist may use enactment to identify the structures which are maintaining the problem behaviours. In difficult cases the experienced structural therapist may resort to a range of techniques to create unbalance in the structure of the existing family system in an attempt to precipitate change.

Disengaged families

Minuchin observed that disengaged families like enmeshed families could be identified in groups from relatively poor socio-economic backgrounds as well as in more middle-income backgrounds. These styles of functioning are not just a reaction to poverty. In disengaged families there is a marked absence of strong emotional connections and relationship ties are relatively weak or absent. Nevertheless this style is different from that found in 'chaotic' families. Disengaged families are often found to have rigid structures. Sometimes they appear to be headed by the mother's single-handed decision taking even when there may be a partner present.

Reframing

Although many families seek help for a family member, often a child, who has been identified as a patient or having problems, the family therapist will want to set the symptoms in the context of the family structure and pattern of functioning.

Often the origin of the symptom in the child is that some chance characteristic has somehow been singled out and amplified, increasing the contrast between that individual and the rest of the family. This can be a mutual causal process. An example of a process which amplifies deviance in the (sick) child is when the symptom is deviation-counteracting in the marital dyad (parents). For the child the symptom behaviour seems to keep the parents together and for the parents having a child with problems may well take precedence over conflicts.

Understanding the symptoms becomes more complicated when the circumstances which led to symptom formation have changed but the symptom carrier has taken on a more general role of scapegoat in the family. The structural family therapist often takes on the task of helping the family members to understand that their initial perceptions of the problem and of reality can be expanded or modified. The different perceptions of the symptoms and of the symptom carrier's position in the family may be challenged. Frequently the reframing of the problem behaviour will attempt to remove its pathological connotation and interpret it as an exaggerated form of normal and age-appropriate functioning.

Strategic models of family therapy

Strategic approaches to family therapy place an emphasis on finding solutions to the presenting problem. Early developments of the techniques at the Mental Research Institute (MRI) at Palo Alto drew on Bateson's work on communication patterns in families and were also influenced by innovative practices of Milton Erikson on the uses of problem solving in individual therapy (Cade, 1987; Haley, 1973, 1976; Jackson, 1975).

Some strategic therapists regard the symptom as a failed attempt at finding a solution to another problem in the family. Eventually the symptom itself becomes the dominant problem. Haley saw symptoms as reflecting problems or ambiguities in the hierarchical organisation of the family across generations. The term perverse triangle refers to a cross-generational coalition in which two members of the family at different levels form a coalition, with a third member of the family being excluded, e.g. mother–son coalition may exclude father. Haley has identified all possible triangles in a family of 2 parents + 2 children where each parent also has two parents: there are 21 triangles (an unknown number may be warring).

In strategic therapy the symptom might be reframed as a behaviour which has a meaning within the systemic functioning of the family. In this way the symptom might be normalised and de-pathologised. Alternatively the therapist might express curiosity about how the family will function if the symptom is taken away (Papp, 1984). Strategic therapy is often directive. As in structural family therapy the therapist has clear views on family hierarchies, boundaries and the relative positions of parents and children. The therapist develops goals for the family and devises positive and creative techniques to allow the family to attain them (Haley, 1976; Madanes, 1981, 1984).

Brief solution-focused therapy as developed by De Shazer and his colleagues can be viewed as a development of strategic therapy. The therapist seeks to identify solutions which the individual or family have not tried. Uncommon solutions are seen as a way of interrupting the pattern of symptom behaviour and allowing the family to perceive that a difference is possible. Solutions, it is suggested, have more in common than the problems they solve so it is possible to develop a number of formula interventions (De Shazer, 1985; De Shazer *et al.*, 1986).

The Milan systemic approach

The originators of the Milan approach to systemic family therapy were Selvini Palazzoli, Boscolo, Cecchin and Prata. All four were psychiatrists with background experience in the use of psychoanalytic methods. They acknowledged having been influenced by the writing of Bateson (1972) and by the ideas on patterns of communication developed at the MRI (Watzlawick *et al.*, 1967). Working as a team with observers behind a one-way screen being in a sense meta to the therapy they were able to obtain a 'double description' of the problem. The original approach was of a rigid adherence to a five-part session:

1. A pre-session discussion of 15–20 minutes during which the team discussed the possible meaning of the problem and formulated preliminary hypotheses.

2. The therapy session which may be 50–60 minutes.

3 A discussion break of 10–25 minutes used to evaluate the interview against the original hypotheses and generate an intervention.

4. The intervention usually delivered to the family in not more than 5 minutes often with the intention of challenging belief systems or generating new patterns of relating.

5. A post-session discussion during which the reactions to the intervention by family members are noted and plans for further sessions are discussed.

The Milan approach has itself undergone changes over the years, but throughout it has shown a concern with relationship patterns – as they existed before and after the emergence of symptomatic behaviour in one of the family members. An extremely influential paper by Selvini *et al.* (1980) outlined important guidelines for the would-be conductor of a family therapy session under the headings of hypothesising, circularity and neutrality. On the basis of the referral information the therapy team formulate a hypothesis prior to the start of the session. It is claimed that the hypothesis has functional value in guaranteeing an active position for the therapist in the conduct of the session. The hypothesis is seen as neither true nor false, but rather, more or less useful – it helps to organise the overwhelming mass of clinical data and as a useful basis for interventions. In the light of information obtained in the session the hypothesis may be modified or changed. The hypothesis must be systemic and this will include all components of the family.

Underlying circularity are the ideas taken from Bateson on difference and change in relationships (Bateson, 1972). By using the technique of circular questioning the therapist elicits information from each family member about perceived relationships between two other family members, e.g. a son might be asked to comment on some aspect of the relationship between his sister and his mother. Through circular and reflexive questioning a systemic understanding of the problem gradually emerges. The study of meaning in communication for hypothetical multiple levels of context has been summarised by Cronen and Pearce (1985).

The Milan group's view of neutrality also draws on Bateson's cybernetic circularity and can be best understood as an attempt to attribute equal weight to all parts of a system. The therapist might be said to have achieved neutrality if at the end of the session all members of the family felt they had been sided with equally.

In a major re-evaluation of concepts, neutrality was redefined as the creation of a state of curiosity in the mind of the therapist (Cecchin, 1987). By gathering a plurality of alternatives the therapist is able to maintain curiosity and seek explanations for relationship difficulties in more neutral ways. Recent research evidence based on outcome evaluation indicates that the Milan approach is an effective method of therapy (Carr, 1991; Simpson, 1991).

A strong criticism of the Milan group's position on neutrality is that it has failed to take account of gendered imbalances within families. It is argued that this is particularly true in attempts at intervention in the areas of child abuse and family violence (Goldner, 1985, 1993).

Communication and interaction styles

There has been a great deal of research into patterns of communication in both normal families (those with no declared psychopathology) and families in which one or more members are symptom carriers or suffer from a physical illness. Attention is drawn to the functions of a family and attempts have been made to measure how well these functions are being met.

The McMaster Model of Family Functioning (see summary by Barker, 1992) considers six aspects: problem solving, communication, roles, affective responses, affective involvement and behavioural control. Two examples will illustrate the level of detail studied. Problem solving tasks are divided into basic, developmental and crisis. Basic tasks for the family include activities like the provision of food, shelter, health care and other essentials for survival in society. Developmental tasks focus on the healthy progression of the family and individuals through the life cycle stages and need to be appropriate to the ages of the children. Crisis tasks refer to the ways the family deals with unexpected or unusual events and major stresses, e.g. illness, bereavement, redundancy. The model also distinguishes between instrumental and affective problems: instrumental being mainly the provision of physical resources and affective being concerned with feelings and possible distrust between family members.

Taking behavioural control as a second illustration the model recognises four styles of control: rigid, flexible, *laissez-faire* and chaotic. Rigid control is high on predictability and may work for the performance of day-to-day activities, but has difficulty with developmental tasks. Flexible control styles, as the term implies, can adapt to changes in circumstances and encourage identification with family ideals. *Laissez-faire* styles tend to be low on constructiveness and lead to inertia which may result in the children being insecure or attention seeking in a new environment (e.g. starting school). Chaotic styles of control are unpredictable switching from rigid to flexible.

Much work has been done on the study of communication. Micro-analytic techniques have looked at both content and process. Who says what and to whom? How was it said? What were the non-verbal cues? Not communicating is an important communication. What is the proportion of positive and negative attributions in communication? Macro-analytic studies focus on the more general patterns of style of functioning.

Measuring family style

The circumplex model developed by Olson and colleagues provides a good example of an attempt to measure aspects of family style (Olson, 1993). The proposed model involves two dimensions, each of which have four categories. Families are assessed on adaptability with an ordering of categories as: chaotic; flexible; structured; rigid. Family adaptability is defined as the ability of a system to change its power structure, role relationships, and relationship rules in response to situational and developmental stress.

On the cohesion dimension the categories are ordered as: disengaged; separated; connected; enmeshed. Family cohesion is defined as the emotional bonding that family members have for one another. The FACES III test provides an estimate of family functioning on these scales.

The Beavers' model provides an alternative method of classification by measuring family competence and style in families labelled as successful in their functioning (Beavers and Hampson, 1990). It is able to account for both optimal and pathological levels of functioning.

Second-order cybernetics

Increasingly family therapists have become concerned to understand and interpret the role of the therapist and of the therapist's meaning system in the therapy process. The therapist is seen as inescapably part of the system. The family and therapists become the problem-determined system (Anderson and Gooloshian, 1988). Through the use of language and conversation a shared meaning system for the problem is created. The therapists remain the experts in the system but the emphasis has changed to one of helping the family create solutions for its own problems.

Arising in part from the second-order perspective and partly from a self-conscious attempt to view families as clients there has been a gradual move away from the systemic metaphor of family functioning to the use of narrative and other techniques in therapy (Hoffman, 1990, 1992).

Social constructionism

In post-modern thinking 'self' is perceived as a narrative, a developing story about life which becomes the basis for identity. We are thought to create our reality within the context of discourse with others. However, since many of us have a range of interactions with different others in the contexts of family, work and social activities, there is more than one discourse and more than one reality. For many, perhaps for everyone, there is also the narrative which is not shared with others. The child and often the adolescent will at first rely on the stories which parents, teachers and others have made for them, but problems arise when they find these stories too constraining or subjugating.

Social constructionism holds that beliefs about the world are social inventions (Hoffman, 1990). Rather than working with the model of the family as a social system, therapy takes the form of conversations which construct alternative narratives. Some therapists refer to re-discovering the individual within the family. The task of co-constructing a reality is much more complicated than leading the family towards a solution the therapist feels might be appropriate for them.

Michael White and externalisation

White and colleagues working in Adelaide have developed a distinctive approach to family therapy which incorporates aspects of social constructionism and the use of narratives with reflexive questioning and a pattern of interventions which include first order change (White, 1986, 1989). In the available space it is only possible to take the technique of Externalisation as an illustrative example of White's work.

Externalisation offers clients a way of viewing themselves as having parts which are uncontaminated by the symptom. The technique entails establishing a linguistic separation of the problem from the personal identity of the labelled patient. Conceptually it seems simple, but the selection of terms which will be acceptable to the patient and family involves considerable therapeutic skill.

White gives an example of a child with a history of faecal soiling who was engaged by being asked to resist being tricked by 'Stinky-poo'. The impulsive and aggressive adolescent might be asked 'How is it that anger keeps getting you into trouble?' After personifying the problem the therapist identifies instances or situations which were problem-free and a plausible alternative narrative is developed for the sufferer. The technique involves a unique combination of strategic problem-solving and a variation of recursive questioning within a structural framework.

Epston who works in New Zealand and has collaborated with White has made extensive use of narrative letters to individuals and families following therapy sessions. In the letters he summarises the interactions and places an emphasis on the positive aspects of the abilities of the individuals to cope with the presenting problems. Epston claims that the time taken to generate the letters is more than justified by a reduction in the number of therapy sessions required when letters are used (Epston, 1994).

Reflecting teams

Team consultation has been an important part of family therapy practice and training. The early Milan team's five-part therapy session clearly demarcated the therapists from the family and involved the therapist-team in sometimes lengthy discussions away from the family (Tomm, 1984a,b). An exciting and challenging variation in the use of the team which has been pioneered in Norway is to simply reverse the lights and allow the family to observe and listen to the discussions of a reflecting team (Andersen, 1987). It is emphasised that the team concentrates on the family and does not talk behind the screen, although the team members may request a discussion observed by the family at any time.

Andersen (1992) comments on the need for the team to talk positively and to empower the family and stresses that functioning in this way turned out to be much easier than he had expected. The strong influence of the Milan approach is recognised, but the team try to avoid forming initial hypotheses and avoid prescriptive interventions. Instead the therapy team offer the family a variety of perspectives on the presenting problem. A recent research evaluation of the approach in Austria found that 80% of respondents were 'very satisfied' with their experience of reflecting teams (Hoger *et al.*, 1994).

Gender and cultural issues in family therapy

These are important topics which deserve far more than a brief mention at the end of a chapter. In recent years there has been a strong call for a greater awareness of gender inequalities in family functioning (see for example Perelberg and Miller, 1990). It is suggested that family therapy very frequently adopts a neutral position on gender and power inequalities within families and consequently lends support to a male-dominated value system. In particular it is stressed that neutrality on gender issues should not be maintained when there are issues connected with violence and abuse. The therapy system needs to take a more interventionist position to further the rights of women and children.

Finally family therapy, of all the therapies, needs to acknowledge the importance of cultural factors and ethnicity on family life and of the functioning of families within the wider community. A second-order perspective helps to make the therapist aware of his or her own position in attempts to create shared meaning systems when there are cultural differences and other perceived inequalities between the therapists and the family. This also raises the important ethical issue of the nature of the intervention in family therapy with all families. There is a temptation for the therapist to attempt to lead families to a position of safe certainty, but it is far more appropriate to help them discover for themselves a position of safe uncertainty (Mason, 1993).

Concluding remarks

Family therapy is more than just working with families. The different approaches briefly summarised in this chapter all take a systemic perspective. Problems are seen as belonging to the family system and not just individuals. Interventions involve facilitating change in the system. The differences between approaches based on different models of family therapy have diminished as therapists of most persuasions have adopted either a second-order perspective or become more concerned about the impact of therapy on individual family members. Particularly in social constructionism and narrative therapy there is a sense of rediscovery of the individual in the family without losing the systemic perspective.

Evaluating outcome during and following family therapy is a complex process. The insider views of therapy sessions obtained from different family members, their separate short- and longer-term evaluations of the effects of change, the views of the original referrer, and the views of the therapists are just some of the variables which need to be considered. Reimers and Treacher (1995) provide some good examples of consumer surveys of degree of satisfaction with family therapy. Whilst there is a need for much more research and evaluation of the ways in which different components of family therapy influence outcome measures, it is clear that family therapy has become the intervention method of choice for many problems involving the behaviour and care of children and adolescents.

References

Andersen, T. (1987) 'The reflecting team: Dialogue and meta-dialogue in clinical work', *Family Process*, **26**, 415–28.

Andersen, T. (1992) 'Reflections of reflecting with families'. In Mcnamee, S. and Gergen, K.J. (eds) *Therapy as Social Construction*. London: Sage.

Anderson, H. and Gooloshian, H.A. (1988) 'Human systems as linguistic systems: Preliminary and evolving ideas about the implications of clinical theory', *Family Process*, **27(4)**, 371–93.

Ashby, W.R. (1960) *Design for a Brain: The Origin of Adaptive Behaviour* (2nd edn.) London: Chapman and Hall.

Barker, P. (1992) *Basic Family Therapy*. Oxford: Blackwell.

Bateson, G. (1972) *Steps to an Ecology of Mind*. New York: Ballantine Books.

Beavers, W.R. and Hampson, R.D. (1990) *Successful Families. Assessment and Intervention*. New York: Norton.

Byng-Hall, J. (1985) 'The family script: A useful bridge between theory and practice', *Journal of Family Therapy*, **7(3)**, 301–305.

Cade, B. (1987) 'Brief/strategic approaches to therapy: A commentary', *Australian and New Zealand Journal of Family Therapy*, **8(1)**, 37–44.

Carr, A. (1991) 'Milan systemic family therapy: A review of ten empirical investigations', *Journal of Family Therapy*, **13**, 237–65.

Carter, E.A. and McGoldrick, M. (eds) (1989) 'Overview: The changing family life cycle: A framework for family therapy.' In *The Changing Family Life Cycle: A Framework for Family Therapy*. Boston: Allyn and Bacon.

Cecchin, G. (1987) 'Hypothesizing-circularity-neutrality revisited: an invitation to curiosity', *Family Process*, **26(1)**, 3–14.

Cronen, V. and Pearce, B. (1985) 'Toward an explanation of how the Milan method works: an invitation to a systemic epistemology and the evolution of family systems.' In Campbell, D. and Draper, R. (eds) *Applications of Systemic Family Therapy: The Milan Approach*. London: Grune and Stratton.

DeShazer, S. (1985) *Keys to Solution in Brief Therapy*. New York: Norton.

DeShazer, S., Berg, I.K., Lipchik, E., Nunnally, E., Molnar, A., Gingerich, W. and Weiner, D.M. (1986) 'Brief Therapy: Focused solution development', *Family Process*, **25**, 207–22.

Epston, D. (1994) 'Extending the conversation', *Family Therapy Networker*, **Nov/Dec**, 31–63.

Erikson, E.H. (1959) 'Identity and the life cycle', *Psychological Issues*, **1**, 1–171.

Ferreira, A.J. (1963) 'Family myth and homeostasis', *Archives of General Psychiatry*, **9**, 457–63.

Frude, N. (1991) *Understanding Family Problems: A Psychological Approach*. New York: Wiley.

Goldner, V. (1985) 'Power and hierarchy: Let's talk about it!', *Family Process*, **32**, 157–62.

Goldner, V. (1993) 'Feminism and Systemic Practice', *Journal of Strategic and Systemic Therapies*, **10**, 3–4.

Haley, J. (1973) *Uncommon Therapy: The Psychiatric Techniques of Milton Erickson*. New York: Norton.

Haley, J. (1976) *Problem-Solving Therapy: New Strategies for Effective Family Therapy*. San Francisco, CA: Jossey-Bass.

Hoffman, L. (1981) *Foundations of Family Therapy: A Conceptual Framework for Systems Change*. New York: Basic Books.

Hoffman, L. (1990) 'Constructing realities: An art of lenses', *Family Process*, **29(1)**, 1–12.

Hoffman, L. (1992) 'A reflexive stance for family therapy'. In Mcnamee, S. and Gergen, K.J. (eds) *Therapy as Social Construction*. London: Sage, pp.7–24.

Hoger, C., Temme, M., Reiter, L. and Steiner, E. (1994) 'The reflecting team approach: Convergent results of two exploratory studies', *Journal of Family Therapy*, **16**, 427–37.

Holmes, T.H. and Rahe, R.H. (1967) 'The social readjustment rating scale', *Journal of Psychosomatic Research*, **2**, 213–18.

Jackson, D.D. (1975) 'The question of family homeostasis', *Psychiatric Quarterly Supplement*, **31**, 79–90.

Madanes, C. (1981) *Strategic Family Therapy*. New York: Basic Books.

Madanes, C. (1984) *Behind the One-Way Mirror*. San Francisco: Jossey-Bass.

Mason, B. (1993) 'Towards positions of safe uncertainty', *Human Systems: The Journal of Systemic Consultation and Management*, **4**, 189–200.

Minuchin, S. (1974) *Families and Family Therapy*. Cambridge, MA: Harvard University Press.

Minuchin, S. (1984) *Family Kaleidoscope*. Cambridge, MA: Harvard University Press.

Olson, D.H. (1993) 'Circumplex model of marital and family systems: Assessing family functioning'. In Walsh, F. (ed.) *Normal Family Process*. London: The Guilford Press.

Papp, P. (1984) *The Process of Change*. New York: Guilford Press.

Perelberg, R.J. and Miller, A.C. (eds) (1990) *Gender and Power in Families*. London: Routledge.

Reimers, S. and Treacher, A. (eds) (1995) *Introducing User-friendly Family Therapy*. London: Routledge.

Selvini Palazzoli, M.S., Boscolo, L., Cecchin, G. and Prata, G. (1980) 'Hypothesizing-circularity-neutrality: three guidelines for the conductor of the session', *Family Process*, **19**, 3–12.

Simpson, L. (1991) 'The comparative efficacy of Milan family therapy for disturbed children and their families', *Journal of Family Therapy*, **13**, 267–84.

Stierlin, H. (1973) 'Group Fantasies and Family Myths: Some theoretical and practical aspects', *Family Process*, **12**, 111–25.

Tomm, K. (1984a) 'One perspective on the Milan systemic approach: Part I. Overview of development, theory and practice', *Journal of Marital and Family Therapy*, **10**, 113–25.

Tomm, K. (1984b) 'One perspective on the Milan systemic approach: Part II. Description of session format, interviewing style and interactions', *Journal of Marital and Family Therapy*, **10**, 253–71.

von Bertalanffy, L. (1968) *General Systems Theory*. New York: Braziller.

Watzlawick, P., Beavin, J.H. and Jackson, D.D. (1967) *Pragmatics of Human Communication*. New York: Norton.

White, M. (1986) 'Negative explanation, restraint and double description. A template for family therapy', *Family Process*, **25(2)**, 169–84.

White, M. (1989) 'The externalizing of the problem and the re-authoring of lives and relationships', *Dulwich Centre Newsletter*, **Autumn**, 3–21.

Chapter Eight

Enhancing the effectiveness of parents: Applications of psychology

Sheila Wolfendale

This chapter spotlights the concept of families and our understanding of parenting; looks at models of parenting and ways of intervening with family functioning, with a view to effecting change. The emphasis is upon the notion of parenting skills and child rearing practice and underlying value bases to these forms of intervention. The dominant discipline perspective will be applications of psychology to enhance the effectiveness of parents.

Concepts of the family

There are as many views on what families are, what they represent, how they enhance or inhibit development as there are people. Most of us have been brought up in families, of all kinds of composition. Those who have not still hold a view of families. Furthermore, those professionals who work with families, who administer to them, support them, who legislate for them, also hold views and values about them. No discipline in the social sciences has a monopoly on pronouncing upon families or offering a theoretical, ideological stance on families.

Psychological perspectives upon family functioning cannot but be informed by and have reference to broader societal contexts, such as family policy formation, welfare and benefits targeted at families. Effective family functioning, as well as dysfunctioning families have to be appraised within these socio-political economic frameworks (see Chapter 10).

The United Nations view of the family is that it is the smallest democracy at the heart of society; the notion that the family is at the core of the society nexus and therefore is an unique and precious resource was the fundamental premise of the 1994 International Year of the Family: 'What is quite clear is that families matter and their wellbeing and strength is intrinsic to the social and economic well-being of the country as a whole'. This quotation is taken from page 5 of the Report of the All Party Parliamentary Group on Parenting and the International Year of the Family Parliamentary Hearings (1995). The Parliamentary hearings focused on four themes – work, relationships, poverty and resource, and parenting. The inter-relationship between these themes and their influence upon future directions of family policy was made explicit in the Report, which states that 'unless these basics are right, families will not be able to thrive' (p.6).

It is the *parenting* theme of the four themes with which this chapter is concerned, although parenting and families are not always easily separable within the literature. Martin Richards (1995:70) is emphatic that psychologists should redress a noted imbalance in their research, namely that 'the family ... receives little mention in writing by psychologists'. He identifies three conceptions of family: the first is household, the second is the nuclear or close family, and the third is kinship. He suggests that these constructions could facilitate future research into family relationships and interactions and their effects. His article constitutes a plea to research psychologists that this is an area wherein they bring their own incomparable experiences and insights to the research endeavour.

Vetere and Gale, as research psychologists, who 'lived' with a family for the best part of a year, as semi-participant researchers (1987) say that the reasons why there has been little first-hand research into family life is quite obvious. Family life is for all of us a sacred domain, with even relatives and friends entering the family nucleus by invitation. Likewise, professionals – such as teachers, health visitors, social workers, educational and clinical psychologists – can only 'intrude' into the family by invitation.

The 'family' is a macro-term for what describes a myriad of temporary or permanent permutations: small unit/nuclear, with no children, one or more children; extended with wider kin networks; mono or dual parent/carer families; separated, divorced, widowed, unmarried parent(s); parents with sole/shared custody; birth-parent carers; foster, adoptive parent(s); multigenerational family units. Then there are family units where one or two parents work full time, part time, or who are not in waged employment, who go out to work or work at or from home, or who study (for contemporary statistics on these compositions see Pugh *et al.*, 1994).

We presuppose that there are, nevertheless, some enduring characteristics and contributions of family life that impact onto and affect children's development and progress.

The contribution of the family to development and learning

There is a longstanding view of the family as having a profound role in educating and socialising children, whilst at the same time providing for adults' needs (Wolfendale, 1983, 1992). The American psychologist Kagan (1979) takes three perspectives in his consideration of the functions of the family – the state's, the parent's and the child's. From the parent's perspective, he asserts, the family can be a 'locus of solace and psychic relief ... it provides each adult with an opportunity to feel needed and useful ... it offers parents an opportunity to validate the value system they brought to adulthood' (p. 211). In Kagan's view, for the child the family offers a model for identification, a source of protection and target of attachment, a setting wherein he or she will be in receipt of information and guidance, a place in which skills can be gradually acquired and competence achieved.

Judy Dunn, a British psychologist tells us (1989:78) that research indicates that the familiar world of the family, and especially conversation with an affectionate parent 'provide contexts of especial value for very young children's intellectual development'.

The Royal Society of Arts Report *Start Right* (1994) promotes a model wherein the family's prime educative function needs to be supported and encouraged by the community and the state – the responsibility is therefore corporate. For a comprehensive, multi-disciplinary (e.g. sociology, social policy, psychology, social psychology) text on the family see Muncie *et al.* (1995).

Conceptions and constructions of parenting

Out of sheer curiosity, I checked in *Apt and Amusing Quotations* (Lamb, 1986) headings entitled 'Children' and 'Parents' and of the many pithy quotations, felt that two epitomised an ambivalent attitude towards children and an equivocal stance on parenting:

> Far from cementing a marriage, children more frequently disrupt it. Child-rearing is on the whole an expensive and unrewarding bore. Nigel Balchin, the writer (p. 45)

> Parents are the bones upon which children sharpen their teeth. Peter Ustinov, the actor (p. 135)

Parenting (used in this chapter to denote care taking and care giving functions carried out by any combination of adults centrally involved in and taking responsibility for child rearing) is a full-time occupation but not a skilled trade in the sense that society demands and provides for the requisite prior training. On the whole a significant number of adults take on the status and duties of parents ignorant of many aspects of child development, early learning processes, the rigours and routines of baby and child care, and the procedures by which to obtain information and support for their new role.

It seems self-evident, as Pugh *et al.* express it (1994:39), that 'to do any job well, it helps to know what is expected, an understanding of why the job is important, the skills to do it and the bare necessities and circumstances to get started'. In fact, these authors, almost tongue in cheek, imagine what an advertisement for the position of parent might look like (p. 40).

Parenting can be defined by looking at what parents actually do. In Wolfendale (1983, 1992) a list of parenting functions is given which encompasses meeting children's primary and secondary needs, physical, emotional, social, learning. The actuality and reality of what parents do when parenting can be at odds with an internalised and idealised model of what a 'good' parent should be doing, as any parent can attest. Attributes of the 'good' parent are reinforced by media images (e.g. television advertisements) and baby and child-rearing books which advise and exhort 'correct' child-rearing practices (Hartley-Brewer, 1994; Marshall, 1991). Parents can and do easily feel anxious and guilty that their own parenting behaviour falls short of this ideal blueprint.

Yet parents evolve their own 'style' of parenting and child-management (see Gross, 1989; Pugh *et al.*, 1994; Wolfendale, 1992, for descriptions of such styles) which undoubtedly have a profound effect upon their children, as we can all attest to. At the extremes (i.e., too authoritarian, or too lax regarding discipline) outcomes (i.e., adult behaviour) have been linked to socially deviant and criminal behaviour (Farrington, 1995; Rutter and Smith, 1995).

One way of attempting to reconcile the ideal and the reality is to posit the view that, on the whole, parents do their best and want the best for their children – this notion has been powerfully conceptualised by the psychologist Bruno Bettelheim (1987) as 'good enough parenting'. The underlying assumption is that there is not and cannot be a sole 'right' way to bring up children. Bettelheim has been at pains to reduce the moral imperative upon parents that presupposes that there is one child-rearing blueprint (which is surely elusive!) whilst at the same time acknowledging that parents need guidance and support to exercise their parenting functions and duties in such a way as to promote and enhance their children's well-being and emotional growth, and maximise their potential. As we shall see later in this chapter, this is the core aim behind many parenting skills/parent support programmes.

Campion explores the ideal-actual conception of parenting and presents her 'Ideal Model and Actual Model of Fit Parenting' in great detail (1995, Chapter 17). She is essentially critical of the ideal model, defined as the traditional family and which 'represents the family as a very self-contained and closed unit within the confines of the home environment' (p.277). Within this conception, the duties and responsibilities of adult and child family members were identifiable and clear cut. By contrast her Actual Model is the more contemporaneously realistic, and is an 'open and fluid one with few clear cut rules or boundaries' since 'the vast majority of parents today are thus raising their children in very different circumstances to the ones in which they were raised themselves' (p. 280).

Parenting as a 'job' is taken very seriously by Campion, who offers a job analysis checklist (1995:293) and by Pugh *et al.* (1994) who offer an agenda for action for parent education and support. There is a growing consensus that 'the need to support parents is incontrovertible' (Walker, 1995:40). This same author, in her Royal Society of Arts lecture, from which this end-quote is taken, refers to the assertion made by Edgar (reference in Walker: 1995:32) that:

> the most profound change in family life over recent decades is that the meaning of parenthood is being transformed in concert with the reconstruction of marital relationships.

These and other writers examine the changing role of mothers and fathers in different cultural contexts in relation to work patterns and opportunities, marital breakdown and changing family composition, and child access arrangements (Barnes, 1995; Burman, 1994; Phoenix *et al.*, 1991; White and Woollett, 1992) within a context of an evolving life cycle (Duvall, 1971).

Parenthood: Testing for fitness and the notion of parenting skills

Walker quotes George Bernard Shaw's aphorism (Walker, 1995:29) 'Parentage is a very important profession, but no test of fitness for it is ever imposed in the interest of children'. Increasing attention has been paid, in recent years, to the notion of fitness for parenthood, with commensurate examination of the requisite skills needed to be an effective parent, and ways of developing and supporting these from the transition to parenthood to the 'state' of being a parent (Michaels and Goldberg 1988, Parr 1995). This section looks at the idea of parenting skills primarily derived from a psychological perspective.

Textbooks of psychology devote considerable space to a consideration of the differing models of skill acquisition which have been proposed over many years of empirical psychological work. Essentially skill can be defined as an item of behaviour. Annett (1989) identifies three characteristics of skill: it is directed towards the attainment of a specific goal; the behaviour is intended to be achieved with economy of time and effort; and thirdly, the behaviour is acquired by training and practice.

Hayes (1994) in expounding Annett's theory of skill acquisition, explains the hierarchical nature of this model and describes how a learning curve representation of skill acquisition can denote those areas of speedy, efficient learning, times of apparent standstill, or plateau, typical when any of us learns a new skill. Two key features of skill acquisition, elaborated by Hayes, common to learning at any age or stage are the effects of practice, and knowledge of results. Readers of this chapter will be able to relate to these key features, as they think of any skill they have sought to acquire at any time, be it typing. learning to drive, electrical wiring, knitting, etc.

Turning now to the area of parenting skills, how have writers and workers in the field conceptualised and defined these? Some examples include:

- Braun and Schonveld (1993:9) in introducing the aims of their resource pack for parents, they view each partner, parent and worker as having equal status, whilst acknowledging that each has different skills and knowledge: 'parents know about themselves, their circumstances, their child; workers know about child development. Only by putting together the specific and general knowledge can individual parents be supported to change and develop'.
- Wolfendale (1992) reports upon series of workshops she had undertaken over a number of years, exploring the dimensions of skills parents bring to the act and experience of parenting. From the wealth of data generated from parent and professional groups, the skills were grouped into domains – experience, knowledge and specific skills or techniques. This approach comprised a mix of tangible skill areas – e.g. child management techniques, household and craft skills – and more abstract areas, such as knowledge of child development, helping children's early learning.
- Earlier in this chapter, reference was made to the hypothetical job description put forward by Pugh and colleagues (1994). Within this advertisement these necessary skills were listed: stress management and conflict resolution, negotiation and problem-solving, communication and listening, budgeting and time management, decision-making, ability to set boundaries and priorities as well as providing loving support (p.40). This list comprises a number of domains, which presumably can be broken down into small sub-units of behaviour according to psychological models of skill acquisition, such as that advanced by Annett and cited above.

These three approaches to parental skills tend to be couched in broad domain terms, rather than invoking learning hierarchies or indeed specific psychological models of skill acquisition. However, a domain or area view of skills involved in parenting is tenable as a conceptual starting point, a framework from which empirical work can be derived, and from which hypotheses can be generated.

But before we take a look at parent training and support intervention approaches, we need to see what ideological premises these are based on and what assumptions are made about parents and their alleged need for such training and support.

Towards a value base for developing parenting skills

Earlier in the chapter Janet Walker was quoted as saying that there is a growing consensus that the need to support parents is incontrovertible. Parenting programmes adopt that view implicitly or explicitly and indeed, it (that view) provides the *raison d'être* for most if not all the programmes. However, there are various ideological shades to that rationale. A parenting programme could adopt one or more of these stated goals which reflect an ideological stance:

1. to empower parents/carers to be in control of their lives and decisions

2. to support parents to effectively exercise their responsibilities for children (a key principle in the 1989 Children Act)

3. to share the expertise that parents have on a basis of equality

4. to foster and develop parenting skills

5. to reflect the differing rights of parents and children

6. to value and address diversity in child-rearing practice

7. to welcome and incorporate a range of differing family compositions

8. to operate a wealth rather than a deficit model of family functioning

This last goal is the most contentious: elsewhere this author (Wolfendale, 1995) refers to the origins of the deficit model, which was rooted in many American Head Start programmes which were predicated upon the notion that targeted educational programmes could compensate for socio-economic deprivation. This model assumed that children and families disadvantaged by their deprived status could be positively assisted, via educational intervention and family focused programmes, to combat their situation, and become enabled, even empowered, to compete on equal terms with their less socio-economically deprived peers.

This 'compensatory intervention' approach has moved on to embrace a broader view which perceives the child to be part of a viable, vibrant dynamic family unit that is socially and culturally valid (even if economically deprived) and which acknowledges the 'equivalent expertise' of parents as primary educators (Meisels and Shonkoff, 1990). Hence a 'wealth' model which assumes a value position that children are the inheritors and inhabitants of a family domain with its own rich, cultural, linguistic traditions.

This model would be reflected in those parenting skills programmes which particularly emphasise goal numbers 3, 5, 7, 8 in the list above.

Yet another ideological shade to the underlying rationale for parent support and training is epitomised within programmes targeted to and for parents of children with special needs. One of these in particular is identified and referred to later in the chapter. These tend to adopt a constructive-positive stance as they perceive parents as active educators and agents of change, who can become empowered, enabled and competent in identifiable skill-areas, working towards agreed sets of goals focusing upon meeting identified special educational needs of their children.

This realm of parent programmes invokes an ideology espoused in Wolfendale (1992) and expressed in these words by Hornby: 'a working relationship based on equality of value of contribution from parent and teachers ... this involves acknowledging the different responsibilities but shared accountability of both parents and teachers within a working alliance formed on behalf of children' (Hornby, 1995:15).

There needs to be built into any evaluation of parenting programmes effectiveness criteria that can determine the viability of the underlying principles and value-base matched with the instructional model.

Applying psychology to parent training

The chapter now moves on to identify a number of parent training/parenting skills programmes which are predicated on applying psychology. What these have in common and what distinguishes them from a wider gamut of such approaches are these features:

- Hypothesis testing: programme designers/operators set out to test the effectiveness of a given instructional model, applied in certain, specified settings or conditions.
- Research-based: programme designers/operators are influenced by existing or prior research that has already demonstrated effectiveness or a particular approach and they may be seeking to replicate research studies in similar or even different circumstances, or with similar or different samples.
- Theoretical premises: programme designers/operators may be impressed by the apparent intactness of a theoretical approach that links in with a clear value system of parent training and support and may wish to explore the ideas empirically.

In reality any one or more of these three major features may be present in one programme.

The whole parent education and parent training field is extensive and so parameters have to be drawn for the purposes of and space available in this chapter. Related areas are excluded from consideration – the reader is referred to Wolfendale and Topping (1996) for description and review of psychological applications to family literacy, to Wolfendale (1990, 1993) regarding the involvement of parents in assessment, to Hornby (1995) and Wolfendale (1989) for essentially school-based parental involvement programmes such as High Scope, and to Braun and Schonveld (1993) and Pugh *et al.* (1994) for transition to and preparation for parenthood (see also Chapters 7 and 9).

The parameters of parent education and parent training adopted for this chapter are defined as: programmes for parents, organised and run usually by professionals (ones cited in this chapter are mostly run by educational and clinical psychologists), including groups of parents engaged in developing their skills and confidence so that they can provide an enriched upbringing for their children. This short definition is taken and adapted from the Open University *Parents and*

Under Eights programme, currently under development, and referred to later in this chapter (also see definition in Fine, 1980).

The approaches listed below are necessarily selective, but hopefully they exemplify psychological applications in this area. They are clustered under these headings:

1. Parent training/child intervention:
   (a) Special Educational Needs
   (b) Behaviour management/behaviour change

2. Parent training and support (with a view to promoting child development and boosting parental confidence in child rearing and child management).

Parent training/child intervention

(a) Special Educational Needs

The prime example is the Portage project, the main aim of which is to develop parents' skills so that they can work with their young children on specific skill-areas within the home (e.g. areas might typically include independence in feeding, language skills, cognitive functioning). The programme comprises: a checklist of developmental skills; teaching cards; activity charts; books of readings; regular (usually weekly) home visits from the Portage worker. The model is behavioural, both for the initial parent training and child-oriented learning sequences. Portage has been in the UK since the late 1970s, is widespread nationally and internationally. The Portage scheme has been subjected to a number of evaluation studies (e.g. Kiernan, 1993). For a longer description see Hornby (1995, Chapter 7).

(b) Behaviour management/behaviour change

Two examples:

1. *The ABC of Behaviour* (Hinton, 1993). This booklet accompanies workshop series based in Surrey since 1982. The theoretical base is described as social learning/behaviour (e.g. the *ABC* stands for an antecedents–behaviour–consequences analytical and problem-solving framework). The author reports reduction in behaviour difficulties as parents' knowledge of behavioural strategies increases.

2. *Assertive Discipline for Parents* (Canter and Canter, 1988). This approach is related to the authors' Assertive Discipline for Schools programme. It is based within a social learning/behavioural/solution-focused framework and consists of materials for use in workshops for parents which deal with skills to promote being in control and managing child behaviour at home. It is being tried out in the UK.

A text which blends psychologically-based research with intervention strategies for working with parents in the area of behaviour disorders and difficulties is

Webster-Stratton and Herbert (1994).

In this area, the behavioural/social learning model is predominant, encompassing the parent-training itself as well as the suggested strategies for child management. The behaviour-change, problem-solving theoretical underpinnings robustly stand up to empirical use; the techniques are transferable and generalisable; results are visible; success itself is reinforcing and can be therefore self-sustaining. Parents can become tangibly empowered and can gain or regain control over their own actions and decision-making.

Parent training and support

There are four examples in this section:

1. *Positive Parenting* (Miller, 1994). This programme, developed by an educational psychologist, covers six training modules in various child rearing skill areas. The materials come in stout, ring-binder form. The objectives are stated to be to empower parents to recognise their existing skills and to prioritise and work systematically towards clear, planned targets. A strong problem-solving approach underpins the programme, which emphasises positives and works towards short- and long-term goals. The programme has been evaluated (Dawson, 1995).

2. *Everyday Problems in Childhood* (EPIC) (Clench). EPIC, developed by Clench, an educational psychologist, is described as an open learning course and is delivered though workshops. The materials come in the form of leaflets which cover 12 topics which are perceived to be everyday issues facing all parents in child rearing and child management. Again the approach is described as social learning/behavioural.

3. *Newpin* (Pound, 1994). Newpin is a voluntary organisation working with parents who suffer from depression and feelings of isolation. The programme aims to break the cyclical effect of destructive family behaviour. It has been running for some 10 years at around 20 Newpin centres in different parts of the country. The theoretical base of the programme, which was initiated by a clinical psychologist, is described as humanistic, social learning, as well as psychoanalytic, systemic, eclectic and feminist. Its particular strength might well lie in this careful mix of a number of theoretical elements and areas of psychology.

4. *Parents and Under Eights Programme* (Open University, K504). A new course, to replace highly successful OU courses on parenting and childcare, is under development and trialling. As before it will be targeted at thousands of parents through distance learning and localised support, using materials which are being tested comprehensively, at the time of writing. The programme would combine child development and personal skills acquisition perspectives.

This is a highly selective and condensed review of a number of parent education and parent training programmes. Each of them has a stated theoretical rationale, each is supported by materials and utilises a collaborative, group workshop approach. Their underpinning value systems emphasise the programme providers (often psychologists) as equal partners with parent recipients and stress that the programmes aim to empower parents. Programme content is usually a mix of specific skills promotion in areas of child rearing and child management and instructional techniques include: role play, modelling, situational problem-solving, focused discussion.

Two recent surveys provide a wealth of information on the plethora of parenting courses currently available:

1. The small study by Cocks (1994) concentrated on analysing features of upwards of a dozen such programmes designed and delivered by educational psychologists.

2. The national survey of 38 parenting programmes carried out by Smith (1995), which constitutes the first ever such national survey.

Both these studies confirm that the overwhelming majority of these programmes use social learning/behavioural theoretical bases (28 out of 38 in Smith's study). Other frameworks used are: humanistic (13/38); psychoanalytic (6/38); family systems (11/38); eclectic (11/38). Evidently some programmes used one or more theoretical framework in combinations.

Various domains of the discipline of psychology are much in evidence. Other disciplines can lay legitimate claim to this crucial area within society (e.g. sociology, anthropology, etc.) but a distinctive contribution comes from developmental and child psychology, instructional psychology/psychology of learning, social psychology, organisational psychology. It looks as if a number of these academic, research and applied psychology interests are beginning to cohere and come together – for example, a group of upwards of 100 psychologists in the UK are founder members of a newly formed (during 1994–95) *Promoting Parenting Skills* network (contact address at the end of this chapter). Many of these psychologists are actively involved in the realm of parenting training and parental involvement.

Intervening with families: practice and policy

It is evident from the literature and surveys that there is indeed a growing coalition in favour of societal intervention with family life and family functioning. The formation during 1995 of the Parenting Education and Support Forum (contact address at the end of this chapter) also attests to growing realisation that in the absence of a commitment at government level to a 'Family Policy' other initiatives could address a number of identified needs. The Forum brings together those concerned with or working in the field of preparation, education and support for parents. This coalition aims to raise awareness of the importance of parenting, create a supportive network for those involved with this area, collate and provide information on research, training and good practice, promote these interests in public domains including the media and take forward policy, practice, training and research on a co-ordinated front. To that extent the Forum constitutes a pressure group, and a representative lobby.

Another call for co-ordination and policy formation in this area comes from Alexander and Clyne (1995) who have conceptualised this whole area as *Family Learning* which includes: informal learning within the family; family members learning together; parenting education. Crucial aspects of their formulation of family learning embrace connections between families and societal institutions, expressed by Alexander and Clyne (1995:6) thus:

> ... learning how to understand, take responsibility and make decisions in relation to wider society, in which the family is a foundation for citizenship and ... learning how to deal with agencies that serve families, such as schools, health service, social services, voluntary organisations and the criminal justice system. Most of these agencies have distinct agenda or concerns which they impart to families with whom they work.

We have seen in this chapter rationales and justification for intervening in family life. To return to a phrase used at the beginning of this chapter this ideology is one of shared and corporate societal responsibility. Although there is a tradition in this country of social intervention, recently and currently exemplified in government funded projects such as Urban Aid, City Challenge, regeneration grants to those areas deemed to be in such need, these initiatives tend to be piecemeal. There is a longer and more extensive tradition in the USA of larger-scale intervention projects involving families, many of which have been subjected to research and evaluation (Meisels and Shonkoff, 1990; Mitchell and Brown, 1991; Pence, 1988; Rapoport, 1987).

Replication of many of these studies could be undertaken in the UK. We need to find out what works, what are effective and less effective features of parent training/support programmes, and what is cost-effective. That is, we need to apply hypothesis-testing and evaluation methodologies to such programmes. Rapoport (1987) contains a useful discussion of action-research methods, and Mitchell and Brown (1991) discuss principles of programme evaluation and propose an operational model. Interestingly, in the light of earlier discussion in this chapter on underpinning values, these authors state (1991:299):

> evaluation of a programme should not only focus on fact questions, but should not *only* focus on fact questions, but should also be concerned with value questions. This expansion of the notion of programme evaluation into the domain of values has led to a recent interest in evaluating the quality of early intervention programmes' operations relative to criteria of best practice.

Such systematic approaches to parenting programmes, which aim to enhance the effectiveness of parents, have clear implications for policy at local and national level. It was hoped by those involved in the *International Year of the Family* initiative, referred to at the start of this chapter, that this would have influenced government thinking and to have influenced formation of and commitment to such a policy. That the dearth of government action in this area is ultimately harmful to society is a pervasive theme in Leach (1994:xiii), who says 'all of us are shareholders in society's children'.

This chapter has sought to effect connections between burgeoning provision in the area of parenting training and parent support, in which applications of psychology play a significant part, and the broader canvas of families in society and how human potential can be more effectively realised when families are actively supported in these ways.

References

Alexander, T. and Clyne, P. (1995) *Riches beyond Price, Making the Most of Family Learning*. Leicester: National Institute of Adult Continuing Education.

Annett, J. (1989) 'Skills'. In Colman, A.M. and Beaumont, J.G. (eds) *Psychology Survey*. London: Routledge and the British Psychological Society.

Barnes, P. (ed.) (1995) *Personal, Social and Emotional Development of Children*. Oxford: Basil Blackwell in association with The Open University.

Bettelheim, B. (1987) *A Good Enough Parent*. London: Thames and Hudson.

Braun, D. and Schonveld, A. (1993) *Approaching Parenthood, a Resource for Parent Education*. London: Health Education Authority.

Burman, E. (1994) *Deconstructing Developmental Psychology*. London: Routledge.

Campion, M. J. (1995) *Who's Fit to be a Parent?* London: Routledge.

Canter, L. and Canter, M. (1988) *Assertive Discipline for Parents*. London: Harper Row and Behaviour Management Ltd.

Clench, H. (undated) *Everyday Problems in Childhood* (EPIC). Hove: The Parent Company.

Cocks, R. (1994) *Parent Education Courses and an Analysis of Educational Psychologists' Involvement*. Unpublished MSc Educational Psychology dissertation, Psychology Department, University of East London.

Dawson, J. (1995) *Positive Parenting, an Evaluation*. Unpublished study, Postgraduate School of Psychology, University of Nottingham.

Duvall, E.M. (1971) *Family Development*. Philadelphia: J.B. Lippincott.

Dunn, J. (1989) 'The family as an educational environment in the preschool years'. In Desforges, C. (ed.) *Early Childhood Education*. Edinburgh: Scottish Academic Press and the British Psychological Society.

Farrington, D. (1994) 'Early developmental prevention of juvenile delinquency', *Royal Society of Arts Journal*, **November**, 22–35.

Fine, M. (ed.) (1980) *Handbook of Parent Education*. London: Academic Press.

Gross, J. (1989) *Psychology and Parenthood*. Milton Keynes: Open University Press.

Hartley-Brewer, E. (1994) *Positive Parenting, Raising Children with Self-esteem*. London: Mandarin Paperbacks.

Hayes, N. (1994) *Foundations of Psychology, An Introductory Text*. London: Routledge.

Hinton, S. (1993) *The ABC of Behaviour – Troubleshooting for Parents of Young Children*. Surrey Education Department.

Hornby, G. (1995) *Working with Parents of Children with Special Needs*. London: Cassell.

Kagan, J. (1979) *The Growth of the Child*. London: Methuen.

Kiernan, C. (1993) *Survey of Portage Provision 1992/1993*. London: National Portage Association.

Lamb, G.G. (1986) *Apt and Amusing Quotations*. Surrey: Paperfronts.

Leach, P. (1994) *Children First*. London: Michael Joseph.

Marshall, H. (1991) 'The social construction of motherhood: an analysis of childcare and parenting manuals'. In Phoenix, A., Woollett, A. and Lloyd, E. (eds) *Motherhood, Meanings, Practices and Ideologies*. London: Sage, Chapter 4.

Meisels, S. and Schonkoff, S. (eds) (1990) Handbook of Early Childhood Intervention, Cambridge, Cambridge University Press

Michaels, G. and Goldberg, W. (eds)(1988) The Transition to Parenthood, Cambridge, Cambridge University Press

Miller, S. (1994) *Positive Parenting*. Newcastle upon Tyne: FORMWORD.

Mitchell, D. and Brown, R. (eds) (1991) *Early Intervention Studies for Young Children with Special Needs*. London: Chapman and Hall.

Muncie, J., Wetherall, M., Dallos, R. and Cochrane, A. (eds) (1995) *Understanding The Family*. London: Sage.

Parr, M. (1996) *Support for Couples in the Transition to Parenthood*. unpublished PhD thesis, Psychology Department, University of East London.

Pence, A. (ed.) (1988) *Ecological Research with Children and Families from Concepts to Methodology*. London: Teachers' College Press.

Phoenix, A., Woollett, A. and Lloyd, E. (eds) (1991) *Motherhood, Meanings, Practices and Ideologies*. London: Sage.

Pound, A. (1994) NEWPIN: *A Befriending and Therapeutic Network for carers of Young Children*. London: HMSO.

Pugh, G., De'Ath, E. and Smith, C. (1994) *Confident Parents, Confident Children*. London: National Children's Bureau.

Rapaport, R. (1987) *New Interventions for Children and Youth, Action-Research Approaches*. Cambridge: Cambridge University Press.

Report of the All Party Parliamentary Group on Parenting and International Year of the Family UK (1995) *Parliamentary Hearings*, **September**.

Richards, M. (1995) 'Family relations', *The Psychologist*, **February**, 70–72.

Royal Society of Arts. *Start Right: the Importance of Early Learning* (1994) London: Royal Society of Arts.

Rutter, M. and Smith, D. (eds) (1995) *Psychosocial Disorders in Young People*. Chichester: John Wiley.

Smith, C. (1995) *Learning to be a Parent: a survey of group-based Parenting Skills Programmes*. London: National Children's Bureau.

Vetere, A. and Gale, A. (1987) *Ecological Studies of Family Life*. Chichester: Wiley.

Walker, J. (1995) 'Parenting in the 1990s: Great expectations and hard times', *Royal Society of Arts Journal*, **Jan/Feb**, 29–42.

Webster-Stratton, C. and Herbert, M. (1994) *Troubled Families – Problem Children*. Chichester: Wiley.

White, D. and Woollett, A. (eds) (1992) *Families, a Context for Development*. London: The Falmer Press.

Wolfendale, S. (1983) *Parental Participation in Children's Development and Education*. London: Gordon and Breach Science Publishers.

Wolfendale, S. (ed.) (1989) *Parental Involvement, Developing Networks between School, Home and Community*. London: Cassell.

Wolfendale, S. (1990) *All About Me*. Nottingham: NES-Arnold

Wolfendale, S. (1992) *Empowering Parents and Teachers – Working for Children*. London: Cassell.

Wolfendale, S. (ed.) (1993) *Assessing Special Educational Needs*. London: Cassell.

Wolfendale, S. (1996) 'Transitions and continuities in home school reading and literacy'. In Wolfendale, S. and Topping, K. (eds) *Family Involvement in Literacy: Effective Partnerships in Education*. London: Cassell.

Useful addresses

Exploring Parenthood, 194 Freston Road, London W10 6TT.

Open University K 504, *Parents and Under Eights*, School of Health and Social Welfare, Open University, Walton Hall, Milton Keynes MK7 6AA.

Parenting Education and Support Forum, National Children's Bureau, 8 Wakley Street, London EC1V 7QE.

Promoting Parenting Skills. Contact David Scott, Psychology Department, Chester College of Higher Education, Cheyney Road, Chester CH1 4BJ.

Chapter Nine

Working together to protect children from abuse and neglect

Anna Harskamp

This chapter defines abuse, clinical and developmental implications, research findings and professional frameworks. Practice issues and interventions are outlined, as well as prevention plans.

Introduction

Child abuse and neglect has a long history; child protection is relatively recent. The 'Cruelty Act' or 'Children's Charter' was passed in the UK in 1889 making ill treatment, neglect, exposure and abandonment of children a punishable offence.

Protecting children and young people from abuse and neglect is inextricably linked with the rights of the child. In 1991 the UK government agreed to be bound by the United Nations Convention on the Rights of the Child (DoH, 1993), which enshrines the rights of children and young people to:

- protection from violence and harmful treatment (article 19 and 37)
- protection from exploitation, which includes sexual abuse (article 34).

These rights apply to all children whatever their race, sex, religion, language, disability or family background (article 2). Decisions which affect children should be made in the best interests of the child (article 3) and the views, thoughts and feelings of the child should be carefully listened to (article 12).

Setting the scene: research evidence

Definitions of child abuse and neglect vary according to clinical practice, research needs, beliefs and value systems and legal requirements. Four types of child abuse are usually referred to:

- neglect
- physical injury
- sexual abuse
- emotional abuse.

These four categories are referred to in *Working Together under the Children Act 1989* (known as *Working Together*; HMSO, 1991) and are the basis of the registration of children on a Child Protection Register. They correspond largely with the definition of 'significant harm' in the Children Act. It is important to note that many children who are abused will experience more than one type of abuse.

According to *Working Together* abuse is defined as:

- *Neglect:* The persistent or severe neglect of a child, or the failure to protect a child from exposure to any kind of danger, including cold or starvation, or extreme failure to carry out important aspects of care, resulting in the significant impairment of the child's health or development, including non-organic failure to thrive.
- *Physical injury:* Actual or likely physical injury to a child, or failure to prevent physical injury (or suffering) to a child including deliberate poisoning, suffocation and Munchausen's syndrome by proxy.
- *Sexual abuse:* Actual or likely sexual exploitation of a child or adolescent. The child may be dependent and/or developmentally immature.
- *Emotional abuse:* Actual or likely severe adverse affect on the emotional and behavioural development of a child caused by persistent or severe emotional ill-treatment or rejection. All abuse involves some emotional ill-treatment.

Accurate figures regarding the actual incidence of abuse are difficult to determine. An analysis of Child Protection Register (CPR) figures show national registrations of abuse or suspected abuse. In 1994, there were 34,900 registrations of child abuse and neglect in England representing just over 3 per 1,000 of the population under 18 years (DoH, 1995).

Types of abuse and impact on development

All types of abuse and neglect include some aspect of emotional abuse. Not infrequently, different types of abuse occur together, e.g., a child who is sexually abused may also be subject to physical assault, as well as to emotional threat to keep the abuse secret. There are, however, important practice implications in teasing out some of the particular effects of different types of abuse.

Neglect

Gross neglect, particularly of babies and small children, can lead to death. Neglect can be of a physical or emotional kind. Skuse (1989) has highlighted developmental difficulties and delay in neglected and emotionally abused children at different age groups. Neglect is seen as affecting a child's development because of both a lack of physical care and supervision and a failure to attend to the developmental needs of the child. As well as actual growth problems, 'nonorganic failure to thrive', neglected children may show serious difficulties in developing social and motor skills, receptive and expressive language. Sometimes it is only when abuse and neglect have been substituted with sensitive care that more appropriate growth and development can be observed in the child.

Reporting of interventions with families showing neglect to their children have been few in number. Of those that have been reported, the results are not very encouraging. Skuse and Bentovim (1994) refer to an extensive review of treatment work in the USA, in over 3,000 families. Researchers found that at least one-third of parents continued to mistreat their children whilst engaged in the programmes and over half of the families were considered likely to continue to mistreat their children after completing the programme. However, Skuse and Bentovim (1994) refer more positively to Lutzker's work in the USA where with families referred for neglect, the focus was on personal cleanliness, nutrition, home safety and cleanliness and demonstrations of feelings during child–parent interaction, improved physical health and cognitive stimulation.

Physical injury

Physical abuse may be a result of direct injury or result in indirect consequences, e.g. shaking can lead to brain damage in babies and infants. Speight (1989) has highlighted some pointers, within a medical context, to help determine whether injuries may be non-accidental.

Particularly unusual types of physical abuse which have been reported in recent years include deliberate poisoning, suffocation and Munchausen's syndrome by proxy (Skuse and Bentovim, 1994). Because accidental poisoning is fairly common in young children, deliberate poisoning has been hard to detect and occurs mainly with children under 2 years.

Munchausen's syndrome by proxy described by Meadows in 1977, is when a parent, most often a mother, fabricates illness in a child and presents the child to medical specialists. Types of illness found in this condition include smotherings, poisonings, seizures, apparent bleeding from various orifices, skin rashes and cuts, high temperatures and high blood pressure (Skuse and Bentovim, 1994).

The results of physical abuse on children and young people may have short- or long-term effects and vary according to different types of abuse and the child's age at the abuse. Many children who have been physically abused have difficulties with social/emotional adjustment and show reactions to adults which can range from total avoidance to being over-friendly. Some children will act out the physical assaults they have experienced, others will show their distress by withdrawal. Some children with a history of physical punishment feel themselves responsible for their 'punishment' and this may have an impact on self-esteem.

Much of the research in this area is inconclusive or contradictory. Even where there is evidence to show the negative impact of physical abuse and neglect on cognitive development and subsequent school performance, it is often difficult to separate this out from the effects of a family living in particularly disadvantaged socioeconomic conditions.

However, clearer conclusions have emerged from the work of Patterson and colleagues in the US, as Skuse and Bentovim (1994) point out, where home visiting and support have been seen as an effective means of preventing or decreasing incidents of physical abuse and neglect.

Sexual abuse

There is an enormous amount of research and clinical work in the area of child sexual abuse (CSA). Definitions of CSA vary in emphasis. Several definitions point to the imbalance of the power relationship an adult has with a child. CSA is seen as an abuse of power, authority and trust, where the child is sexually abused for the adult's sexual gratification. Feminist views of CSA have a long and well-recorded history and refer to notions that males maintain their power over females by a kind of 'sexual terrorism' (Adams, 1992). Other definitions refer to the notion of the exploitation of a relationship, regardless of the age of the person abused. Children from all age groups, including babies, are sexually abused. All studies have shown higher rates of abuse against girls than boys, although abuse against boys may be under-reported. Smith and Bentovim (1994) cite Finkelhor's work in the mid-1980s. Reviewing the CSA data available at that time, he calculated that 71% were female and 29% male.

The National Childrens' Home (1992) Report into *Children and Young People who Sexually Abuse other Children (1992)* cites one in three sexual abusers being under the age of 18. The vast majority of perpetrators of CSA are male. Smith and Bentovim (1994) estimate that 85–95% of abusers are male, although many clinicians would suggest the rate is higher. Significant differences in the typologies of male and female sexual offending behaviour are becoming clearer, e.g. women less often use violence, and they tend to be more willing to take responsibility for the abuse than men (Matthews, 1993).

Most of the CSA brought to the attention of child protection agencies is perpetrated within the family or by people known to the children concerned. Some studies have shown rates of 75% of cases seen clinically are of children abused within the household, mostly by fathers (46%) or step-fathers (27%) (Smith and Bentovim, 1994). A number of recent studies have looked at the characteristics of the abusive experience and short- and long-term effects of CSA.

Kendall-Tackett *et al.* (1993) surveyed 45 studies, investigating the effects of abuse on children. Although the overall picture provided is tentative, a few general conclusions were borne out. In those studies where CSA involved a close perpetrator, a high frequency of sexual contact, a long duration, the use of force, sexual acts which included oral, anal or vaginal penetration, this increased the number of symptoms in the children. The lack of maternal support at the time of disclosure also led to increased difficulties in children coping. A key variable in recovery was maternal and family support, which was demonstrated through believing the child and acting in a protective way towards the child and getting support. Crisis intervention and specialised therapy were associated with children showing the best recovery rates. About a third of children in the studies showed no apparent symptoms of abuse. Despite the lack of a particular single symptom that occurs in a large majority of CSA cases, both sexualised behaviour and behaviours associated with Post Traumatic Stress Disorder (PTSD) were noted with relatively high frequency. Longer term effects of CSA have been reviewed by Beitchman *et al.* (1992).

Childrens' capacity to cope with CSA may lie on a continuum from positive to negative coping. Positive coping may include a child being able to choose confidants or having a supportive home, school or peer environment. However, what may appear as positive coping can also be seen in some cases, and at a later stage of development, as dissociative responses which may be triggered by stressful periods or key life events. Negative coping may include dissociation, amnesia, personality problems, self-destructive attitudes, which can include self-hate and poor body image. Smith and Bentovim (1994) quote a number of studies relating a higher than expected rate of CSA in children and young people with eating disorders. A high correlation (95%) of sexually and physically abused children and young people using solvents and other substances in a solitary setting has been observed in clinical work in an east London area (Cripps, 1995)

Emotional abuse

As previously stated, all other types of abuse, including neglect, have an element of emotional abuse. Skuse (1989) refers to emotional abuse as 'the habitual verbal harassment of a child by disparagement, criticism, threat and ridicule and the inversion of love'. Skuse has highlighted the link with emotional abuse and delay in growth, both physical and developmental, and with associated feeding difficulties, e.g. pica and foraging in dustbins for food. Issues around the identification, assessment and treatment of emotional abuse have already been noted. Glaser (1995) identified six types of emotional abuse and warns against the reluctance of agencies to intervene unless there is physical abuse or other forms of harm to the child. By breaking down the all-encompassing nature of the term 'emotional abuse', it is possible to tackle specific behaviour and intervene more effectively.

The effect on a child of continued emotional abuse can permeate virtually every aspect of a child's development, functioning and welfare. Because emotional abuse is often a component of physical and sexual abuse and neglect, there has been relatively little work addressing ways of remediating the effects of primarily emotional abuse on children.

A framework for practice

The child protection context – multi-agency co-operation

The context within child protection work is embedded operates at a variety of levels (Figure 9.1):

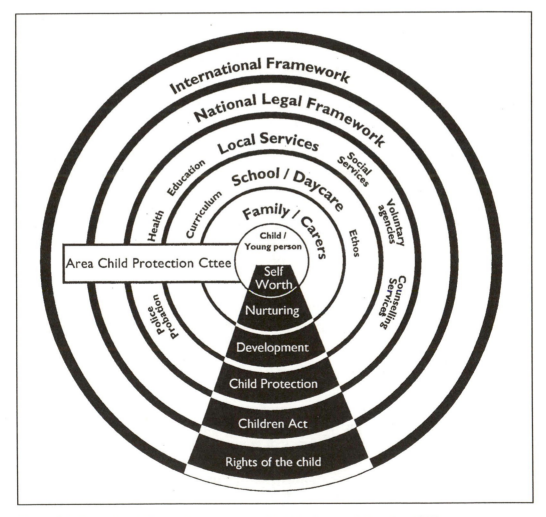

Figure 9.1 Protecting children and young people (Bird Harskamp and Knowles, 1995)

1. International Framework

The rights of the child and the UN Convention were referred to earlier (DoH, 1993).

2. National Legal Framework

The safety, well-being and development of the child or young person is central to all aspects of child protection work and is enshrined in the Children Act (1989). This far-reaching comprehensive legislation contains principles which underpin child protection work with children and families.

Following events in Cleveland in the 1980s, the urgent need for inter-agency co-operation was well documented and led to a key publication *Working Together under the Children Act 1989* (HMSO, 1991). This outlines the essential role of the Area Child Protection Committee (ACPC): 'Every ACPC should establish a programme of work to develop and keep under review local joint working and policies and procedures'. The main emphasis is on agencies working together to protect children.

Working Together (HMSO, 1991) although clearly 'not a detailed practice guide' gives valuable information regarding working together on individual cases and a core view of essential elements in child protection work.

3. Local Services

Whilst national and general developments are referred to in *Working Together* there are many local differences in the smaller detail of internal agency structures and indeed the range of agencies, particularly voluntary agencies available locally. Everyone engaged in child protection work must be fully conversant with both national and legal developments, as well as locally based practice, procedures and resources. *Working Together* outlines inter-agency procedures to protect children and also to the internal procedures of each of the agencies referred to.

4. The School Context

The essential role of schools and the education service in protecting children and young people from abuse and neglect is clear. Virtually every child has some experience of school and apart from time at home spends most time within an educational setting (or the under-5s within a day care or nursery setting). Key documents and publications referring to the role of the education service in this area normally address two aspects: (a) child abuse issues, e.g., signs and indicators of abuse, procedures for reporting alleged abuse or suspicions of abuse, working with the child who has been abused; and (b) wider child protection issues, e.g. the ethos of the school, prevention of abuse, the impact of the educational curriculum, and education for parenthood.

Publications which have helped shape or have been referred to in the development of child protection work in schools and the wider educational context are: DES *Circular 4/88* (DES, 1988); DfEE *Circular 10/95* (DfEE, 1995);

Working Together (HMSO, 1991); the *Handbook for the Inspection of Schools* (Technical Paper 9) (OFSTED, 1994); and the *Code of Practice on the Identification and Assessment of Special Educational Needs* (DfE, 1994).

- Circular 4/88. In 1988, the then Department of Education and Science (now Department for Education and Employment), issued a circular recommending that each LEA and each school designate staff with identified responsibilities in this area.
- *Working Together under the Children Act 1989* (HMSO, 1991).
  This guide acknowledged the key role teachers and school staff and professionals from support services, such as EWO and EPs and Youth Workers have due to their day-to-day contact with children.

- *Handbook for the Inspection of Schools* (Child Protection), Technical Paper 9. With regard to pupils' welfare and guidance, inspectors have to judge the effectiveness of the school 'in promoting the welfare, health, safety and guidance of its pupils'. The paper makes it clear that the inspectors will look for evidence of the impact of the school's child protection policy and procedures and the extent to which they comply with national requirements. It outlines the necessary procedures schools should follow.
- The *Code Of Practice* (DfE, 1994) addressing the identification of special educational needs refers to the importance of information as to whether a child is on the child protection register and to joint assessment and planning for a child's needs.
- The most recent Circulars are 10/95 and 11/95 (DfEE, 1995a,b).

5. Role of Governors
The role of school governors in child protection was highlighted in *Circular 4/88* and also in *Croner's School Governor's Manual* (Croner, 1992). Governors should ensure that the requirements of *Circular 4/88* and *Working Together* (HMSO, 1991) are met in schools for all staff, including teaching and non-teaching. Governors are advised to ensure that the school has a comprehensive child protection policy consistent with ACPC and LEA guidelines (Croner, 1992).

6. The Family
Clinical work with families and training workshops will be described in a later section. Extensive media coverage regarding child abuse has led to a general level of awareness in the public. However, the vast majority of detailed published information regarding child protection is meant for professional users, e.g. teachers, as documented above. Whilst essential principles in the Children Act (1989) are the concept of parental responsibility and partnership with parents and other family members, there is a relative dearth of information directly geared to the needs of parents and families (and perhaps less so carers).

A noteworthy exception is the NSPCC/Family Rights Groups booklet *Child*

Protection Procedures – What They Mean for Your Family (NSPCC, 1992) which provides a model format for a Child Protection Plan Agreement involving appropriate family members as fully as possible.

7. The Child/Young Person

An essential principle of the Children Act (1989) is that a child's views be taken into account regarding safety and welfare issues in the light of age and understanding. The Act also stipulates that careful consideration be given to a child's racial origin, religion, language and culture.

Helping children understand child abuse investigations and procedures is a complex task. Published material on this subject is developing, e.g. the NSPCC booklet *Child Abuse Investigations – A Guide for Children and Young People. The Child Witness Pack* (NSPCC, 1993). This is for children who are called to court to testify in child abuse cases, and even has a cardboard cut-out of a Crown Court with pop-up figures of the judge, lawyer, witnesses, etc.

For children, families and other members of the community the increasing availability of telephone helplines, e.g. Childline, demonstrates the widespread need for easily accessible support and information regarding child abuse concerns.

Practice and professional issues

There are three main areas of professional intervention in the areas of child abuse and child protection:

1. Direct work carried out with the individual child or young person who has been abused, and his/her family.

2. Wide-scale preventative work carried out with community groups or organisations such as schools.

3. Inter-agency work centred around investigation of abuse, management of abuse cases, e.g. liaison, policy development, joint training, research initiatives.

Each of these three areas links up with, impacts on, and influences the other two.

1. Direct work with children, young people and families

Direct work covers a wide range of interventions and is sometimes referred to as 'treatment', counselling, therapy or support and can be carried out by a variety of agencies in a number of settings. Direct work can be at an individual, family or group level or a mixture of these and be extremely short in duration (from one or two sessions) to highly extensive (over several years or more). The regularity of the input also varies enormously. The theoretical framework within which the intervention takes place shows the widest possible span of approaches including psycho-dynamic, cognitive-behavioural, person-centred, counselling and family systems approaches. (Family therapy is the subject of Chapter 7.) Sometimes a number of workers may be involved in joint work or providing intervention at a number of levels with the same family, e.g.:

- A family therapist and social worker working with the family members.
- The child who has been abused also sees a worker on their own, e.g. play therapist, psychotherapist, psychologist or victim support counsellor.
- The perpetrator of the abuse taking part in a group with, for example, a probation officer and social worker.
- Ongoing links with the child's school made by, for example, a psychologist or counsellor.
- Ongoing family visiting by the health visitor where there are younger children.

Most of this direct work is focused on the time-scale following investigation of abuse or allegations or evidence of abuse. However, sometimes children and families will be involved in ongoing work around other issues when the abuse comes to light. It needs to be acknowledged that other traumatic events unconnected to the actual abuse can occur.

Case example (A): Ann

Ann was 8 years old when her father died following a long illness. Ann and her three older sisters had been sexually abused over many years by a neighbour who was regarded as a friend by the family. Each sister had kept the abuse secret because of threats and intimidation from the abuser. Ann was 9 when she disclosed the abuse to her mother. When Ann and her mother asked for help following the social services and police investigations, feelings around both the death and the abuse had to be explored and worked through.

The reaction of non-abused siblings of children who have been abused will sometimes only emerge in family work or in an indirect way.

Case example (B): Darren

Darren was referred because of reading difficulties. Darren's younger sister had been sexually and physically abused by her mother's boyfriend and then 2 years later by an uncle. Darren's mother had experienced abuse and neglect as a child and was, at that time, unwilling to use the support or therapeutic services offered to her daughter, herself and her other children. However, she was very concerned about Darren's school achievements and his lack of confidence which had led to referral. Darren, who had apparently not been directly abused, was in turmoil about the powerlessness and anger he had felt about hearing his sister being abused in the next room. He felt let down and ignored by those around him. In many ways Darren's emotional development and well-being had been neglected.

In those families where the abusers are family members, clinicians have found a number of factors which influence the progress of the intervention. Skuse and Bentovim (1994) describe factors which they argue are essential to the assessment of outcome as 'hopeful, doubtful or hopeless'.

These predictions of the outcome of intervention can change over time. It is not unusual for direct work to be carried out in distinct phases, often with different referral patterns in a family's history.

Given the paucity of resources in many areas or the prevalence of waiting lists for direct work, a full range of services may not always be available for children and families. Sensitive matching or awareness of gender or cultural or linguistic background is a particularly important factor with case work. Some practices such as female genital mutilation (FMG) raise specific issues which need to be addressed extremely sensitively (LBWHAP, 1991).

Increasingly, the possibility of a heightened vulnerability of some children and young people with special needs or with a disability is becoming apparent (Brown and Craft, 1989; Kelly, 1992). Particular emphasis needs to be placed on matching communication systems between child and the support worker, e.g. Makaton, British Sign Language. Frequently, specialist workers may need to be drawn in or specialist skills developed in other workers to make direct work meaningful for some children.

Case example (C): Yemi
Yemi was 9 years old when her teacher observed her highly sexualised behaviour on a school trip. Yemi has severe learning difficulties and communicated the abuse she had experienced through acting it out, through the use of gesture, a few spoken words and Makaton symbols. Her teacher, whom Yemi trusted and could communicate with, was asked to help the police and social services in conducting their investigation. The perpetrator(s) of the abuse has not been discovered but medical assessment confirmed extreme long-term sexual abuse. To provide appropriate direct individual work with Yemi, a specialist therapist was appointed to work with her in the school setting.

Group work with children or young people who have been sexually abused has sometimes been provided alongside family work. Some of the group work has had a focus on educating abused children skills to prevent recurrence of abuse. (Bentovim *et al.*, 1987). Peake (1989) has produced a helpful resource pack which includes guidelines and materials for group work with sexually abused children.

A comprehensive modular pack addressing a number of therapeutic issues has been produced by the NSPCC (1992) dealing with therapeutic work with children and young people, work with non-abusing parents, with offenders, with survivors and carers.

Direct work supporting individuals or families such as Homestart or Newpin can be seen by the subjects of this support as extremely valuable (Skuse and Bentovim, 1994). There are also a number of self-help or survivors groups, particularly for adult survivors of child sexual abuse which have strong, clear messages for today's work with children. Ainscough and Toon (1993) describe adult survivors' accounts of a range of feelings and experiences children who are abused have, including 'silent ways of telling', flashbacks and intrusive thoughts.

From time to time those working directly with children who have been abused may become involved in providing reports for courts or other settings, as well as supporting children who give evidence in court as witnesses. As Flin (1990) points out, child witnesses find the long wait and inadequate preparation before court appearances extremely stressful.

Some children and young people who have been abused are eligible to apply to the Criminal Injuries Compensation Board (CICB) and those working directly with them may be asked to write a report outlining the psychological damage induced by the abuse. The CICB guide (CICB, 1990) refers to 'personal injury directly attributable to ... a crime of "violence"'. Personal injury can include 'mental injury'.

Clinical models of working with children and young people who sexually abuse are starting to develop as more young abusers are coming to the attention of agencies (see Tavistock Project). There are particular issues which need to be addressed when planning direct work with young abusers who frequently have themselves been abused – the child or young person is also victim, survivor and abuser.

2. Preventative work

Professional preventative strategies in the area of child abuse can be classified predominantly as either at a primary or secondary level. Primary prevention is aimed at the general population as a whole e.g. wide-scale publicity campaigns, whilst secondary prevention is targeted more specifically at those considered 'at risk' in the hope of eliminating or reducing the incidence of the problem. In practice, secondary prevention refers to work with families where there is already a child with experience of abuse. The context within which most primary prevention takes place is within community groups and specific organisations like schools, whereas secondary prevention is focused more on work with children and families by a variety of agencies, e.g., social services, therapeutic centres (see above, direct work). Inter-agency liaison and development influences both types of interventions.

This section deals with primary prevention strategies.

Community based prevention programmes
Many of these strategies involve awareness raising with a variety of publicity targets and methods, such as using leaflets, campaigns, roadshows, etc., to inform children and adults about child protection matters, e.g. *Working Towards a Child-Safe Newham* and *Don't Shake Your Baby* (London Borough of Newham, 1993, 1995, respectively).

Preventative work in schools
Over the last 5–10 years there has been a rapid increase in the amount of work

carried out and materials produced for schools to use in the area of primary prevention of abuse. Much of it has had child sexual abuse at the core of the prevention programme but increasingly a wider approach encompassing all forms of abuse is being taken. Kidscape materials are often known in schools even if not always used directly (Elliott, 1989). Evans (1991) has produced two comprehensive packs, specifically for use in schools, using a strong curriculum approach to prevention. Plans for workshops with school governors and parents are also included.

'The Listening School' provides materials for the 'preventative curriculum' where children's emotional needs are addressed as well as their educational needs (Gilmore and Dymond, 1993).

Inter-agency work

It is essential for each worker to be clear about his or her own role and responsibilities and the procedures which apply before effective inter-agency work is really possible. Good channels of communication, clarity of line management issues and access to support and supervision within the work setting are also pre-requisites to developing effective inter-agency work. Specific responses to child abuse cases and child protection work have been mapped out by many agencies e.g. in relation to schools (Maher, 1987). The perception of agency worker's roles is often unclear to other workers (Birchall and Hallett, 1995).

One of the perils of working in isolation has become known as 'professional dangerousness'. Defining inter-agency co-ordination, co-operation or collaboration is complex (Hallett, 1995). Perhaps continuum approaches are most helpful here such as that put forward by Gough *et al.* (1987), where inter-agency work is described as existing on a continuum from working separately to being part of a team (Chapter 1 addresses effective team working).

There is a need for ongoing, updated training for individuals within each of the main agencies – social services, health, education, police, probation service and the voluntary sector. There is a wide range of training materials available geared both to inter-agency joint training, as well as specific agencies (Braun, 1988; Elliott, 1989; Holdsworth, 1994; Paley, 1990).

Recent studies have shown enormous variation in the extent of knowledge about signs and indicators of abuse, assessment of risk issues, how to respond to cases of child abuse and professional roles in child protection plans. With reference to teachers, Hallett (1995) suggests that evidence from the research study indicates a need to raise the level of awareness and knowledge of how to respond to child abuse as well as spelling out the teacher's role more clearly in child protection plans. The increasing complexity of information used in raising awareness regarding, for example, signs and indicators of abuse, is shown by a review of the literature of signs and indicators associated with child sexual abuse. Lamers-Winkelman (1995) found 102 signs and indicators in a survey of American, British and other European studies. Inter-agency training should also address the preparation for and presentation at a child protection conference, as well as the most appropriate form of debriefing afterwards. Sometimes agency workers at case conferences can feel a 'lone voice' and need to be able to find a constructive way of expressing their views about a child's situation with regard to assessment of risk.

Agencies working together need to allow time to reflect on complex case work issues and learn from them in a forum where different skills and perspectives are valued. Tufnell *et al.* (1993) describe a model for the development of a consultation workshop within a Child and Family Consultation Service.

Conclusions

Everyone involved with children and young people has a duty to be well informed about child abuse and neglect, know how to respond to abuse and work towards preventing it. Kempe and Kempe (1984) assert that the whole community is involved in protecting children.

It is every child's and young persons' right to be free from abuse and to be cared for and looked after. These rights need to be asserted and children and young people made aware of them. They also should be made aware of what to do and who to go to when these rights are violated. Appropriate, accessible and effective support must be made available for children and their families or carers as quickly as possible following abuse and in a sensitive way that respects their background and current situation. Abuse may lead to a child experiencing extreme and profound feelings which may impact on many areas of their life currently and in the future. Powerful emotions experienced by the child might include anger, resentment, grief, confusion, betrayal and self-loathing (Alsop, 1993). Those who are in positions to listen to children who have been abused need to find better ways of understanding what is being communicated so that, with appropriate support, children can increasingly define themselves not as victims but as survivors.

References

Adams, J. *et al.*, (1992) In O'Donohue, W. and Geer, J.H. (eds) *The Sexual Abuse of Children: Theory and Research*. Hove: Lawrence Erlbaum Associates.

Ainscough, C. and Toon, K. (1993) *Breaking Free: Help for Survivors of Child Sexual Abuse*. London: Sheldon Press.

Alsop, P. (1993) In Alsop, P. and McCaffrey, T. (eds) *How to Cope with Childhood Stress: Guide for Teachers*. Harlow: Longman.

Beitchman, J.H., Zucker, K.J., Hood, J.E., da Costa, G.A, Akman, D. and Cassaria, E. (1992) 'A review of the long-term effects of child sexual abuse', *Child Abuse and Neglect*, **16**, 101–18.

Bentovim, A., Boston, P. and Elbury, A. (1987) 'Child sexual abuse – children and families referred to a treatment projects and the effects of intervention', *British Medical Journal*, **295**, 1453–57.

Birchall, E. and Hallett, C. (1995) *Working Together in Child Protection.* London: HMSO.

Bird, J., Harskamp, A. and Knowles, M. (1995) unpublished child protection training materials for a variety of needs, e.g. articled teachers, newly qualified teachers, whole-school staff, CP coordinators, governors, trainee educational psychologists: Educational Psychology Service. London: London Borough of Newham.

Braun, D. (1988) *Responding to Child Abuse. Action and Planning for Teachers and other Professionals.* London: Bedford Square Publishers.

Brown, H. and Craft, A. (1989) *Thinking the Unthinkable. Papers on Sexual Abuse and People with Learning Difficulties.* London: Family Planning Association Education Unit.

CICB (1990) *A Guide to the Criminal Injuries Compensation Scheme.* Glasgow: CICB.

Cripps, C. (1995) Personal Communication. Coordinator Youth Awareness Programmes for Network Drugs Advice Projects. London: Borough of Newham.

Croner (1992), *Croner's School Governor's Manual.* Kingston-upon-Thames: Croner.

Department for Education (1994) *Code of Practice on the Identification and Assessment of Special Educational Needs.* London: DfE.

Department for Education and Employment (1995a) Circular 10/95. *Protecting Children from Abuse – The Role of the Education Service.* London: DfEE.

Department for Education and Employment (1995b) Circular 11/95. *Misconduct of Teachers and Workers with Children and Young Persons.* London: DfEE.

Department of Education and Science (1998) Circular DES 4/88. *Working Together for Protection of Children from Abuse. Procedures within the Education Service.* London: DoH.

Department of Health (1993) *Guide to the United Nations Convention: The Rights of the Child.* London: DoH/Children's Rights Development Unit.

Department of Health (1995) *Children and Young People on Child Protection Registers Year Ending 31 March 1994, England.* London: DoH.

Eaton, L. (1994) 'Slaughter of the innocence'. *Guardian.* 2 November.

Elliott, M. (1989) *Dealing with Child Abuse.* London: Kidscape.

Evans, G. (1991) *Child Protection. A Whole Curriculum Approach.* Bristol: Avec Designs.

Flin, R. (1990) 'Child witnesses in criminal courts', *Children and Society,* **4(3)**, 264–83.

Gilmore, J. and Dymond, P. (1993) *The Listening School – Creating a Preventative Curriculum,* and *The Listening School – A Positive Response to Child Sexual Abuse.* Pontesbury: Links Educational Publications.

Glaser, D. (1995) 'Emotionally abused children - a report of the Young Minds Conference', *Young Minds Newsletter,* 20 January.

Hallett, C. (1995) *Interagency Coordination in Child Protection.* London: HMSO.

HMSO (1991) *Working Together under the Children Act 1989.* London: HMSO.

Holdsworth, R. (1994) *Multi-Disciplinary Communication in Child Protection.* London: NSPCC.

Kelly, L. (1992) 'The connections between disability and child abuse: a review of the research evidence', *Child Abuse Review,* **1(3)**, 157–67.

Kempe, R.S. and Kempe, H.C. (1984) *The Common Secret. Sexual Abuse of Children and Adolescents.* New York: Freeman.

Kendall-Tackett, K., Williams, L.M. and Finkelhor, D. (1993) 'Impact of sexual abuse on children: A review of synthesis of recent empirical studies', *Psychological Bulletin,* **113(1)**, 164–80.

Lamers-Winkelman, F. (1995) *Seksueel misbruik van kinderen.* Amsterdam: VU Uitgever.

LBWHAP (London Black Women's Health Action Project) (1991) *Is Female Circumcision Child Abuse?* London: LBWHAP.

London Borough of Newham (1993) *Working Towards a Child-Safe Newham.* London: London Borough of Newham.

London Borough of Newham (1995) Don't Shake Your Baby. London: London Borough of Newham.

Maher, P. (ed.) (1987) *Child Abuse. The Educational Perspective.* Oxford: Blackwell.

Matthews, J. (1993) In Elliott, M. (ed.) *Female Sexual Abuse of Children: The Ultimate Taboo.* Harlow: Longman.

National Children's Homes (1992) *Summary of Report of Committee of Inquiry into Children and Young People who Sexually Abuse other Children.* London: National Children's Homes.

NSPCC (1992b) *Child Protection Procedures: What They Mean for Your Family.* London: NSPCC/Family Rights Group.

NSPCC (1992a) *Working with the Aftermath of Child Sexual Abuse.* London: NSPCC.

NSPCC (1993) *The Child Witness Pack – Helping Children to Cope.* London: NSPCC.

OFSTED (1994) *The Handbook for the Inspection of Schools.* London: OFSTED.

Paley, J. (ed.) (1990) *Child Protection Adviser's Resource Pack.* London: NSPCC.

Peake, A. (1989) *Working with Sexually Abused Children: A Resource Pack for Professionals.* London: The Children's Society.

Skuse, D. (1989) 'Emotional abuse and neglect', *British Medical Journal,* **298**, 1692–95.

Skuse, D. and Bentovim, A. (1994) 'Physical and emotional maltreatment'. In Rutter, M., Taylor, E. and Hersov, L. (eds) *Child and Adolescent Psychiatry – Modern Approach.* 3rd edn. Oxford: Blackwell Science.

Smith, M. and Bentovim, A. (1994) Sexual abuse. In Rutter, M., Taylor, E. and Hersov, L. (eds) *Child and Adolescent Psychiatry – Modern Approach.* 3rd edn. Oxford: Blackwell Science.

Speight, N. (1989) 'Non-accidental injury', *British Medical Journal,* **298**, 879–82.

Tavistock Clinic Young Abusers Project. Tavistock Clinic, 120 Belsize Lane, London NW3 5BA.

Tufnell, G. *et al.* (1993) Child abuse and neglect: The development of a consultation workshop', *ACPP Review and Newsletter,* **15(1)**, 7–14.

Chapter Ten

Growing up in non-nuclear families

Andrea Pecherek

Most children are brought up within a family; however, not all families are constituted in the same way and not all families remain together. Whilst it is the adults who make decisions as to how to live and how to order their family life, the children are directly influenced by whatever arrangement is made.

This chapter will address the effects on children of the disruption of a marriage or marriage-type relationship in terms of various factors, both interpersonal, emotional, practical and political.

What is the family?

The family, and the concept of the family, in addition to being seen as the vessel for human security and bonds of affection, is highly political. It also figures strongly in religious dogma, and is the inspiration for great works of art. But what is it? What do we mean by a family?

The stereotype of the family which is adopted in Western society is that of the 'nuclear family', which is the norm. The family also presupposes the presence of children, more specifically, dependent children. The nuclear family is a group consisting of two adults who are mother and father to one or more children who are of dependent age, living with them because they are not yet independent adults. The political debate has heightened as this norm appears to be being violated – often voluntarily.

Do exceptions disprove the rule? Are there are alternative ways of defining 'family life'? Can there be a family without children?

In effect, in 1995 one household in four consisted of a married couple with dependent children and one in three cohabiting households have dependent children who may be stepchildren. (Statistical data in this chapter are from Utting, 1995.)

The incidence of lone parenting is increasing. In 1971, one in thirteen families was headed by a single parent, i.e. 8% of families. In 1995 this had risen to one in five – 21%. Divorce is only one of the explanations for this sharp rise. Other explanations include:

- a decrease in fertility;
- increased propensity for women with children to establish independent households outside marriage;
- an increase in remarriage;
- an increase in non-marital births.

In addition, there has been a rise in what has been called the 'companionate marriage' (Elliott and Richards, 1991), rather than marriage based on economic, religious or social factors. These partnerships probably see childbearing as a matter of personal choice and negotiation, rather than as an automatic course of events.

When examining issues surrounding the care and upbringing of children, there is no neutrality. We all have feelings about it – not only those who are parents. People who do not have children or do not work with children, have feelings and opinions about how they should be treated, and how they should be brought up.

Parents who divorce, separate or who bring up children on their own often believe that there is a stigma attached to them, that in some way they are not 'doing the right thing'. There is an accumulation of evidence within our society that this is the case. Michael Argyle (1994) quotes Abrams *et al.* (1985) and Brown (1985) in their findings that working-class people place more value on the family than do the middle classes and that middle-class people think divorce is too easy.

1994 was designated The Year of the Family; it was an international attempt to reinstate the family as a valued and valuable inter-personal and political unit. Martin Richards (1995) suggests that despite this initiative being a proactive and positive event, concurrent UK Government actions included stigmatisation of single parents, rejection of EC proposals on paternity leave, and having a UK record as the country in the European Community with the fastest growth rate of poverty.

The structure and functioning of the family can be defined in three ways (Richards, 1995):

1. The **household**, which consists of a group of people – of any ages – who share the same dwelling and who usually eat together and share other intimate domestic arrangements. This structure includes children born to the adults. Within our culture it would usually be two people – one of each sex – who determine the culture and rules and who brings up the children. They may or may not be married.

2. On the other hand, it is affinity by 'blood' which determines the **nuclear** nature of family life rather than its legal status, although in British Law (Children Act 1989) a blood father who is not married to the child's mother does not have the same rights as he would if they were married. In addition to this blood relationship, our culture would assume that this nuclear group fulfils the more important emotional relationships and stability.

3. **Kinship**, which implies a shared set of beliefs which thereby determines action and lifestyle. Kinship embraces more than the immediate relationship of and between the procreators and can be multi-generational.

The nuclear family has been generally perceived as being the arrangement which secures the mental health (Bowlby, 1958) and social stability of the members (Gorman, 1991).

They can be disrupted in one of two ways, either by death or by the separation of the adult partners. Increasingly, in families with children, it is separation or divorce which causes the family to end. There has been a six-fold increase in the annual divorce rate since 1961. If current trends continue, four out of ten new marriages will end in divorce. One in four children can expect to have experienced parental divorce or separation at age 16.

Research issues

Most of the research available to us comes from studies of the effects of divorce or separation on children. This emphasis has come about for three reasons:

1. The recent increase in research has come about because of the escalating divorce rate.

2. Through the necessity to dispel some of the myths surrounding the effects of divorce.

3. To highlight those factors which have a strong bearing on children's development.

It is clear, however, that research has not kept pace with the changes in family structure.

One of the problems inherent in research in the human sciences is the problem of adequate sampling. In the case of looking at families, which families do you choose? Families are private. How do we access their thoughts, feelings, motivations, etc.? The most rigorous and wide-ranging research, for example the work of Wallerstein and Kelly (1980), attracts a self-selecting group who feel comfortable with this method

Once the families are identified, how do we find out about them? Do we use interviews or use questionnaires or observational approaches? Who do we talk to or observe, the adults, the children, or both? Separately or together?

Often, research presents a snapshot of the here and now. Human dynamics dictate that people in groups change, and as they change individually, so the group changes as a whole. Particularly with children, we need to acknowledge that their natural increasing maturity and understanding will change reactions and dynamics between adults. Children with the same experiences within families, for example, divorce or poverty, do in fact have different reactions to and interpretations of their surroundings (Utting, 1995).

These considerations do not necessarily negate the findings of such studies which offer us pointers rather than absolutes.

Most of the research concentrates on trying to identify the negative effects of disrupted families or to validate the appropriateness of lone-parenting. In most cases this disruption refers to divorce. Separation and divorce are not entities, they constitute a process, there are events that happen before it and situations that occur after. The effects which these events and situations have upon children is dependent on a combination of factors such as temperament, relationships with both parents, stability and wealth, or lack of it. How do we monitor the disintegration of a family and measure the effects of this process?

Some of the most extensive research has followed large samples followed over a period of time, such as that by Wallerstein (1985) and Hetherington, Cox and Cox (1982).

The effects on children of divorce and separation

Most children whose parents separate or divorce are clearly affected in some way for at least a period of time (Burgoyne *et al.*, 1987). These changes are varied and depend upon the age of the child, the circumstances of the separation, and the conditions in the home following the separation. Table 10.1 shows some consistent findings on the effects of divorce on children of different ages. It is compiled from a combination of developmental research and research looking specifically at divorce.

There have been no divorce studies focusing on children aged under 2 years. Infants normally develop their first attachment bonds to a parent early in life (Bowlby, 1969; Rutter, 1978). It is not clear when the infant may be affected by changes in relationships in the family, though in some cases severe reactions have been found in children aged under 5 (Hetherington *et al.*, 1983).

In general, boys seem to demonstrate more prolonged problems than girls (Hess and Camara, 1979). This is possibly because children are usually placed with their mothers, and boys may feel the loss of a gender model (Haley, 1976; Hetherington, 1979). An alternative explanation is that boys are more likely than girls to demonstrate challenging behaviour and overt expressions of anger; an extension of this which comes about as a reaction to divorce may be seen as problematic. However, girls tend to show more disturbance in adolescence (Amato and Keith, 1991).

Table 10.1 The effects of divorce on children of different ages (based on data collated by Longfellow, 1979)

Age of child (years)	Behavioural and psychological effects
Preschool	Frightened, confused, self-blaming
5–6	Some understanding of what divorce means, protest, withdrawal, detachment
7–8	Sadness, fear, insecurity
9–10	Better understanding, outward expressions of anger
13–18	Engagement in examination of family relationships and their own values and concepts

Many children demonstrate a lowering of self-esteem and there is also a high statistical incidence of children developing conduct disorders and symptoms of psychological distress, difficulties of adjustment and lowered academic achievement (Amato and Keith, 1991; Hetherington, 1989). However, Richards (1995:84) points out that:

> The differences in educational attainment measures for middle class children who have and have not had the experience of parental divorce are of the same order as the differences between children from homes without divorce from middle class and working class backgrounds.

Therefore, divorce is *one* of many factors which cause academic difficulties.

The effects of these negative changes may be short or longer term. Again, the research shows differences. For example, Wallerstein (1984) found effects of disturbance 5 and 10 years after the divorce. Hetherington (1988) found that these tended to have diminished by 5 years. One possible explanation for these different findings is that Wallerstein's sample consisted of participants prepared to engage in counselling, and who were, perhaps, more likely to perceive enduring difficulties. No offers of support were made in the Hetherington sample. This illustrates the need for care in interpreting research findings in this sensitive area.

Stepparenting

The 1994 Office of Population Censuses and Surveys showed that in the UK there were 500,000 stepfamilies, with 800,000 stepchildren.

In 1995, 7% of households with children included stepchildren, three out of four of these children came from women's previous relationships.

The National Children's Bureau conducted a survey of all children born during one week during 1958. They found that 5% were members of stepfamilies at age 16 and the ratio of those living with mothers rather than fathers was 3:1.

Hetherington (1988) found that within their sample, 6 years after divorce 70% of women and 80% of men had remarried.

As with divorce, stepparenting carries a wealth of myths, such as 'the wicked stepmother' and 'the abusing stepfather'. It is important to differentiate fact from fiction. Table 10.2 illustrates those factors which, either singly or in combination, are likely to make for success or failure of adjustment within stepfamilies.

Table 10.2 Factors likely to affect the success or otherwise of stepfamilies (adapted from Schaffer, 1990)

Factor	Likely to succeed	Less likely to succeed
Sex of stepparent	Father	Mother
Sex of stepchild	Girl	Boy
Length of relationship	18 months +	Less than 1 year
Relationship with non-custodial parent	Good	Erratic or poor
Siblings	With own siblings	Parted from siblings
Number of family members	Four or less	More than four
Complexity of stepfamily	Straightforward	Many members, complex relationships

Furstenberg (1987) began a National Survey of Children in the USA in 1976 with a representative sample of 2,279 children between the ages of 7 and 11. Five years later children from divorced families were seen again, together with a random sub-sample of children from non-divorced families. The majority of stepchildren were positive in their evaluations of closeness, tension, and sharing in the family, though they did not respond as favourably as children in nuclear families. He goes on to point out, however, that the statistical differences were due largely to the responses of those children living in stepmother families. These families are consistently found to have more difficulties in adjustment than those with a stepfather.

Another important determinant of the success of stepfamilies is the amount and quality of contact which the child has with the absent birth-parent (Wallerstein, 1987).

Other factors are whether the child is with natural siblings, the number of children in the family, the complexity of the new family structure and age of the child at remarriage.

In a study conducted by Santrock *et al.* (1987), it was found that on a variety of measures of competence in physical, social and cognitive skills, children in stepfather families fared similarly to children living with both biological parents. This finding was confirmed by direct observation and by reports from teachers. However, the stepchildren did tend to have a rather more negative view of themselves than did other children.

The fact that so many stepparenting families are successful is undoubtedly due to a feeling of well-being on the part of the parents. In the Hetherington study, the remarried parents commented on their diminished loneliness, anxiety, economic concerns and household disorganisation, and was reflected in their relationships with their children, to the advantage of all.

Schaffer (1990:178) comments that in regards to the relationships between stepchildren and their new families:

> What is clear is that children *can* form proper relationships; there is nothing in human nature to prevent this occurring. Under optimal conditions these can be close and satisfying: the fact that in a certain proportion of cases they fall short of this ideal makes it all the more important to search for the factors that prevent this occurring, as only then can appropriate action be taken.

Children with lone parents

The mythology about children of parents who have separated includes beliefs about the effects of paternal absence. These have been stated as including effeminate or juvenile delinquent behaviour in boys and promiscuity in girls (Longfellow, 1979; Nye, 1957). It was also believed to have an impact on mental health and stability. More recent research however suggests that there is no support for these suggestions (Bernard and Nesbitt, 1981; Herzog and Sudia, 1973). Lowery and Settle (1985:455) state:

> A direct causal link between divorce and a variety of children's problems has not been supported by more recent, better controlled studies.

Rather than divorce itself being a causal factor in children's emotional and psychological development, factors such as positive communication and preparing the child for the inevitable changes are seen as paramount (Noller and Callan, 1991) We know this also from other studies which have looked at the effects of overt family conflict. These studies have shown that most of the negative effects on children, such as juvenile crime, behaviour problems, acute stress and anxiety and academic problems, which are often assumed to be the result of divorce are in fact more likely to have been caused by other factors, such as domestic tension or conflict. (Booth and Amato, 1994; Farrington, 1992).

Elliott and Richards (1991) suggest that it may be the attitudes towards divorce on the part of the parents, the children and the community which colour views of its consequences for children.

Another very important factor which changes for families after divorce or separation is income and relative wealth. The pattern of single parent poverty appears to be rising dramatically. In 1975 one-third of lone parents with dependent children were receiving Supplementary Benefit; in 1995 7 out of 10 such parents were receiving Income Support (the current equivalent). The change in financial status is usually for the worse; 25% of divorced women fall into poverty for some time during the first 5 years after divorce (Morgan, 1989). As most lone parents are women, this has led to what has been called the 'feminisation of poverty'. A study by Duffy (1986) showed that among divorced women, financial stability was their primary consideration. Whilst UK Governmental policies have tried to address this factor by the establishment of the Child Support Agency, the evidence suggests that the current scheme makes very little difference to the incomes of households of divorced women and their children (Children's Society, 1994). Poverty has effects on most areas of children's lives, from diet and health to emotional well-being and achievement (Huston, 1991).

With divorce or the separation of parents, the lives of adults and children are disrupted. The adults may show mood-swings and experience problems with employment or poor health (Hetherington, 1989). It has been shown that these effects are less severe when there is another adult in the household, such as a friend or someone from the extended family (Dornbusch, 1985). This suggests that a two-adult system in a family may be more stable or easier to manage.

Another major factor in how the adults cope with their change in life-style is social support. Simons (1993) found that single mothers with little education had low access to social network support and reported high exposure to negative events and low social support.

Whilst it is more common for mothers to have the care of the children after divorce, this is not always the case. A study in Kentucky conducted by the Displaced Homemaker Program at Northern Kentucky University which interviewed a selection of lone fathers found them to be confident in their role but felt that some of society's expectations of fathers were unrealistic.

Models for explaining the process of divorce

In the opening section of this chapter it was noted that we all have belief systems which influence the way explain and deal with family systems, arrangements and organisation. One useful way of taking stock of these beliefs is to examine various models, or paradigms, and to take comfort that our own instinctive interpretations and methods of working with children and families does in fact have a basis within some theoretical framework. As with most theoretical frameworks used to describe behaviour and relationships, most practitioners acknowledge that in reality we tend to hold views which encompass more than one of these models.

Family systems model

This approach emphasises the fact that after divorce or separation the relationship between the parents does not end, it merely changes, even when one of the parents has no contact. The absent parent is seen as continuing to exist within the family through the child. Professionals who work with families will be familiar with the scenario where the parent who has care of the child (usually the mother) comments that the child reminds her of the absent father – often in terms of the fathers less appealing traits or characteristics!

Adherents to this model (e.g. Hess and Camara, 1979; Huntington, 1982; Musetto, 1978) would concentrate on helping the parent come to terms with the effects which the previous relationship continues to exert, thereby, hopefully, freeing the child to be perceived as an individual, free of 'malign contagion'.

Family systems interventions are discussed further in Chapter 7.

Political model

The rationale behind the political model is defined by Stainton Rogers (1992:108) as:

> The family's purpose is to provide a location for growing up, and the purpose of growing up is to provide children who will go on to provide new families.

This, of course, means that the family must be encouraged to resist all contingencies which might disrupt it. This is achieved by the legislative process, which makes dissolution difficult, and by religious and social mores.

The political model encompasses positions based on religious beliefs, which hold that any alternative to the nuclear family is inherently flawed. If the purpose of the family is to provide a location for growing up and the purpose of growing up is to provide children who will parent new families then the family system has to endure and resist disruptions.

Williamson (1987:116) comments as follows:

> The representations of the family as an autonomous emotional unit cuts across class and power relations to imply that we all share the same experience. It provides a common sexual and economic goal; images of family life hold out pleasure and leisure as the fulfilment of desires which, if not thus contained, could cause social chaos.

Practitioners within this paradigm would emphasise that making things better within the family is the most providential course of action, and would also highlight the harmful effects which divorce, separation and lone parenting have on children and society.

Cumulative stress model

This paradigm is the one which most succinctly brings together evidence, opinions and subjective experiences. It seems to reflect common knowledge and commonsense.

The cumulative stress model proposes that the process of any one, or more than one, member of the family experiencing unhappiness within a relationship to the point of desiring its dissolution, is the culmination of more than the inter-personal dynamics of the adults. Likewise, the effects on children are cumulative (e.g. Hodges *et al.*, 1979).

According to the cumulative stress model, it:

> assumes that there is a threshold of stress that can be exceeded either by a single event that is extremely stressful or by the occurrence of several events of a less stressful nature within a short period of time, not allowing for enough time between events to recover.
>
> (Lowery and Settle, 1985:456)

There is some disagreement over the interpretation of the dynamics of multiple stressors associated with divorce. Shaw *et al.* (1994) found a linear pattern between family stress and children's adjustment, whereas Rutter *et al.* (1978) found a multiplicative effect, in that the interaction of two or more stressors was greater than their sum.

Desforges (1994) supports the linear perspective in that he points out that there are economic, legal and emotional ties that break down at different times. There seems to be no accessible research which has looked at the relative effects on children of these various factors.

Factors considered to be significant are:

- the amount of preparation which has been afforded to the child;
- the amount of ambiguity expressed;
- the duration and extent of conflict;
- the strength of the remaining social networks;
- the material comfort of the caring parent and children.

In a paper presented to the Annual Convention of the American Psychological Association in 1991, Judith Worell suggests that psychological disruption observed in children of recently divorced parents may be, in part, related to the quality of the custodial mother's adjustment to her changed life circumstances. These may include loss of attachment bonds, changes in daily living patterns, excessive role strain and the amount of continuing interpersonal conflict. This stress on the part of the carer may foster negative and coercive childrearing practices which are reflected in the disrupted behavioural and developmental progress of the children.

The problems experienced within the marriage or cohabitation prior to the separation of parents may be equally responsible for any post-separation disturbance observed in the children (Hetherington *et al.*, 1985). This coincides with the findings of Rutter *et al.* (1975a,b) that there is an increase in the probability of children exhibiting a behavioural disorder as a function of multiple family stressors. These stressors may include poor marital functioning, parental warmth, mental adjustment, and poverty.

Supporting children of non-nuclear families

The evidence discussed above all indicates that there is no blanket evidence that children of non-nuclear families are inherently disadvantaged on a permanent basis because of the single factor of divorce or separation. It is therefore not possible or sensible to assume that intervention 'X' is appropriate when the child has experienced 'A'. Professionals who work with children and families have to be sensitive to individual and family needs, and to rely on clinical judgement which, when taken together, constitutes good practice. This good practice can take place with the children themselves, with the families, within schools and within the community.

Good practice with children

The way in which the child perceives events within the family will be determined by a variety of factors from individual temperament to the amount of explanation and communication which has taken place with them about what is happening in the family. Children have opinions about their parents and about parents' behaviour and actions. A study conducted by Mazur (1990) looked at children's attitudes about marriage and divorce. The children were aged from 6 to 9, and were from both divorced and non-divorced families. Mazur found that whilst most of the children expected to marry and believed that marriage is a positive experience, the children were surprisingly accepting of divorce as a solution to an unhappy marriage, even in cases involving young children. Perhaps not surprisingly, she also found that children with divorced parents were more likely than children with still-married parents to view divorce as a possibility for themselves.

Herbert (1988) found that children viewed some aspects of the divorce process as more disturbing than others. These were: parents who were not able to talk to them about the break-up in a reasoned way; not getting on with one of the parents after the divorce, and acrimonious or unsatisfactory custody arrangements. These observations highlight particular aspects of concern for children; it is possible for those adults working with children and families to be aware of the specific cause of observed disturbance. It also has implications for social policy. Cowie and Pecherek (1994) suggest that the most difficult situation for children is where they are used as pawns in the parental conflict. Again, this has implications for direct work with families.

Good practice in schools

As we have seen, stressful environmental experiences such as divorce can compromise children's receptivity to learning and, in some cases, their attitude towards school.

Teachers have an understanding of child development of the children in their classes, if not in its complexity. They are aware of abnormal reactions to life events such as divorce (Desforges, 1994), and are in a prime position to monitor and intervene in cases of children showing distress or academic difficulties.

For these reasons it is important for the school to be a welcoming place for parents. Since 1981 the phrase Parents as Partners has been enshrined in school policies and legislation. Wolfendale (1992) describes effective ways in which parents and teachers can work together. On an everyday level, this means being available to support parents in regards to their children whenever necessary.

Schools have knowledge of and access to other agencies such as child psychiatry, the educational psychological service and social services. They can direct parents towards appropriate courses of action. The Code of Practice (1993 Education Act) has as a requirement that schools work with parents of pupils with special educational needs in this partnership.

On a curricular level, the school can help to support children either suffering through the trauma of parental separation or living in hardship with a lone parent, by ensuring that teaching materials and examples reflect their own situation, rather than emphasising the 'normality' of the nuclear family.

It is important for schools to question how effectively they have adjusted to the changing patterns of family life such as single-parents and stepfamilies. Shea (1982:146) suggests that:

> Accompanying the recent rise in non-nuclear families is a gap in teachers' knowledge of, and skills dealing with these families, due in part to the general socialisation of teachers in a society which compares non-nuclear families unfavourably with traditional ones.

The Children Act (1989) now makes it law for schools to take 'all reasonable steps' to ascertain who has parental responsibility for the child. Schools pastoral policies need to reflect good and open communication with these individuals, and school staff need to be able to explain to the child who is receiving what information about them and for what purpose.

There are various illustrations of school programmes devised specifically to help the children of separated and divorced parents. One example of such a project is described by Crosbie-Burnett (1990) who devised an eight-session school-based model of group intervention for children of divorced or separated parents, and Carlucci (1988) who worked jointly with a schools psychologist in a programme of structured support for children and parents. These examples come from the USA. There is no comparable literature for the UK. Desforges (1994) suggests that schools may be culpable of less than sympathetic dealings with divorced or lone parents.

Good practice in the community

The public at large need to appreciate how family life has changed in recent years. To a certain extent this has happened; single parents are now no longer discriminated against in, for example, housing or employment law. Although there are alarmingly regular examples of malpractice, this is now illegal under UK and EEC mandate.

On 8 December 1994, the Rt. Hon Virginia Bottomley, MP, then Secretary of State for Health, in her response to 'Agenda for Action', recognised that almost all Governmental Departments handle policies which are of direct relevance to families and that the Cabinet should bear this in mind. To facilitate this, it was decided that ministers would meet 'periodically to examine the impact of government policies as a whole on the family'.

On 23 February a question was posed in the House of Commons to Mrs Bottomley:

> ...how often since 8 December 1994 have Ministers met to examine the impact of Government policies as a whole on the family; how often Ministers will be meeting for this purpose; and what assessment she has made of the outcomes to date?

The response was:

> Frequently. Such meetings contribute to overall policy making. They are not assessed in the way described.
>
> (*Hansard*, 1995)

Conclusions

Divorce and separation is, more often than not, a difficult and painful process. It brings about emotional as well as practical changes. What the research indicates is that there is no one factor or set of factors which indicate a more or less successful outcome for the children or the adults concerned. Many of the myths surrounding children of divorced or separated parents have been challenged. This opens up the field for new myths to be expounded. For this reason, it is of paramount importance that open-minded and critical studies of the effects of parental behaviours on children's development and well-being are encouraged and noted.

References

Abrams, M., Gerard, D. and Timms, N. (eds) (1985) *Values and Social Change in Britain*. Basingstoke: Macmillan.

Amato, P.R. and Keith, B. (1991) 'Parental divorce and the well being of children. A meta analysis', *Psychological Bulletin*, **110**, 24–46.

Argyle, M. (1994) *The Psychology of Social Class*. London: Routledge.

Bernard, J.M. and Nesbitt, S. (1981) 'Divorce: An unreliable predictor of children's emotional predispositions', *Journal of Divorce*, **4**, 31–41.

Booth, A. and Amato, P.R. (1994) 'Parental marital quality, parental divorce and relations with parents', *Journal of Marriage and the Family*, **56**, 21–34.

Bowlby, J. (1958) 'The nature of the child's tie to his mother', *International Journal of Psychoanalysis*, **39**, 350–73.

Bowlby, J. (1969) *Attachment and Loss: Attachment*. New York: Basic Books.

Brown, J. (1985) 'Marriage and the family'. In Abrams, M. Gerard, N. and Timms, N. (eds) *Values and Social Change in Britain*. Basingstoke: Macmillan.

Carlucci, J.P. (1988) 'Increasing elementary school based interventions for children of divorce by utilising faculty and parent workshops and developmental student groups'. Ed.D Practicum, Nova University, Ontario Canada.

Children's Society (1994) *Losing Support – Children and the Child Support Act*. London: The Children's Society.

Cowie, H. and Pecherek, A. (1994) *Counselling: Approaches and Issues in Education*. London: David Fulton.

Crosbie-Burnett, M. (1990) Paper presented to the annual convention of the American School Counsellor Association. Alexandria, VA.

Desforges, M. F. (1994) 'Separation, Divorce and the School'. In Best, R. (ed.) *Pastoral Care and PSE: Entitlement and Provision*. London: Cassell.

Dornbusch, S.M. *et al.* (1985) 'Single parents, extended households, and the control of adolescents', *Child Development*, **56**, 326–41.

Duffy, M.E. (1986) *The Transition of Divorce: An Analysis of Public Policy*. Paper presented at the annual conference of the National Council on Family Relations: Dearborn, MI, November.

Duffy, M.E. and Jorgensen, K. (1986) *The Transition of Divorce: An Analysis of Public Policy*. Paper presented at the Annual Conference of the National Council on Family Relations (Dearborn, MI, November 3–7)

Elliott, B.J. and Richards, M.P.M. (1991) 'Children and divorce: educational performance and behaviour, before and after parental separation', *International Journal of Law and the Family*, **5**, 258–78.

Farrington, D. (1992) 'Juvenile delinquency'. In Coleman, J. (ed.) *The School Years: Current Issues in the Socialization of Young People*, 2nd edn. London: Routledge.

Furstenberg, F.F. (1987) 'The new extended family: the experience of parents and children after remarriage'. In Pasley, K. and Ihinger-Tallman, D. (eds) *Remarriage and Stepparenting*. New York: Guildford.

Gorman, T. (1991) 'Empowering children' paper presented to the Libertarian Alliance Conference on Children's Rights', Albermarle Hall, London.

Haley, J. (1976) *Problem Solving Therapy*. San Francisco: Jossey-Bass.

Hansard PQ 2100/1994/95. Thursday 23 February 1995. Written Answer Wednesday 1 March 1995.

Hetherington, E.M., Cox, M. and Cox, R. (1983) 'Effects of divorce on single parents and children'. In Lamb, M.E. (ed.) *Non-Traditional Families: Parenting and Child Development*. Hilldale, NJ: Lawrence Eribaum.

Herbert, M. (1988) *Working with Children and their Families*. Leicester: BPS Books.

Herzog, E. and Sudia, C.A. (1973) 'Children in fatherless families'. In Caldwell, B.M. and Riccuiti, H.N. (eds) *Review of Child Development Research*. Vol. 3 *Child Development and Child Policy*.

Hess, R.D. and Camara, K.A. (1979) 'Post-divorce family relationships as mediating factors in the consequences of divorce for children', *Journal of Social Issues*, **35**, 79–96.

Hetherington, E.M. (1979) 'Divorce: A child's perspective', *American Psychologist*, **34**, 851–58.

Hetherington, E.M. (1988) 'Parents, children and siblings: six years after divorce'. In Hinde, R.A. and Stevenson-Hinde, J. (eds) *Relationship Within Families: Mutual Influences*. Oxford: Clarendon Press.

Hetherington, E.M. (1989) 'Coping with family transitions: Winners, losers, and survivors', *Child Development*, **60**, 1–14.

Hetherington, E.M., Cox, M. and Cox, R. (1982) 'Effects of divorce on parents and children'. In Lamb, M.E. (ed.) *Nontraditional Families*. Hillsdale, NJ: Erlbaum.

Hetherington, E.M., Cox, M. and Cox, R. (1985) 'Long-term effects of divorce and remarriage on the adjustment of children', *Journal of the American Academy of Child Psychiatry*, **28**, 399–415.

Hodges, W.F., Wechsler, R.C. and Ballantine, C. (1979) 'Divorce and the preschool child. Cumulative stress',

Journal of Divorce, **3**, 55–69.

Huntingdon, D.S. (1982) 'Attachment loss and divorce: A reconsideration of the concepts'. In Messinger, L. (ed.) *Therapy with Remarriage Families*. Rockville, MD: Aspen systems.

Huston, A.C. (1991) *Children in Poverty: Child Development and Public Policy*. Cambridge University Press.

Longfellow, C. (1979) 'Divorce in context: Its impact on children'. In Levinger, G. and Moles, O.C. (eds) *Divorce and Separation*. New York: Basic Books Inc.

Lowery, C.R. and Settle, S.A. (1985) 'Effects of Divorce on Children: Differential Impact of Custody and Visitation Patterns', *Family Relations*, **34**, 455–63.

Mazur, E. (1990) '"Why stay married if you're unhappy being married': Children's attitudes towards marriage and divorce". Paper presented at the Biennial Conference on Human Development (11th Richmond, VA, March 29–31).

Morgan, L.A. (1989) 'Economic well-being following marital termination: A comparison of widowed and divorced women', *Journal of Family Issues*, **10**, 86–101.

Musetto, A.P. (1978) 'Evaluating families with custody or visitation problems', *Journal of Marriage and Family Counselling*, **4**, 59–65.

Noller, P. and Callan, V. (1991) *The Adolescent in the Family*. London: Routledge.

Nye, F.I. (1957) 'Child adjustment in broken and in unhappy unbroken homes', *Marriage and Family Living*, **19**, 356–61.

Office of Population Censuses and Surveys (1994a) *1992 Marriage and Divorce Statistics: England and Wales*. London: HMSO.

Richards, M. (1995) 'Family Relations', *The Psychologist*, **8(2)**, 70–73.

Rutter, M. (1978a) 'Early sources of security and competence'. In Bruner, J.S. and Garton, A. (eds). *Human Growth and Development*. London: Oxford University Press.

Rutter, M. (1978b) 'Family, area and school influences in the genesis of conduct disorders'. In Hersov, L.A. and Schaffer, D. (eds). *Aggression and Anti-social Behaviour in Childhood and adolescence*. Oxford: Pergamon Press

Rutter, M., Cox, A., Tupling, C., Berger, M. and Yule, W. (1975a) 'Attainment and adjustment in two geographical areas: 1. The prevalence of psychiatric disorder', *British Journal of Psychiatry*, **126**, 493–509.

Rutter, M., Yule, B., Quinton, D., Rowlands, O., Yule, W. and Berger, W. (1975b) 'Attainment and adjustment in two geographical area. 3. Some factors accounting for area differences', *British Journal of Psychiatry*, **126**, 520–33.

Santrock, J.W. and Sitterle, K.A. (1987) 'Parent–child relationships in stepmother families'. In Pasley, K. and Ihinger-Tallman, M. (eds) *Remarriage and Stepparenting*. New York: Guilford.

Schaffer, H.R. (1990) *Making Decisions about Children – Psychological Questions and Answers*. London: Blackwell.

Shaw, D.S., Vondra, J.I., Hommerding, K.D., Keenan, K. and Dunn, M. (1994) 'Chronic Family Adversity and early child behaviour problems: A longitudinal study of low income families', *Journal of Child Psychology and Psychiatry*, **35**, 1109–22.

Shea, C.A. (1982) *Schools and Non-Nuclear Families: Recasting Relationships*. Missouri: Geographic Books.

Simons, R. (1993) 'Stress, support and antisocial behaviour trait as determinants of emotional well-being and parenting practices among single mothers', *Journal of Marriage and the Family*, **55(2)**, 385–98.

Stainton Rogers, R. and Stainton Rogers, W. (1992) *Stories of Childhood – Shifting Agendas of Child Concern*. Hertfordshire: Harvester Wheatsheaf.

Utting, D. (1995) *Family and Parenthood: Supporting Families, Preventing Breakdown*. London: Joseph Rowntree Foundation.

Wallerstein, J.S. (1984) 'Children of divorce: preliminary report of a ten-year follow-up of young children', *American Journal of Orthopsychiatry*, **53**, 230–43.

Wallerstein, J.S. (1985) 'Children of divorce – emerging trends', *Psychiatric Clinics of North America*, **8**, 837–55.

Wallerstein, J.S. and Kelly, J.B. (1980) *Surviving the Breakup*. New York: Basic Books.

Wallerstein, J.S. (1987) 'Children of divorce: report of a ten-year follow-up of young children', *American Journal of Orthopsychiatry*, **57**, 199–211.

Williamson, J. (1987) *Consuming Passions*. London: Marion Boyar.

Wolfendale, S. (1992) *Empowering Parents and Teachers: Working for Children*. London: Cassell.

Worrell, J. 1991. Sex-role components of maternal stress and children's well-being following divorce. Paper presented at the Annual Convention of the American Psychological Association (89th Los Angeles, CA, August 24–26).

Chapter Eleven

Adoption and fostering: New perspectives, new research, new practice

Alan Rushton and Andrée Rushton

Children transferred into the care of families who are unrelated to them will enter the lives of strangers and, despite the lack of biological ties, will normally become absorbed into the new family. How complete is the integration, how satisfactory the new relationships and how rapidly children recover from earlier adversity are important and intriguing psychological questions. We set out here the extent to which these questions have been answered.

Many of these children would formerly have remained in institutions, but now every effort is made to ensure they experience normal family life. Some children in need of permanent care may not be suitable for family placement, because their behaviour is too disturbed or because emotional distress prevents them, at the stage in question, from coping with family life, but most children who cannot live with their birth families can be found another home. These new families need to be well equipped to cope with the demands the children make, backed by professional help which has kept pace with new thinking and new research evidence.

The placement of children who present a special challenge is our main focus. In recent years, interest has shifted from the adoption of healthy infants to ways of securing a permanent family home for older children with special needs. These may arise from physical and intellectual disabilities or emotional or behavioural problems or the children may be part of a sibling group or come from ethnic minority backgrounds.

We have ourselves adopted children with special needs and undertaken child care social work. One of us is currently conducting research into the outcomes of late placements. We therefore bring a consumer, practitioner and research perspective to our task.

Research into permanent family placement

Adoption by relatives or foster parents

The increase of divorce and remarriage has led to an increase in the adoption of the children of a new relationship by the birth parent together with the new stepparent. Such adoptions now account for about half the total number. As the children are living in the family permanently and adoption helps to build the new family, they do not have a high profile in the child mental health field. Only isolated studies exist (see Masson, 1984), but we know that adoptions where the child does not move home or family are more stable than moves to an entirely new family (Barth and Berry, 1988; Rowe *et al.*, 1984).

Infant adoption

The total number of adoptions has declined dramatically from a peak of over 24,000 a year in the 1960s to the most recent figure of just over 7,000 a year. The fall is mainly due to the fact that infants now remain with their birth mothers. Research interest in infant adoption has waned as a consequence but we are beginning to profit from prospective studies which have followed UK samples beyond adolescence (Maughan and Pickles, 1990). Bohman and Sigvardsson (1990) had access to a large sample of adopted infants which they have followed through to adulthood. They found that the long-term prognosis for adopted children was no worse than that for children in the general population. Indeed, adoption reduced the risks for these children, given the levels of maladjustment in their birth parents.

Such studies make it reasonable to conclude that infant adoptions are largely stable and successful. Current interest now focuses on open adoption, the childrens' varying needs for knowledge of their background and the prospect and experience of reunion with birth parents (The Children's Society, 1995; Sachdev, 1992).

Inter-country adoption

Inter-country adoption has provided couples with a source of babies, and sometimes older children, from countries in poverty and political turmoil. The practice is criticised for severing children from their country of origin and as primarily a service to childless couples. Discussion of these issues and reviews of the research evidence are found in Bagley *et al.* (1993), Tizard (1991), and Thoburn and Charles (1992).

The most recent evidence of the outcome of inter-country adoption arises from following a large sample of very deprived children in The Netherlands into adolescence (Verhulst and Versluis-den Bieman, 1995). The authors reported a significant rise in total problem scores and a decrease in competence scores greater than that for adolescents from the general population. However, anti-social behaviour and social withdrawal were attributed to the confluence of challenges faced in adolescence, rather than to adverse pre-adoption experiences.

A new and intensive study is investigating a population of malnourished and emotionally deprived Romanian children adopted from institutional care into families in Britain. The study will investigate developmental outcomes and parental handling of the children's difficulties (Rutter *et al.*, 1995).

Issues arising in family placement

Infants are now very rarely available for adoption but, by contrast, disturbed and handicapped children in the care of local authorities queue for a scarce supply of prospective parents willing to take on the challenge.

Children with learning and physical disabilities

Experience shows that families can be found for children with learning and physical disabilities. Wolkind and Kozaruk (1986) in a 3-year follow-up study reported low disruption rates and, despite the difficulties, a high level of satisfaction in the adopters. Catherine Macaskill's study (1985) concluded that professional attitudes towards handicap were more of a barrier to progress than finding suitable families.

Clearly essential is a full and sensitive explanation to the new family, covering the medical facts and behaviour associated with the condition and the child's background. Important too is co-ordinated support from health professionals and social workers. Effective contact needs to be established between the new parents and the school and other educational services like education welfare and psychology. Children who are HIV positive or have developed AIDS and who need permanent placement may require a wide range of services. In all cases of permanent placement of children with disabilities, it is necessary to try to anticipate future needs as well as understand present difficulties.

Good practice in the case of children with severe to profound physical and mental disabilities relies on the preparation of carers and provision of post placement support (BAAF, 1991). Social workers also need guidance on assessing the developmental needs of children with disabilities (Del Priore, 1984).

Sibling groups

The Children Act 1989 advises placing sibling groups together wherever possible, reflecting the importance of sibling ties. To children attaching to new parents, the presence of birth siblings can be mutually supportive. However, there are limits to the number of families willing to take on sibling groups as tensions are likely to be greater. Where one sibling is responsible for sexual abuse or chronic hostility or where siblings have different wishes about future care, separation (perhaps with contact with each other) may be indicated.

The examination of placement patterns in one small-scale study showed better outcomes for the sibling placements, although this could have been because the children placed singly were more disturbed (Rushton *et al.*, 1989). Findings from the only recent British study focusing specifically on sibling placements have reinforced the conclusion that closeness in age to younger children in the new family predicts instability in the placement (Wedge and Mantle, 1991). Little research is available of the outcome of placing siblings in different configurations but one study is currently examining these questions more systematically (Rushton *et al.*, 1995).

Children from ethnic minorities
In Britain, consideration of racial matching is now a legal requirement of the 1989 Children Act. Guidance explains that: 'in the great majority of cases, placement with a family of similar ethnic origin and religion is most likely to meet a child's needs as fully as possible' (DoH, 1990).

In the eyes of its critics, especially many black professionals, the circular has not gone far enough, because it fails to make race matching the overriding priority in a decision about placement. While wishing to stress the need for attention to ethnic origins and a positive racial identity, we are also aware of the complexity of racial groupings and associated questions of class, generation, gender and the dynamic nature of culture. Consideration of all these factors, which space prevents us from discussing in detail, leads us to conclude that trans-racial placements should not be ruled out altogether.

Agencies placing children in permanent homes have improved their recruitment of families to match the race of children in their care (Arnold, 1982). A recent survey of the views of principal adoption officers (Rushton, 1994) reported that trans-racial placements have become rare or are made only in special circumstances, for example, where a child with multiple difficulties had been waiting a long time for a family. Earlier failures to attend to questions of racial identity are now being remedied and progressive agencies have developed detailed guidance on conditions that must be satisfied in trans-racial placements.

A number of studies have examined placement outcome for black children placed in white families: mainly in the USA (Feigelman and Silverman, 1984; McRoy and Zurcher, 1983; Simon and Altstein, 1987) but also in Britain (Charles *et al.*, 1992; Gill and Jackson, 1983). The studies have shown that most trans-racially placed children achieve good levels of emotional and social adjustment and self-esteem. These generally optimistic conclusions are at variance with criticisms that the studies fail to deal adequately with the assessment of identity in black children (Barn, 1993). Ways of promoting the positive identity of black children are being developed (Banks, 1992).

Families with adopted or fostered children of another race may require professional support and intervention. It is also especially important to provide ethnically sensitive support for black and Asian families taking on same-race and mixed-parentage children.

Contact with birth families

Complete severance from the past was once advised so that attachments could form unimpeded to the new family. More recent emphasis on preserving emotional links with the birth family is designed to help counter the child's sense of loss and rejection and promote satisfactory identity formation. Contact may, however, be stressful for the child especially if the birth parent is functioning poorly, is mentally disordered or seeks to undermine the placement. It may create divided loyalties, or cause tensions between the two sets of parents or the children themselves may not wish contact to continue.

Whether preserving contact reduces the security of the placement or has an effect on the child's adjustment is a complex research question. The child's view may change with time. It will also be influenced by the form and frequency of contact and the nature of the meetings. It is important to know what proportion of contact arrangements wither away. Recent reviews of the research literature (Berry, 1991; Gross, 1993; Triseliotis, 1991) have concluded that the evidence favours contact, although lack of representative samples precludes any very firm conclusions. Some much needed longitudinal data examining the outcomes of such arrangements are just beginning to emerge. Fratter (1995), in her 4-year follow-up of 22 new families with older children involved in varying degrees of contact with birth relatives, found that such arrangements could work successfully.

Late placements

In 1991 in England and Wales, a total of 2439 children were adopted from care, of whom 701 were aged between 5 and 9 (DOH/PSS/LAS, 1993). This group is a major concern of Social Services Departments. It is harder to discover how many non-relative permanent placements are being made for older children. An estimate based on 20 authorities suggests an annual figure of about 500 children of 5–9 years old (Quinton *et al.*, 1995). Social Services record keeping does not yet allow easy access to accurate national information on the numbers of older children who are *waiting* for permanent family placement.

Older children will have many positive attributes, but they characteristically bring a number of serious problems to a permanent placement. They tend to come from disadvantaged backgrounds and to have suffered the effects of poverty. They are known to have more medical problems than children in the general population. They have often been physically or sexually abused. They are likely to exhibit behavioural problems, typically in clusters rather than singly. For example, bed-wetting, indiscriminately affectionate or emotionally distant behaviour, aggression, unco-operativeness, stealing, lying and destructiveness are common. Such problems are of course seen in children in the general population; the difference is that those children do not also have to contend with making new attachments.

Many older children are now being placed permanently but without the legal security of adoption. Where continuing contact with significant people from the past is indicated, permanent fostering is often chosen. One recent example from current research illustrates the distance travelled from the traditional closed model of placement. In this case, there was no evidence that the birth parents had abused their two children, but the children's physical and intellectual development aroused grave concern. Enough evidence was finally accumulated to indicate that the children were suffering from deficient parenting. With parental consent, they were then placed in a foster family. Very frequent contact between the children and the birth parents was negotiated, including regular weekends home. The foster parents provided the attention and care the children needed and the relationship with the birth parents continued. Although the aim was permanence, there was no plan to adopt. Shared parenting arrangements such as this are likely to become more common and should be carefully monitored.

Research into outcomes of late placement

Unravelling the multiple influences on late placements offers a challenge to research. Practitioners must keep abreast of new findings and social workers, in particular, need more training to develop a critical appreciation of the published results. The 1980s and 1990s have seen the growth of larger and more detailed empirical studies of the adjustment, development, educational progress and attachment of adopted children. The most recent British data come from a study by Fratter *et al.* (1991) of over 1000 voluntary sector placements. Following up children between 18 months and 6 years after placement, they found an overall disruption rate of 21% with older age at placement predicting less favourable outcomes.

Barth and Berry's large-scale, Californian study of late placements (1988) is a retrospective evaluation of modern practice, based on placements made between 1980 and 1984 and showing a breakdown rate of only 10%. A greater risk of disruption was associated with:

- later age at placement;
- previous adoption breakdown;
- the level of the child's disturbance;
- the new mother's educational level.

A longer stay in foster care prior to adoption was associated with greater stability of placement. The presence of the foster parent adopters in this sample may have reduced the rate of disruption compared with samples drawn from entirely fresh placements.

Implications for practice

Research has so far therefore delivered some broad correlates of adoption and fostering disruption. Age at placement and level of behavioural difficulty are recurring predictors whereas the ethnicity and gender of the children and the characteristics of parents are not consistently associated with placement outcome, and some findings may be sample specific. Festinger (1986) regards the possible disruption of the placement as a 'necessary risk'. As most late placements are stable, practitioners should think positively of late family placement for children who cannot live with their birth parents.

It is clearly necessary to think of ways of reducing the disruption rate further, both by preventive and crisis work. When a placement falters or fails it can be harrowing for the children, parents and professionals. Elbow and Knight (1987) argue for skilled professional attention for all concerned and sensitive handling of the accompanying feelings of disappointment, loss and guilt.

Developmental recovery

Breakdown is not necessarily the most informative indicator of placement outcome. We also need to know about the effects of adversity on continuing placements. The recent review by Skuse and Bentovim (1994) looked at the impact of maltreatment on emotional, cognitive and educational performance and concluded that it raised the risk of depression and led to poorer educational performance. Problems arise, however, in disentangling the direct effects of maltreatment from other material privations and psychological stresses.

Hodges and Tizard (1989) have produced valuable evidence based on a research design that was both prospective and comparative. A group of children adopted from residential care fared better than children who returned home or remained in residential care. Although good attachments had been formed to the new parents, difficulties in peer relationships were found to have persisted for the adopted group.

Some progress is being made, using attachment theory (Bowlby, 1988), in understanding the capacity of maltreated children to form new emotional ties. One recent study has shown, in a sample of continuing adoptions, that pre-placement abuse was a significant predictor of low trust and anxious relationships in the new placements (Groze and Rosenthal, 1993).

A small sample of boys, placed between the ages of 5 and 9, almost all of whom had suffered abuse and neglect, has been followed-up on five occasions until adolescence, using detailed parental accounts and standardised scales (Rushton *et al.*, 1988, 1995). The 19% disruption rate found over 8 years is comparable with similar UK samples (Borland *et al.*, 1991; Fratter *et al.*, 1991). Of the surviving placements, 85% had made a substantial recovery in their secure new homes. They were largely free of problems or else were demonstrating manageable difficulties. Fifteen per cent of the boys in the continuing placements persisted with high levels of disturbance. The group with disrupted placements and very poor outcomes had experienced a combination of greater adversity prior to placement and less positive parenting in their new homes. Problems continued long after placement with weak attachments, overactive and restless behaviour and poor peer relationships, indicating a need for continuing professional monitoring and intervention (Rushton *et al.*, 1993).

Below are vignettes of two contrasting placements from the 8-year follow-up of this sample. Names have been changed.

Good outcome after a difficult start

Carl was taken into care with his older brother, following inadequate care from his lone-parent mother. When he was 6, he and his brother were placed with permanent foster parents whose own son had died of cancer at 18. From the beginning, Carl was moody, withdrawn, immature and craved affection. His habitual enuresis continued for a year into the placement. Intense sibling conflict became a great strain on the foster parents and led to disagreements between them about handling the children.

Access – granted by the court – was rescinded after a year because it was jeopardising the placement, which was close to breakdown. As a result, Carl relaxed: the enuresis ceased, his play became more imaginative and the sibling rivalry diminished. Five years into the placement, the new parents stated that Carl was attached to them and by the 8-year follow-up, the foster parents reported that he was more open and, with remedial help, was making progress at school.

Continuing difficulties

Jimmy, one of six children, was received into care at 3. A neglected child, exposed to marital violence, he was thin, ravenous and enuretic. At 5, he went to live with prospective adoptive parents who had no previous experience of children. At first he thrived. His new parents were relieved that he was not too taxing. They found him intelligent and attractive, but he was tense, had disturbed nights and was sometimes cruel to animals.

By the 8-year follow-up when he was 13, Jimmy had become sullen and unco-operative. He spent all his time with friends and was not affectionate at home. His concentration was poor and he made little effort at school. He was truanting and stealing and was often irritable. His adoptive parents worried about him, but, undemonstrative themselves, they accepted his lack of affection. He was receiving some individual psychiatric help and his adoptive parents were hopeful of progress.

New data from an extension of this early study, based on 61 late permanent placements of boys and girls followed through the first year of placement, will report on predictors of outcome and progress in the placements (the Maudsley Adoption and Fostering Study: Quinton *et al.*, 1996).

Professional services: before and after placement

In Britain, adoption and fostering services are still largely the preserve of statutory and voluntary social work agencies. Local authority Adoption and Fostering Units are engaged in family finding, preparing parents, placing children and providing post placement support. Independent agencies like Parents for Children, Barnardo's, the Catholic Children's Society and NCH Action for Children now concentrate mainly on placing special needs children. Other professionals play an important part, but social workers have the major role.

Preparation and support for new parents

The new parents may have endured arduous investigations of infertility and many years of debate about assisted conception, childlessness and adoption (Houghton and Houghton, 1984). They may also have refused children they thought too much of a challenge, leaving them with uncomfortable memories. On the other hand, many will now have experience of parenting. Despite the greater flexibility of recruitment – more latitude towards sexual orientation (see Post Adoption Centre paper, 1990) or single-mother or single-father placements (Owen, 1994) – the new parents are still most likely to be married couples.

New parents are entitled to more specific information and greater honesty about the extent of a child's problems – whether behavioural or medical, intellectual or educational. If given sensitively, it will not frighten away prospective adopters and foster parents. A list of key factors in a child's life and a current psycho-social profile should be routinely provided.

Parenting late placed children is different in significant ways from parenting birth children (see Shaw, 1986). The new parents may not receive much return of affection from the child and may have to develop special strategies for handling disobedience in children from deprived backgrounds (Batty, 1991). They may have to accept that problems persist and show a great deal of flexibility and a capacity to modify expectations.

Placement agencies should provide comprehensive support so that new parents know what to expect and where necessary are referred for professional help in handling difficult behaviour (Webster-Stratton, 1991) or the promotion of a fresh attachment in the child (Delaney, 1991). It may seem obvious, but it needs to be said that adoptive and permanent foster parents are seeking some acknowledgement that the difficulties do indeed exist. Well-meaning reassurance from family and friends is not always helpful. Reassurance has its place, but it can too easily fail to give due weight to the unhappy parents' feelings. Professional help can provide this acknowledgement and then direct intervention at specific targets on the basis of thorough assessments of the children and family (Rushton, 1989). Some problems may need little more than reinforcement of parental authority, suggesting the development of management strategies; others may need closer analysis of the family system and sustained intervention. Early intervention is strongly recommended, before negative patterns become established.

The literature on effective parenting is not well integrated with the field of permanent substitute family care (Hill, 1991), but defiant behaviour and weak attachment appears to be the most challenging combination of problems facing parents of late placed children. Some agencies now run workshops on effective substitute parenting, aimed at understanding the effects of losses and trauma suffered by children and how to develop constructive responses.

Adoptive and foster parents may wish to benefit from links with other such families. This can be done either informally or with the help of the agency. Such links are likely to be a useful source of mutual aid which may reduce pressure on professional services. The provision of respite care may also be essential for preserving placements in difficulty.

Case example of professional intervention

A family was referred to a Child and Family Consultation Centre with continuing problems in their 13-year-old adopted daughter. The parents had taken on a group of three siblings aged under 5 and help was first sought 5 years later. The parents complained of severe and unrelenting sibling conflict, mostly generated by this middle child. The child was also rejecting the mother, bed wetting, soiling and stealing and hiding food.

The child was given cognitive and psychological assessments, the parents were interviewed jointly and the siblings seen together. A diagnosis of mixed conduct and emotional disorder was established, and the family was reassured that their daughter was not suffering from a psychiatric disorder as they had feared. The girl was seen individually by a child psychiatrist with the aim of helping her understand her situation and place in the family.

The couple were seen together for help as parents, and also to explore hints from the children about marital conflict. It became evident that the mother's vulnerability had made her especially sensitive to rejection by her new daughter.

Subsequently the team treated the family together, both to avoid scapegoating the referred child and to teach the parents management strategies to help them handle the sibling conflicts.

The help has continued over 3 years. On two occasions the placement disrupted, but the daughter in question was rehabilitated in the family. The mother has a better understanding of her own reactions and is feeling better able to cope. Initial problems have abated, and although the sibling disputes continue the parents have improved their parenting skills and adjusted to some of the persisting problems.

Preparation of the child for permanent placement

Children in the care system can be helped to come to terms with their lives or to adapt to a new placement by Life Story Work. The literature is especially influenced by American child psychotherapists (Fahlberg, 1994), but it has also been championed and developed in the UK (Ryan and Walker, 1993). However, there is no standardised Life Story Work programme. Where specially trained social workers are contracted to do a specific piece of work it is probably practised more systematically (see Corrigan and Floud, 1990).

Certain conditions, such as a safe and quiet space and regular appointments, are crucial for individual therapeutic work (Trowell, 1994). The timing must be right for the child and the effect of the therapy on others taken into account. It is often hard, if not impossible, to achieve these conditions in the current, turbulent social services world. No evaluation of the effect of Life Story Work on the transition to the new home or on progress in the new placement has yet been conducted.

A framework for practice

By way of aligning the preceding discussion with adoption and fostering practice we now draw out 10 aspects of crucial importance, particularly in regard to late placements. Before doing so, we must acknowledge that research and practice into permanent family placement exist within a changing legal context. At the time of writing, new adoption legislation is anticipated, arising out of a lengthy review and consultation procedure (DoH, 1992,1993) concerned to harmonise it with the philosophy of the 1989 Children Act, modernise adoption procedures and services and amend the law on open adoption and inter-country adoption (see Cullen and White, 1992).

1. There is a political dimension in adoption and fostering. Many questions are contentious – concerning for example, biology, class, race, religion and sexual orientation. In devising policies, ideology needs to be distinguished from robust research evidence.

2. The Permanency Planning framework for child welfare practice (Maluccio *et al.*, 1986) gives the basis for moving children who cannot live with their birth family into secure alternative families. A minimum of delay should follow this decision.

3. Finding suitable families for these children must be a national priority. Prospective parents should receive a rapid and welcoming response to their enquiry, followed by a sensitive selection process and relevant preparation for the challenges to follow.

4. Detailed, accurate and up-to-date information about the children – their medical, psychological and intellectual status and their backgrounds at the time of placement – is essential in preparing the parents and calculating service needs. Information given to the new parents needs to be carefully managed.

5. It is essential to consult children about any move and to discover their wishes about, for example, contact with parents and siblings. However, the decision and its consequences must still rest with the responsible adults.

6. Practitioners must keep in mind the *triangle* of relationships involved: relinquishing parent/s and family; the placed child or children; and the new parents and family. The birth family may include significant other relatives. Continued professional involvement with the birth parent may be necessary in the case of open arrangements to encourage their positive support for the placement. Furthermore, the new parents may have resident children, both related and non-related, whose interests must be considered.

7. A lifespan view of the child should replace mere consideration of immediate needs and circumstances. The child's perceptions will vary with development and an attempt to anticipate this should be part of the placement planning.

8. Realistic expectations need to be created of the child's emotional capacity, intellectual level and academic potential. The new parents need to be helped to think about the possible impact of these factors.

9. Post-placement and post-adoptive support are essential where the new parents wish it and will require extra funding, better integrated multi-disciplinary practice and more post-adoption centres or equivalent services. Help needs to be more accessible and responsive as well as properly targeted and effective. Psychologists and psychiatrists have a major part to play in intervention and consultation in collaboration with social workers (see Hobday and Lee, 1995).

10. Practitioners and researchers need to be aware of developments abroad, learning from European and international comparisons of cultural norms, policy and practice (see Hoksbergen, 1986).

References

Arnold, E. (1982) 'Finding black families for black children in Britain'. In Cheetham, J. (ed.) *Social Work and Ethnicity*. London: Allen and Unwin.

BAAF (1991) *Permanent Placement of Children with Disabilities*. Practice Note 22.

Bagley, C., Young, L. and Scully, A. (1993) *International and Transracial Adoptions*. Aldershot: Avebury.

Banks, N. (1992) 'Techniques for direct identity work with black children', *Adoption and Fostering*, **16(3)**, 19–25.

Barn, R. (1993) *Black Children and the Public Care System*. London: Batsford.

Barth, B.P. and Berry, M. (1988) *Adoption and Disruption: Rates, Risks and Responses*. New York: Aldine de Gruyter.

Batty, D. (1991) (ed.) *Sexually Abused Children: Making their Placements Work*. London: BAAF.

Berry, M. (1991) 'The effects of open adoption on biological and adoptive parents and the children: the arguments and the evidence', *Child Welfare*, **70(6)**, 637–51.

Bohman, M. and Sigvardsson, S. (1990) 'Outcome in adoption: Lessons from longitudinal studies'. In *The Psychology of Adoption*. Brodzinsky, D. and Schechter, M. (eds) Oxford University Press.

Borland, M., O'Hara, G. and Triseliotis, J. (1991) 'Placement outcomes for children with special needs', *Adoption and Fostering*, **15(2)**, 18–28.

Bowlby, J. (1988) *A Secure Base: Clinical Applications of Attachment Theory*. London: Tavistock.

Charles, M., Rashid, S. and Thoburn, J. (1992) 'The placement of black children with permanent new families', *Adoption and Fostering*, **16(3)**, 13–19.

Corrigan, M. and Floud, C. (1990) 'A framework for direct work with children in care', *Adoption and Fostering*, **14(3)**.

Cullen, D. and White, J. (1992) 'Adoption law review – checklist of changes', *Adoption and Fostering*, **16(4)**, 7–11.

Delaney, R.J. (1991) *Fostering Changes: Treating Attachment – Disordered Foster Children*. Fort Collins, Colorado: Walter J. Corbett Publishing.

Del Priore, C. (1984) 'Assessing needs of the handicapped child', *Adoption and Fostering*, **8(4)**,38–41.

DoH (1990) *Guidelines to Directors of Social Services. Issues of Race and Culture in the Family Placement of Children*. Circular C1(90)2. London: HMSO.

DoH (1992) *Review of Adoption Law: Report to Ministers of an Inter-departmental Working Group*. London: HMSO.

DoH (1993) *Adoption: The Future*. London: HMSO.

Department of Health/Personal Social Services/Local Authority Statistics (1993) *Children in Care of Local Authorities, Year ending 31 March 1991 England*. London: Government Statistical Service, HMSO.

Elbow, M. and Knight, M. (1987) 'Adoption disruption: losses, transitions and tasks', *Social Casework*, **68(9)**, 546–52.

Fahlberg, V. (1994) *A Child's Journey through Placement*. London: BAAF.

Feigelman, W. and Silverman, A. (1984) 'The long term effects of transracial adoption', *Social Services Review*, **December**, 588–602.

Festinger, T. (1986) *Necessary Risk: A Study of Adoptions and Disrupted Adoptive Placements*. Child Welfare League of America.

Fratter, J. (1995) *Perspectives on Adoption with Contact: Implications for Policy and Practice*. Unpublished PhD thesis. Cranfield University. School of Management.

Fratter, J., Rowe, J, Sapsford, D. and Thoburn, J. (1991) *Permanent Family Placement: A Decade of Experience*. London: BAAF.

Gill, O. and Jackson, B. (1983) Adoption and Race. London: Batsford/BAAF.

Gross, H. (1993) 'Open adoption: a research based literature review and new data', *Child Welfare*, **72(3)**, 269–84.

Groze, V. and Rosenthal, J. (1993) 'Attachment theory and the adoption of children with special needs', *Social Work Research and Abstracts*, **29(2)**, 5–12.

Hill, M. (1991) 'Concepts of parenthood and their application to adoption', *Adoption and Fostering*, **15(4)**, 16–23.

Hobday, A. and Lee, K. (1995) 'Adoption: A specialist area for psychology', *The Psychologist*, **January**.

Hodges, J. and Tizard, B. (1989) 'Social and family relationships of ex-institutional adolescents', *Journal of Child Psychology and Psychiatry*, **30(1)**, 77–97.

Hoksbergen R. (1986) *Adoption in Worldwide Perspective: A Review of Programs, Policies and Legislation in 14 Countries*. Lisse, The Netherlands: Swets & Zeitlinger.

Houghton, D. and Houghton, P. (1984) *Coping with Childlessness*. London: Allen and Unwin.

Macaskill, C. (1985) *Against the Odds: Adopting Mentally Handicapped Children*. London: BAAF.

McRoy, R. and Zurcher, L. (1983) *Transracial and Inracial Adoptees: The Adolescent Years*. Springfield, Ill. Charles C.Thomas.

Maluccio, A., Fein, E. and Olmstead, K. (1986) *Permanency Planning for Children: Concepts and Methods*.

London: Tavistock Publications.

Masson, J. (1984) 'Step parent adoptions'. In Bean, P. (ed.) *Adoption: Essays in Social Policy Law and Sociology*. London: Tavistock.

Maughan, B. and Pickles, A. (1990) 'Adopted and illegitimate children growing up'. In Robins, L. and Rutter, M. (eds) *Straight and Devious Pathways from Childhood to Adulthood*. Cambridge University Press.

Owen, M. (1994) 'Single person adoption: for and against', *Children and Society*, **8(2)**, 151–63.

Post-Adoption Centre (1990) *Adoption Issues for Lesbian Women*. London: Post-adoption centre.

Quinton, D., Rushton, A., Dance, C., Dooley, N. and Mayes, D. (1995) *The Maudsley Adoption and Fostering Study: A Prospective Study of Children Late Placed in Substitute Family Care*. London: The Maudsley Hospital. (in press).

Rowe, J., Cain, H., Hundleby, M. and Keane, A. (1984) *Long term Fostering and the Children Act: A Study of Foster Parents who Went on to Adopt*. BAAF.

Rushton, A. (1989) 'Post placement services for foster and adoptive parents', *Journal of Child Psychology and Psychiatry*, **30**, 197–204.

Rushton, A. (1994) 'Principles and practice in the permanent placement of older children', Children and Society', **8(3)**, 245–56.

Rushton, A., Treseder, J. and Quinton, D. (1988) *New Parents for Older Children*. London: British Agencies for Adoption and Fostering.

Rushton, A., Treseder, J. and Quinton, D. (1989) 'Sibling groups in permanent placements', *Adoption and Fostering*, 13(4), 5–11.

Rushton, A., Treseder, J. and Quinton, D. (1993) 'New parents for older children: support services during eight years of placement', *Adoption and Fostering*, **17(4)**, 39–45.

Rushton, A., Treseder, J. and Quinton, D. (1995) 'An eight-year prospective study of older boys placed in permanent substitute families', *Journal of Child Psychology and Psychiatry*, **36(4)**, 687–95.

Rushton, A., Quinton, D., Dance, C. and Mayes, D. (1996) *A Study of Siblings Late Placed in Permanent Substitute Family Care*. London: The Maudsley Hospital. (in press).

Rutter, M., Hay, D. and Quinton, D. (1995) *A Study of Children Adopted from Romania*. London: MRC Child Psychiatry Unit, Institute of Psychiatry. (in press).

Ryan, T. and Walker, R. (1993) *Life Story Work*. London: BAAF.

Sachdev, P. (1992) 'Adoption reunion and after: a study of the search process and experience of adoptees', *Child Welfare*, **71(1)**, 53–68.

Shaw, M. (1986) 'Substitute parenting'. In Slukin, W. and Herbert, M. (eds) *Parental Behaviour*. Oxford: Basil Blackwell.

Simon, R. and Altstein, H. (1987) *Transracial Adoptees and Their Families*. New York: Praeger.

Skuse, D. and Bentovim, A. (1994) 'Physical and emotional maltreatment'. In Rutter, M., Taylor, E. and Hersov, L. (eds) *Child and Adolescent Psychiatry*, 3rd edn. Oxford: Blackwell Scientific Publications.

Thoburn, J. and Charles, M. (1992) *Review of Research Relating to Inter-country Adoption*. Background Paper Number 3. Inter-departmental review of Adoption Law. London: DoH.

The Children's Society (1995) *Preparing for Reunion*. London: Edward Rudolf House.

Tizard, B. (1991) 'Intercountry adoption. A review of the evidence', *Journal of Child Psychology and Psychiatry*, **32(5)**, 743–56.

Triseliotis, J. (1991) 'Maintaining the links in adoption', *British Journal of Social Work*, **21(4)**, 401–14.

Trowell, J. (1994) 'Individual and group psychotherapy'. In Rutter, M., Hersov, L. and Taylor, E. (eds) *Child and Adolescent Psychiatry: Modern Approaches*. Oxford: Blackwell Scientific Publications.

Verhulst, F. and Versluis-den Bieman, H. (1995) 'Developmental course of problem behaviours in adolescent adoptees', *Journal of the American Academy of Child and Adolescent Psychiatry*, **34(2)**, 151–59.

Webster-Stratton, C. (1991) 'Strategies for helping families with conduct disordered children', *Journal of Child Psychology and Psychiatry*, **32**, 1047–62.

Wedge, P. and Mantle, G. (1991) *Sibling Groups in Social Work: A Study of Children Referred for Permanent Substitute Family Placement*. Aldershot: Avebury.

Wolkind, S. and Kozaruk, A. (1983) '"Hard to place"? Children with medical and developmental problems'. In Wedge, P. and Thoburn, J. (eds) *Finding Families for 'Hard to Place' Children: Evidence From Research*. London: BAAF.

PART FOUR: Schools

Chapter Twelve

Applying psychology to school effectiveness

Irvine S. Gersch

The focus of this chapter is on applying psychology to school effectiveness.

What one means by 'effective' is, however, a critical matter for researchers and practitioners alike. Indeed Ouston and Maughan (1985) refer to 'outcome' measures and point out that such measures are not value free but rather will reflect the aims of the school. Probably the key indicators of interest to parents and pupils relate to examination results, pupil behaviour and, to a lesser degree, attendance rates. Other outcomes such as preparation for adult life, and becoming a 'good and responsible citizen', would be espoused as important by many, but are much more difficult to measure.

In the first section of this chapter, there are some observations on the work of educational psychologists and the gap between research and practice in the area. Further sections will examine the current context and changes which have taken place within schools, research on school effectiveness, some action research projects and the interaction between the individual child at school and the teaching–learning environment. The final sections hazard some guesses at schools of the next decade and beyond and suggest some implications for professionals working with schools.

Increasingly, educational psychologists are invited to assist schools in solving problems at a whole-school or institutional level in addition to dealing with problems in individual children. Indeed, sometimes where there are frequent referrals to the educational psychologist of a number of children who all present similar difficulties or where there are distinct patterns of referral – for example children who steal, bullying, unmotivated pupils, challenging behaviour or slow progress with reading – it makes sense to enquire further about what the school as a whole is doing to meet such issues. One could ask whether there is a whole-school policy or practice, or a training need for teachers or school rules which require review. School functioning and school effectiveness are therefore at the heart of educational psychologists' practice.

It is argued by Allan Sigston in Chapter 1 that there is a *gap* between the work of practitioners and researchers. It could be argued that such a gap, apart from being inevitable, is not unhelpful. Let the researcher research and the practitioners practise. Provided the practitioners keep up-to-date there is not a problem. However, the view taken in this chapter is that practitioners have much to contribute to the research knowledge base, they can help form the questions which warrant investigation, and an experimental paradigm of action research will have positive outcomes for the client or school as well as to the research community. In short, there would be merit in closing the gap to some degree.

Indeed, one could argue that there are ways of combining research and practice, to the mutual advantage of both enterprises.

Schools of the present

During the past decade there have been some major changes to our schools, as a result of legislation and altered attitudes by headteachers and other educationists.

In the UK the 1988 Education Act gave a much higher degree of management autonomy to governors and headteachers, whose role as Chief Executive became very much clarified. Schools have become more responsible for their own destiny, image, culture and management. The fact that schools are seen as specific organisations, following the same principles and variables as other organisations, has led to a large body of research, utilising methodologies previously reserved for other organisations. It has also led to an exploration of such factors as the school's culture, leadership, management and development. In similar vein, during the past 5 years there has been a change in the culture of many schools, with far greater emphasis on a 'business' culture.

Schools have also become more accountable. They have to publish their examination results, absentee figures, information on special needs for parents and other information, and must undergo a full audit every 4 years by an independent team of inspectors through the auspices of the Office for Standards in Education. Their results and reports are published, for public scrutiny.

This trend has comprised several strands, including (a) increased autonomy for schools and governors and (b) increased accountability through a statutory framework. The underlying stated governmental aim has been to expose schools to parental choice, in the hope that good schools will be popular with parents, and thus will attract more pupils; and poorer ones will shrink, and ultimately close.

During the past 5 years, the educational psychology service within which I am employed as principal has received the following requests which serve as illustrations of what triggers schools to seek outside help:

- Could you help a headteacher prepare an action plan following an appraisal?
- Could you partner another colleague to carry out a headteacher appraisal?
- Could you work with a headteacher to discuss parental concerns over bullying?
- Could you carry out inset with all staff with a view to assisting with a revised Behaviour Policy for the whole school?
- Could you advise about ways of dealing with a high number of referrals to the educational psychologist in one area?
- Could you help reduce truancy rates in several schools?
- Could the service help set up a system to audit all children in schools with special educational needs, so that the budget share could be allocated more fairly from the Local Education Authority?
- Could you set up a system to help schools with the early and orderly assessment of special educational needs, in the light of the 1993 Education Act and Code of Practice?
- Could you help the school develop more effective behaviour management procedures?

It would appear that there is a legitimate and much needed role for such a consultant or educational psychologist to:

- help clarify the problem;
- help determine appropriate processes for change;
- provide research information and perhaps inset, if appropriate;
- help set up appropriate evaluation techniques;
- help the school meet any performance indicators agreed at the commencement of the project, to deal with the specific cause of concern e.g. truancy rates, behavioural outcomes, etc;
- help the school determine appropriate methods for collecting data before and after the change;
- provide external and impartial advice and scrutiny of the school's issues of concern.

In today's business oriented world it is increasingly likely that such consultancy would need to be **paid** for by the school, and thus require careful negotiation, often culminating in a written contract or service agreement. Such payment tends to focus thinking on such matters as clarity about what has been offered, quality, reliability as well as price and competition for the work!

Research on school effectiveness

This section reviews some of the literature on school effectiveness and offers a critique of the concept and the evidence available.

During the past 15 years there has been a growth in literature concluding that differences between schools have a significant effect on pupil achievement, accompanied more recently by commentators drawing attention to criticisms of some of the work and the consequent limitations of the evidence (Purkey and Smith, 1982, 1983; Reynolds, 1976a,b, 1982, 1985a,b; Reynolds *et al.*, 1994a; Rowan *et al.*, 1983; Sammons *et al.*, 1995). Bossert (1988) argued that the concept of effectiveness in schools is diffuse and ambiguous, partly reflecting the multiple and often contradictory missions that schools are expected to fulfil.

In an excellent state-of-the-art review of the findings prepared by the Institute of Education, University of London, Sammons *et al.* (1995) provide a comprehensive critique of the literature and the key characteristics of effective schools (Table 12.1).

Consistent findings are reported by Reynolds *et al.* (1994a) when reviewing the international literature. The seminal British studies are those by Rutter *et al.* (1979) and Mortimore *et al.* (1988), pertaining to secondary and primary schools respectively. Purkey and Smith (1983) advance a 'school culture model', that is, the conception of school as a dynamic social system, in which its organisation structure, process and climate are linked, and the unique mix of interrelated factors (see Table 12.1) at different levels combine to produce its culture and individual personality.

Of particular interest is the study by Rutter *et al.* (1979) which examined 12 secondary schools in London. Perhaps the key conclusion reached was that – as measured by observations, rating scales, questionnaires, interviews and attainment scores – the secondary schools in the sample differed markedly in the behaviour, attendance and attainments of their pupils. This difference could not be accounted for by family background. Physical factors – such as the size of the school, age of the buildings and space available – seemed to make little difference. Similarly, organisation arrangements did not appear to be a significant factor. Mostly, however, the combined and cumulative effect of the various factors 'create a particular ethos, or set of values, attitudes and behaviours which will become characteristics of the school as a whole' (Rutter *et al.*, 1979:179). The variables they found most related to better school outcomes are listed in Table 12.1.

Although Rutter *et al.* (1979) concluded from their correlational study that the pattern of findings was suggestive of a causal connection between pupil behaviour and other school outcomes with school factors, their work has been heavily criticised on statistical grounds, for confusing process and product, and arguments persist over the simplistic definition of behaviour (Johnstone and Munn, 1987; Tizard, 1980).

Table 12.1 Factors and variables associated with effective schools

Sammons et al. (1995)	Purkey and Smith (1983)	Rutter et al. (1979)	Mortimore et al. (1988)
UK review paper	USA school research review	UK research in secondary schools	UK research in primary schools
1. Firm purposive professional leadership 2. Shared and consistent vision and goals by staff 3. An orderly and attractive learning environment 4. Emphasis on teaching, learning, learning time and achievement 5. Purposeful teaching which is well planned, structured and adaptive 6. High expectations 7. Positive reinforcement 8. Monitoring progress and performance of pupils and school 9. Pupils' rights, responsibilities and self-esteem stressed 10. Home–school partnership and parental involvement 11. School based staff development	Key organisational variables: 1. School site management 2. Instructional leadership 3. Staff stability 4. Curriculum articulation and organisation 5. School-wide staff development. 6. Parental involvement and support 7. School-wide recognition of academic success 8. Maximising learning time 9. District support Key process variables: 1. Collaborative planning and collegial relationships 2. Sense of community 3. Clear goals and high expectations 4. Order and discipline	1. Pleasant working conditions for pupils 2. Academic emphasis, including co-ordinated planning of the curriculum, high expectations, setting and marking of home-work, total teaching time 3. Teacher behaviour (e.g. demonstrating punctuality, showing concern for the well-being of the school, and for the children, available to be consulted by pupils, displaying children's work). 4. Prevalent use of rewards and praise. 5. The extent to which pupils held some kind of position of responsibility and participated in the school system. 6. Staff decision-making reflecting a consensus	Purposeful leadership by the head teacher The involvement of the deputy head The involvement of teachers Consistency Structured lessons Intellectually challenging teaching A work-centred environment Lessons organised around a single curriculum area Maximum communication between teachers and pupils Good record keeping Parental involvement Positive climate

Johnstone and Munn (1987:9) also make the interesting point that there is debate about whether 'good schools are good at everything' as is indicated by the work of Rutter *et al.* (1979) or whether schools might be effective differentially with respect to different measures of, for example, behaviour, and examination results, as suggested by the findings of Gray *et al.* (1983) in their Scottish survey.

A major British study by Mortimore *et al.* (1988) of some 50 schools and 2,000 junior school pupils from 1980 to 1987 identified a number of important factors (see Table 12.1).

Finally, Beare *et al.* (1989) remind us of the need to include the notion of culture in any analysis of effective schools. Effective schools, according to Beare *et al.* (1989), appear to share the same world view, or paradigm, as revealed in metaphors, stories and shared language. The corporate culture with its distinct set of values, myths, sagas, ceremonies, legends, rites, rituals, social interactions and symbols (the familiar province of anthropologists) are all applicable to schools.

The concept of school effectiveness

One could certainly agree with Bossert (1988) that whilst the concept of school effectiveness is important theoretically and practically, it is very ambiguous indeed, with studies focusing on everything from teacher satisfaction to school discipline, reflecting the multiple goals and contradictory missions of schools. Achilles (1987) makes the general point that the quest for better schools led to studies of 'good schools' reflecting a positive and optimistic outlook.

In my view, analysis of several factors related to the individual child, the family, the environment and socio-economic status in combination with school factors will probably be required for a sufficient analysis of pupil outcome; but the focus has moved to an investigation of school-related factors.

The concept and definition of 'school effectiveness' is itself problematic. Reid *et al.* (1987) refer to the lack of definition in the literature, and they also provide a lengthy list of the diverse definitions given by teachers, which demonstrates the range of possibilities from instruction to the ethos, parental involvement, access to in-service courses and extra-curricular activities. However, Bossert (1988) (without supportive evidence for his assertion) identifies one key aim of schools, namely instruction in basic skills. Purkey and Smith (1983) in their classic review, and commenting on the weakness of the evidence, regard the quest as not having been overwhelmingly successful. These authors argue that the new literature does not necessarily contradict the earlier research on non-school factors, but rather the new studies look at other variables, and they further conclude that the new studies do not find large differences between schools.

Critique of the evidence

Whilst there appears to be an acceptance that schools do make a difference, much of the research on school effectiveness and the effects of school has been subject to considerable criticism, much repeated in the literature (Goldstein, 1980). Reynolds (1982:7) refers to the 'substantial volume of criticism' attracted by his own and the Rutter study, relating to limitation of controlled variables, inadequate understanding of school processes, neglect of important causal factors, and the 'atheoretical' nature of the work. Bossert (1988) adds to this list other limitations of the research designs, including the facts that:

- they are based on correlational and *post hoc* methods of analysis;
- the definitions of effectiveness and criteria for selection of schools are unreliable;
- school goals are not assessed.

Although critical of many of the case studies, Purkey and Smith (1983) draw attention to the possibility that what has positive effects in one school may not have the same effect elsewhere, and they caution against a simplistic suggestion that schools should simply adopt practices from 'an easy to assemble model taken from the research findings'.

Reviewing the generally similar but not identical results from four major studies (Brookover and Lezotte, 1979; Edmonds and Frederiksen, 1979; Phi Delta Kappa, 1980; and Rutter *et al.*, 1979), D'Amico (1982:61) argues that 'each effective school may be one of a kind' and the mismatches in the research findings probably result from the intricate, perhaps idiosyncratic nature of school process. Lezotte (1982) responds that it would be more sensible to view the ongoing and evolving findings as a framework, not a recipe.

In an extensive critique of the research, Good and Weinstein (1986) draw attention to the conceptual and methodological weaknesses, reliability and validity of the data, mixing concepts such as 'effectiveness' and 'achievement'. Most studies assume a direct linear (positive or negative) relationship between factors, which may not be the case for all variables. Good and Weinstein (1986:1094) give the example of an 'inverted U' relationship whereby too little or too much of a variable (e.g. teacher giving direction) could be unhelpful.

In a detailed evaluation of the research shortcomings, Rowan *et al.* (1983) listed the problems with narrow measures of effectiveness, problems with comparing contrasting 'effective' versus 'ineffective' schools related to their selection (see also Purkey and Smith, 1983), and subsequent limited information about the causal relationships between variables, their relative effects and the generalisability of the results. Most importantly, these reviewers state that:

> A more disturbing problem is that many of the results...may be spurious ... measures of school demographic composition, organisation, climate and achievement are all correlated ... unfortunately, most of the studies we reviewed failed to control for school

demographics and prior school achievement...the result is uncertainty about which specific features...exercise the most important influence on student achievement

(Rowan *et al.*, 1983:28)

Schools are dynamic, organic and developing organisations. Reid *et al.* (1987) aptly question the extent to which schools are in fact consistent over time. Furthermore, it is perhaps worth acknowledging the view of some workers in the field (particularly Cuban, 1983; Ralph and Fennessey, 1983) that some of the research has led to the implementation of school programmes (e.g. Eubanks and Levine, 1983) despite the absence of solid evidence, with reviews referring to earlier reviews as if they were evidence!

Taken together with the lack of statistical data reported, the possibility of observer bias and the lack of control variables, Ralph and Fennessey (1983:691) comment that some of the papers in this area seem to be evangelical, justifying policy recommendations despite 'the paucity of verifiable evidence'. These writers refer to a study by Armor *et al.* (1976) in which the data were unreliable because some children were coached (perhaps inadvertently) for a reading test, later used as an outcome measure. They argue that there is always pressure from 'central office' to raise test scores and that a sceptical interpretation of the results is required, in such a complex area, in which the roles of the scientist and the reformer/practitioner/policy-maker need to be clarified and presumably separated. None the less, this type of action research involving programme evaluation is felt by Purkey and Smith (1983) to be methodologically stronger than case studies and has produced data consistent with the familiar findings.

An important point is made by Firestone and Herriott (1982) who report significant differences between effective elementary (or primary) and secondary schools, with the former professional staff best construed as a work group and the latter teachers as members of a complex organisation. They suggest that our ways of thinking about the two school types (and their leadership) require differentiation. The implication for practice is that somewhat different ways of working will be required in our primary, secondary and indeed nursery schools.

In interpreting the evidence, it is fair to comment that this is a difficult and complex area to subject to controlled scientific study. Some associations, however, do appear to be occurring repeatedly in the literature, and warrant taking seriously, whilst mismatches should not be ignored. A compelling case is argued by several workers that each school is a highly complex 'single case' and that the 'whole may be more than the sum of the parts'; that is, the combination of variables at different levels may be more than simply the sum of a series of individual factors. What is clear, however, is that schools *do* make a difference to pupil outcomes and behaviour in particular.

Characteristics of schools with good discipline

Reid *et al.* (1987), reviewing the evidence, conclude that well-disciplined schools have clearly stated rules, consistently applied. In such schools, classroom management promotes student activity and interest, praise is freely given, pupils are given responsibility for school resources and duties (Rutter *et al.*, 1979), and the disciplinary regime is neither too harsh nor too weak (Reynolds, 1982).

Lasley and Wayson (1982) reporting findings from exemplary schools for discipline describe the five most important features of schools with effective discipline as:

1 The total involvement of the staff in decision-making.

2 The school is seen as a place where success is experienced.

3 Problem solving focuses on causes rather than symptoms.

4 Emphasis on positive behaviours and preventive measures.

5 Strong principal leadership.

These workers stress that there are no simple recipes or solutions, and imply that all the complex factors which contribute towards creating a positive climate need to be considered.

The importance of school leadership: the role of the headteacher

Evidence linking leadership with school effectiveness began to emerge after the 1960s. In a synthesis of the research up until the early 1980s, Sweeney (1982) explored two questions in research he felt was sufficiently rigorously conducted: namely, whether principals make a difference, and if so, which leadership behaviours are associated with positive outcomes?

Citing research by Weber (1971), Madden *et al.* (1976), Wellisch *et al.* (1978), Edmonds (1978), Brookover *et al.* (1979) and Rutter *et al.* (1979), Sweeney concluded that the evidence clearly indicates that principals make a difference, and that the six leadership behaviours shown in Table 12.2 emerged as important.

These studies indicated that effective headteachers were 'quietly everywhere', that is highly visible, they emphasised achievement, they developed an atmosphere conducive to learning, and they were assertive. Sweeney expresses two cautions in respect of how far the findings would apply to different schools and the possibility of complex interactive effects (principals may influence school factors but also be influenced by them).

Murgatroyd and Gray (1982) call upon evidence from an inspection of a 'failing school', and point to seven major leadership qualities which emerged as important through their absence. These qualities are all essentially interpersonal (see Table 12.2). Offering a pertinent reminder that schools may be improved without always relying on the principal, Cawelti (1984) identifies several strands from the research literature describing principals from effective schools (see Table 12.2).

Rutherford (1985) collected observational and interview data on principals from

Table 12.2 Qualities and characteristics of effective headteachers/school principals

Sweeney (1982)	Murgatroyd & Gray (1982)	Cawelti (1984)	Russell et al. (1985a,b)	Gersch (1992)
Review of USA and UK research	UK case study	USA research review	USA High school research	UK Secondary school research
1. Emphasising achievement	1. Visibility	1. Vision: they articulate goals, directions and priorities	1. Measures progress at a school-wide level	1. Setting structures
2. Setting instructional targets	2. High ability to communicate thought and feelings	2. Resourcefulness: obtaining resources from all sources	2. Creates an orderly and studious environment	2. Personal and management styles
3. Providing an orderly school atmosphere	3. Acceptance of others	3. Planning for improvement and valuing staff	3. High emphasis on curriculum articulation	3. Visibility
4. Frequently evaluating pupil progress	4. Openness and genuineness	4. Instructional support: they are visible in every area of the curriculum and school life	4. Supports teachers and instructional efforts	4. Good relationships with and support for teachers
5. Co-ordination of instruction	5. Making explicit intentions and beliefs	5. Monitoring of student progress	5. High expectations and clear goals for students	5. Good relationships with and support for pupils
6. Support of teachers	6. Facing problems directly and learning from them	6. Optimism that constructive change is possible	6. Collaborative planning with staff	6. Direct dealing with behaviour incidents
	7. Resolving problems according to the situation rather than punitively		7. Instructional leadership for teachers	7. Involvement in teaching
			8. Parental involvement	8. Contacts with the community and parents

principals, teachers and students in a variety of types of school, concluding that effective principals have a clear vision, clear goals and implementation plans, they establish school climates which support progress towards these goals, they monitor progress continuously and intervene when necessary. With less effective principals, the interviewers noted that students often spoke without pride or enthusiasm about their school, and teachers tended to work more as individuals. More effective principals gathered information both formally and informally, often going into classes; and interestingly, this appeared to be appreciated by teachers. What emerged from this research is that whilst effective principals display the qualities described, they may demonstrate them in different ways.

Russell *et al.* (1985a,b) conducted a careful and detailed investigation into the relationship between the behaviour and activities of American secondary school principals and school effectiveness, which they defined as high academic achievement, low rates of vandalism and absenteeism, a sense of community and a stable staff. Using characteristics culled from the research as a model, and interviews with staff, parents, students and other observers in 16 schools, these workers used a critical incident technique (whereby interviewees were given actual incidents and asked to rate different behaviours as effective or ineffective). Some 133 ineffective and 202 effective behaviours were finally agreed, which clustered into the eight major categories shown in Table 12.2.

The author's (Gersch, 1992) own work also highlights the relationship between pupil behaviour and school leadership. Situational Theory of Leadership (Hersey and Blanchard, 1988) and a synthesis of the literature on pupil behaviour, school effectiveness, educational management and leadership was used as a framework to investigate effective school disciplinary leadership, and in particular the disciplinary role of the headteacher. According to Situational Theory there is no single best leadership style, rather, effective responses depend upon the situation, the task and the followers; leaders need to be flexible, adaptable and able to vary their style according to different circumstances. The central hypothesis in the study postulated a positive relationship between school leadership and pupil behaviour, as perceived by headteachers, senior teachers, other teachers and children.

A combination of ethnographic, questionnaire and statistical techniques were employed with a view to triangulation of methods, and both qualitative and quantitative data were collected.Within the constraints of the sample size (four schools), the results supported the central and subsidiary hypotheses, identifying some of the key mechanisms and processes through which headteacher influence occurs. The key components of effective disciplinary leadership emerged as setting structures, personal style, visibility, relationships with teachers and pupils, direct dealing with behaviour incidents, involvement in teaching and contacts with the community. A profile of the key personal qualities and management styles associated with successful headteachers was produced.

Finally, within the classroom itself, there is evidence that teaching style, behaviour management skills, organisation and communication (Kounin, 1970), seating arrangements (Ng, 1982; Wheldall *et al.*, 1981), timetabling, lesson planning, and providing help for children with learning difficulties in the context of a whole-school policy on behaviour management (Gillham, 1984) are factors influencing pupil behaviour in school.

What does emerge from the literature surveyed in this section is that schools themselves have a significant influence upon pupil outcomes, including pupil behaviour, but the specific effects of particular school variables, including those related to the headteacher and school leadership, require further detailed investigation. Sammons *et al.* (1995) conclude that between 8% and 10% of pupil variance might be explained by school and classroom factors. It should not be forgotten, however, that individual student background factors still account for a very high proportion of differences.

Some action research projects

Introduction to action research

In this section, some principles of action research and some practical projects in schools undertaken by my colleagues and myself will be outlined.

Action research is described in detail in Chapter 1 of this book. In the area of school effectiveness it is of special value in enabling:

> research involving planned intervention in some social process accompanied by an evaluation of the effects of this intervention. Action research aims to contribute both to the practical concerns of people in an immediate problematic situation and to an increase in knowledge.
>
> (Jupp and Miller, 1980:3)

The following sections outline some examples of research in which I have been involved.

A behaviour systems project in a secondary school

In this project the school was concerned about the level of disruptive behaviour around the school, students seeming to be unmotivated, not completing classwork or homework and generally breaking school rules. In fact, the school initially requested additional counselling help but following negotiation a more direct approach was agreed.

The detailed intervention is reported elsewhere (Gersch, 1986) but included a training session for staff; staff working parties addressing rules, rewards and sanctions; and full decision-making staff meetings. New rules, procedures and a reward system was set up, with some very positive effects. The role of the consultant was to guide the process, assist in resolving disputes and provide external evidence where needed. The project, which took about 12 months, was felt to have been important in the life of the school, to have improved behaviour and importantly to have improved staff morale through joint staff planning. It was particularly important for the school to have found their own solutions to the problems raised.

A systems project involving pupils in a secondary school

A second project in a secondary school followed concern about non-attendance and disenchantment in a Year 11 group. The initial request was for more EWOs to work with the school. As before, the initial request was reframed and a new proposal agreed, namely that a steering group be set up and working parties of teachers and children meet to consider the questions and make recommendations. The questions were:

(a) What was causing the misbehaviour and truancy?

(b) What could the school do to put this right?

(c) What changes would you recommend?

Up to six recommendations were invited from each group.

The details of this project and its evaluation are described elsewhere (Gersch and Noble, 1991). Many useful and practical proposals emerged and were put into effect, greater pupil participation in the running of the school resulted, and overall staff felt that communication had improved (an unplanned for outcome). Attendance figures also improved to some degree. It was difficult to determine the exact effects of this project as opposed to other forces operating at the time, statistically, but overall staff and others rated the project as having been beneficial for the school.

A systems project in a junior school

Following the publication of the above reports a junior school became interested in reviewing its response to pupil behaviour. The use of staff 'quality circles' whereby staff identify the problem areas and make suggestions was utilised. This school ended up with a new policy for behaviour, procedures for teachers, a reward system using 'smiley faces' and plans for improving relevant resources to improve pupil behaviour. Changes in the systems for playtime supervision and important collaboration with mid-day assistants were features of this project.

What was particularly interesting was that some procedures – e.g. the timing of assembly, collection of dinner tickets and the way children came in from playtime – were, on close investigation by staff themselves, seen to be promoting disruption, and capable of being planned differently thus leading to more orderly pupil behaviour. Yet such 'disruptive' systems had been in operation for many years. The project enabled staff to review what was happening within a productive context to allow changes to be made. Simple and small system changes can have a marked effect upon schools and pupils.

A detailed report of this project can be found in Gersch (1990).

A systems project in a primary school to improve the school ethos

In a final example to be outlined here, a primary school headteacher invited our help to improve the school ethos. As with all first contacts, it is important to check:

(a) Who shares this concern, is it just the headteacher? Do we have more general staff concern?

(b) What changes are really wanted?

(c) What is meant by 'ethos'?

In this project a member of the Educational Psychology Service spent some time at the needs analysis stage investigating the context of the concern, who shared it and what was going on generally.

A series of staff meetings, inset preparations and working party work went on, and some practical suggestions were agreed for staff and pupils, many to improve the communication flow. Some years later a follow-up was requested focusing on the school leadership and looking at ways for the headteacher to implement his appraisal plan. In this case, following detailed and sensitive negotiations, it was agreed to meet a sample of staff individually to review the perception of the headteacher's management and produce some recommendations for the headteacher.

A research project on school leadership

Experience in the sort of projects described above gave rise to the strong hypothesis that school leadership was a critical factor, but very little exposed to empirical study and investigation. I interviewed four headteachers, 10 staff in each of their schools and several classes of pupils to examine what made an effective headteacher, from the point of view of pupil behaviour. Some brave and open headteachers permitted such an investigation into their styles and it was possible to determine significant differences in the behaviour of headteachers, and some factors which seemed to be associated with positive pupil behaviour.

A less than successful project

In one project, an acting headteacher wishing to produce rapid change, referred many problems for review including student behaviour, the buildings, the curriculum. A staff survey was produced and I was invited to staff discussions. However, the list of proposals was so long as to be unmanageable, and the timetable so unrealistically short that staff lost confidence and we were not able to provide a useful outcome. With hindsight, it would perhaps have been better not to have started! However, the lessons were clear; don't take on too much, allow a sufficiently long timetable for change (at least a year) and be clear about prioritising problems to work on!

General model and critical stages for systems work

The key stages in all projects have been similar and appear to have wider applicability to general systems work in schools. The steps appear to be as follows:

1. *Preparation* – Usually the plea for help is framed in a way different from that which may be most useful. At this point it is useful to regard such comments, questions and concerns as a cry for help and as a basis for negotiation. It is a good idea at this stage to consult with colleagues.

2. *Planning and setting up* – Here the art of the possible coupled with an understanding of what is needed must be harmonised. Detailed negotiations, further questions and background data collection is vital. The saying 'Fools rush in where angels fear to tread' rings quite a few bells at this stage.

3. *Data collection* – Before going on to produce solutions it is important to collect relevant data. This data could be used for research purposes later, if collected with sufficient control, rigour and care in experimental research procedures.

4. *Prioritising proposals* – Any plans need to be manageable. I have often favoured a full staff meeting for decision taking, with the headteacher having the final right of veto, and the opportunity to take the proposals away for further scrutiny and possibly discussion with governors and the LEA.

5. *Enactment of proposals* – Detailed plans about who is going to do *what when* and *where* need to be specified.

6. *Evaluation and fine tuning* – Any system, however carefully planned, must be exposed to the real world and the fullness of time. Outcomes need to be reviewed, using research methodologies both in the short and long term. I have found that triangulation at this point is very helpful, e.g. surveys, interviews, statistics, output measures and questionnaires. All can have a part to play and moreover together increase confidence in the findings. Any things which do not work well can be modified at this stage and problems arising can be dealt with.

7. *Maintenance* – Consideration needs to be given to the ongoing plans for maintaining the actions planned.

In all of these projects, the implication is that it is not sufficient simply to focus on the child, attempt to change the child but rather to consider the school system, what everybody does, and to change all or some of the system which itself may be the source of the problem.

The individual child at school

Although studies of whole-school effects are important, individual children will almost certainly respond differently to different factors; indeed research work is at the earliest stage in respect of this latter area.

There are, of course, many individual differences between children in respect of rate of learning, abilities, interests and motivation, undoubtedly caused by a combination of early development, teaching environment, social and economic environment and family factors (Docking, 1987).

We do know that teacher expectations and attitudes, pupil self-perceptions and labels are of immense importance. The classic work by Hargreaves (1976) and Lacey (1970) on the effects of streaming are of interest here. We also need more information about the effects of major school variables upon the performance of pupils from different ethnic backgrounds.

Similarly, the work of Maslow (1954) is important in understanding motivation both of pupils, but also of teachers as workers. Maslow argues that we need to understand what people need, and there is a hierarchy of needs, ranging from basic physiological need for food to the need for safety, social interaction, esteem and finally self-actualisation. This framework, which may be criticised for oversimplification, is none the less very helpful in making the point that when practitioners do wish to explore what is going wrong and bring about change in schools it is vital to determine what are the motivations and thus needs of both the children and the staff.

Perhaps the key point is that teachers do need to identify, assess and plan for the needs of individual children carefully, and although whole-school approaches will go a long way to improve the situation for children and hopefully staff in a school, one still needs to carry out action research at the individual child level, perhaps through using similar experimental methods as proposed for schools but on a micro rather than macro level.

Schools of the future

As said earlier there have been marked changes to schools in the past decade, and there does appear to be greater accountability, statutory frameworks, financial autonomy and greater parental say. Such a trend is unlikely to be reversed, in my view, since as schools enjoy self-determination they are unlikely to request a return to more central control. Schools are having to demonstrate responses to parents and children which attract pupils, which ensure sound financial management, which meet statutory requirements, which deliver the national curriculum and have perceived good examination results or other academic outputs, and in which the children are well behaved.

It would appear that schools will increasingly be required to produce *Output data* on its results, with perhaps measures of academic outcomes and attendance being augmented by measures of behaviour and discipline.

With the impact of the information technology revolution, educationists have a true opportunity to review all aspects of learning for children. This might include more specific teaching for individual children, individual programmes, enhanced materials and visual aids (using virtual reality technology) with children actually visiting other countries without leaving their desks, and ways of teaching languages speedily and enjoyably through multimedia presentations. Courses and programmes, assessment and evaluation could all be carried out with fast, sophisticated computers which seem like science fiction at this stage. Within 10 years such technology should be readily available, cheap and regarded as routine.

Travel too should have become easier and there may well be a greater requirement for parents to travel to different countries for employment, necessitating children attending several different schools, in different countries throughout their school life.

The implications for schools are fascinating. Will we have community schools, modular type learning environments, with schools becoming more like universities, offering courses for individual children, with flexible times for attending, distance learning on occasion (although there will always be a need and wish for socialisation) and more sharing across the ages, with adults going on to learn courses, say in the evenings, with their children.

If so, the role of the consultant or educational psychologist will be very different. One can only hazard a guess at the sort of school effectiveness projects which will be required. The concerns might be the same – e.g. behaviour, special needs, poor progress, staff motivation, leadership – and the process of change might be very similar to now, but the content of changes and proposals might be very different.

Educational psychologists and consultants will, in my view, still need to display effective personal and social skills, adaptability, flexibility, and most importantly, listening skills. They will also need to keep up to date with the research literature.

Implications for professionals working with schools

Where problems arise it would be helpful for the consultant to consider the sort of steps listed earlier, and more specifically to take time to explore what the problem is, who is worried and what the aims of change might be.

I have argued in favour of the adoption of a scientific paradigm, including the setting of hypotheses, predictions or thoughts about what is going on, data collection, testing and interpretation of the evidence, evaluation and reporting. A focus on different perceptions of the same problems should always prove to be helpful and constructive. One invaluable text which provides a rich source of techniques for researchers is that of Miles and Huberman (1984).

Some questions might be posed about:

1. How effective is the leadership of the school?

2. How far is there a shared and useful vision and set of aims?

3. What is the quality of the learning environment?

4. What is the quality of teaching, the lessons and learning in the school?

5. What expectations are made about the pupils?

6. How far are positive rewards used and clear rules?

7. How effective are the systems for monitoring pupil progress?

8. How far are pupils and indeed parents involved in the life of the school and sharing responsibility for it?

Reynolds (1994b) makes the excellent point that studies of schools have tended to focus upon successful schools and that researchers have not looked hard enough at schools which have failed. He draws an analogy between failing schools and aeroplanes which have crashed, when there is always a close scrutiny of the black box recorder. It could be that factors relating to failure are not the opposite of the successful ones, and that there are additional problems leading to a 'crashed school' which warrant investigation.

This would encourage any practitioner to look very closely at the whole environment, rather than making a single factor analysis and noting that the whole might well be more than the sum of the parts.

The implications for headteachers and teachers are that it is important to keep up-to-date with research findings, to attend courses, but also to share experiences with others. Using outsiders can be very important.

For advisers, advisory teachers and consultants the above is true but there is also a need to adopt a scientific paradigm, even if this refers to the single case. For educational psychologists, work at the systems level should always be borne in mind. Indeed, although much of educational psychology practice is now dictated by statutory demands and will move towards child-centred work, there will be occasions when it will be more desirable, effective and productive to attempt to help to change a system. The aim is of course to improve prospects for children, whether directly or indirectly, and using the best research knowledge as a basis for so doing.

Acknowledgements

I am grateful to all the schools, children, headteachers, teachers, educational psychologist colleagues and trainee educational psychologist/researchers who took part in the projects described in this chapter, which would not have been possible without the invaluable editing help given by Barbara Gersch. The key stages listed on page 174 are reproduced from Gersch and Noble (1991:143), with the kind permission of the Association of Educational Psychologists.

I am also indebted to education officers within the LEA in which the work took place for their support and encouragement of new ideas. The views expressed in this chapter, however, remain those of the author alone, and do not necessarily reflect those of the employing authority, being the London Borough of Waltham Forest.

References

Achilles, C.M. (1987) 'A vision of better schools'. In Greenfield, W. (ed.) *Instructional Leadership*. New York: Allyn & Bacon, pp.17–37.

Armor, D. *et al.* (1976) *Analysis of the School Preferred Reading Programme in Selected Los Angeles Minority Schools*. Santa Monica, Cal: Rand.

Beare, H., Caldwell, B. and Millikan, R. (1989). *Creating an Excellent School: Some New Management Techniques*. London: Routledge.

Bossert, S.T. (1988) 'School effects'. In Boyan, N. (ed.) *Handbook of Research on Educational Administration*, Chapter 17. Harlow: Longman, pp.341–52.

Brookover, W.B. and Lezotte, L.W. (1979) *Changes in School Characteristics Coincident with Changes in Student Achievement*. Institute for Research on Teaching, College of Education, Michigan State University.

Cawelti, G. (1984) 'Behaviour patterns of effective principals', *Educational Leadership*, **41(5)**, 3.

Cuban, L. (1983) 'Effective schools: A friendly but cautionary note', *Phi Delta Kappan*, **64(10)**, 695–96.

D'Amico, J. (1982) 'Using effective school studies to create effective schools: No recipe yet', *Educational Leadership*, **40(3)**, 60–2.

Department of Education and Science (1988). *Secondary Schools. An Appraisal by HMI*. London: HMSO.

Docking, J.W. (1987) *Control and Discipline in Schools*, 2nd edn. London: Harper and Row.

Edmonds, R.R. (1978) *A Discussion of the Literature and Issues Related to Effective Schooling*. Presented at the National Conference of Urban Education, St. Louis, Missouri.

Edmonds, R.R. and Frederiksen, J.R. (1979) Search for Effective Schools: *The Identification and Analysis of City Schools that are Instructionally Effective for Poor Children*. ERIC Document Reproduction Service, No. ED 170 396.

Eubanks, E. and Levine, D. (1983) 'A first look at effective schools projects in New York City and Milwaukee', *Phi Delta Kappan*, **64(10)**, 697–702.

Firestone, W. and Herriott, R. (1982) 'Prescriptions for effective elementary schools don't fit secondary schools', *Educational Leadership*, **40(3)**, 51–3.

Gersch, I.S. (1986) 'Behaviour modification and systems analysis in a secondary school: combining two approaches', *Educational and Child Psychology*, **3(2)**, 61–7.

Gersch, I.S. (1990a) 'Dealing with disruption', *Special Children*, **June/July**, 7–9.

Gersch, I.S. (1990b) 'Behavioural systems projects in junior and secondary schools'. In Scherer, M., Gersch, I.S. and Fry, L. (eds) *Meeting Disruptive Behaviour: Assessment, Intervention and Partnership*. Basingstoke: MacMillan, pp.206–22.

Gersch, I.S. (1992) *School Leadership and Pupil Behaviour in the Secondary School*. University of East London, Unpublished PhD Thesis.

Gersch, I.S. and Noble., J. (1991) 'A systems project involving students and staff in a secondary school', *Educational Psychology in Practice*, **7(3)**, 140–47.

Gillham, B. (1984) 'School organisation and the control of disruptive incidents'. In Frude, N. and Gault, H. (eds.) *Disruptive Behaviour in Schools*. Chichester: Wiley.

Goldstein, H. (1980) 'Fifteen thousand hours: A review of the statistical procedures', *Journal of Child Psychology and Child Psychiatry*, **21(4)**, 363–66.

Good, T. and Weinstein, R. (1986) 'Schools Make a Difference', *American Psychologist*, **41(10)**, 1090–97.

Gray, J., McPherson, A.F. and Raffe, D. (1983) *Reconstructions of Secondary Education: Theory, Myth and Practice Since the War*. London: Routledge and Kegan Paul.

Hargreaves, D.H. (1976) 'Reactions to labelling'. In Hammersley, M. and Woods, P. (eds) *The Process of Schooling*. London: Routledge and Kegan Paul/Open University Press.

Hersey, P. and Blanchard, K.H. (1988) *Management of Organizational Behaviour*. New York: Prentice-Hall International.

Johnstone, M. and Munn, P. (1987) *Discipline in School. A Review of 'Causes' and 'Cures'*. Edinburgh: The Scottish Council for Research in Education.

Jupp, V. and Miller, P. (1980) *Glossary for the OU Social Sciences Course DE304: Research Methods in Education and The Social Sciences*. Milton Keynes: Open University Press.

Kounin, J. (1970) *Discipline and Group Management in Classrooms*. New York: Holt, Rinehart and Winston.

Lacey, C. (1970) *Hightown Grammar*. Manchester: Manchester University Press.

Lasley, T.J. and Wayson, W.W. (1982) 'Characteristics of schools with good discipline', *Educational Leadership*, **40(3)**, 28–31.

Lezotte, L.W. (1982) 'A response to D'Amico: not a recipe but a framework', *Educational Leadership*, **40(3)**, 63.

Madden, J.V., Lawson, D.R. and Sweet, D. (1976) *School Effectiveness Study*. State of California.

Maslow, A. (1954) *Motivation and Personality*. New York: Harper & Row.

Miles, M.B. and Huberman, A.M. (1984) *Qualitative Data Analysis*. London: Sage Publications.

Mortimore, P., Sammons, P., Stoll, L., Lewis, D., and Ecob, R. (1988) *School Matters. The Junior Years*. New York: Open Books.

Murgatroyd, S. and Gray, H.L. (1982) 'Leadership and the effective school'. In Harling, P. (ed.) *New Directions in Educational Leadership*. Lewes: Falmer Press, pp.39–50.

Ng, Y.Y. (1982) 'The effects of various seating arrangements on a group of ESN(M) children with behavioural problems', *CORE*, **6**, Fiche 1/2.

Ouston J. and Maughan, B. (1985) *Issues in the Assessment of School Outcomes*. In Reynolds, D. (ed.) *Studying School Effectiveness*. Lewes: Falmer Press.

Phi Delta Kappa (1980) 'Why do some urban schools succeed?'. In *The Phi Delta Kappa Study of Exceptional Urban Elementary Schools*. Bloomington, Ind.: Phi Delta Kappa and Indiana University.

Purkey, S.C. and Smith, M.S. (1982) 'Too soon to cheer? Synthesis of research on effective schools', *Educational Leadership*, **40(3)**, 64–69.

Purkey, S.C. and Smith, M.S. (1983) 'Effective schools: A review', *Elementary School Journal*, **83(4)**, 427–52.

Ralph, J. and Fennessey, J. (1983) 'Science or reform: some questions about the effective schools model', *Phi Delta Kappan*, **64(10)**, 689–94.

Reid, K., Hopkins, D. and Holly, P. (1987) *Towards The Effective School*. London: Basil Blackwell.

Reynolds, D. (1976a) 'Schools do make a difference', *New Society*, **29(37)**, 223–25.

Reynolds, D., (1976b) 'The delinquent school'. In Hammersley, M. and Woods, P. (eds) *The Process of Schooling*. London: Routledge and Kegan Paul/The Open University. Chapter 25.

Reynolds, D. (1982) 'School effectiveness research: A review of the literature', *School Organisation and Management Abstracts*, **1(1)**, 5–14.

Reynolds, D. (1985a) 'The effective school'. *Times Educational Supplement*, **20 September**, 25.

Reynolds, D. (ed.) 1985b) *Studying School Effectiveness*. Lewes: The Falmer Press.

Reynolds, D. (1994) *The Future of School Effectiveness and School Improvement*. Paper presented at the 1994 Annual Meeting of the Association of Educational Psychologists, Liverpool.

Reynolds, D., *et al.* (1994) 'School effectiveness research: a review of the international literature'. In Reynolds, D. *et al.* (eds) *Advances in School Effectiveness Research and Practice*. Oxford: Pergamon.

Rowan, R., Bossert, S. and Dwyer, D. (1983) 'Research on effective schools: A cautionary note', *Educational Researcher*, **12(4)**, 24–31.

Russell, J.S., Mazzarella, J.A., White, T. and Maurer, S. (1985a) *Linking the Behaviours and Activities of Secondary School Principals to Schools Effectiveness: A Focus on Effective and Ineffective Behaviours*. University of

Oregon, Centre for Educational Policy and Management.

Russell, J.S., White, T. and Maurer, S. (1985b) *Linking the Behaviours and Activities of Secondary School Principals to School Effectiveness: A Technical Report*. University of Oregon, Centre for Educational Policy and Management.

Rutherford, W.L. (1985) 'School principals as effective leaders', *Phi Delta Kappan*, **67(1)**, 31–34.

Rutter, M., Maughan, B., Mortimore, P. and Ouston, J. with Smith, A. (1979) *Fifteen Thousand Hours: Secondary Schools and their Effects on Children*. New York: Open Books.

Sammons, P., Hillman, J. and Mortimore, P. (1995) *Key Characteristics of Effective Schools. A Review of School Effectiveness Research*. London: Institute of Education for The Office for Standards in Education.

Sweeney, J. (1982) 'Research synthesis on effective school leadership', *Educational Leadership*, **39(5)**, 346–52.

Tizard, B. (ed.) (1980). *Fifteen Thousand Hours: A Discussion*. University of London Institute of Education.

Weber, G. (1971) *Inner-city Children Can be Taught to Read. Four Successful Schools*. Washington, D.C.: Council for Basic Education.

Wellisch, J.B., MacQueen, A., Carriere, R. and Duck, C. (1978) 'School management and organisation in successful schools', *Sociology of Education*, **51(3)**, 211–26.

Wheldall, K., Morris, M., Vaughan, P. and Ng, Y.Y. (1981) 'Rows Versus Tables: an example of the use of behavioural ecology in two classes of eleven year-old children', *Educational Psychology*, **1(2)**, 171–84.

Chapter Thirteen

Changing views of research on integration: The inclusion of students with 'special needs' or participation for all?

Tony Booth

The October 1993 edition of the *European Journal of Special Needs Education* was devoted to a major review of the literature on 'integration' conducted by 'leading experts in five different countries'. Seamus Hegarty, the editor of the journal and Director of the National Foundation of Educational Research, provided an introduction to the review articles, and reading between the lines I think that he found the task problematic. Each article took as its theme a British category of 'special need' such as 'moderate learning difficulty' and 'emotional and behavioural difficulty'. Thus the extent to which category systems differ between cultures was barely explored. He was concerned that this emphasis on categories 'in the eyes of some might be deemed sufficient to discredit the whole enterprise' (Hegarty, 1993:194). He argued that differences in student needs were in part related to 'disability' but that an emphasis on student difficulties as produced by their defects or disabilities deflected attention away from 'the barriers that schools place in the way of their learning' (Hegarty, 1993:199). Thus the format of the review conformed to a much criticised but still vigorous medical model which contrasts with Seamus Hegarty's own notion that 'integration is in the end a matter of school reform' (Hegarty, 1993:199).

He noted too, that much of the reported research was preoccupied with what he and others regard as a failed enterprise; the attempt to compare 'integrated' and 'segregated' settings in terms of their efficacy:

> as with previous reviews of this kind, the conclusions were tentative at best and generally inconclusive...the body of research comparing integration and segregation has limited validity.
>
> (Hegarty, 1993:197)

Twelve years earlier he was arguing against the value of 'comparative studies contrasting integrated and segregated provision' in similar terms:

> The research effort expended in this direction has yielded a comparatively meagre payoff....partly because it is misguided and based on a premise of limited relevance.
>
> (Hegarty *et al.*, 1981:51)

I empathise with any frustration Seamus Hegarty felt at the lack of progress that has been made on this issue in the last 20 years. It would be a pity if, by the year 2005, such major disputes about research on integration were left unresolved. I see this chapter as a contribution to dialogue between contrasting positions on the conception and conduct of research on integration. The review of international research, mentioned above, was conducted without an agreed or explicit definition of integration. In the next sections I will analyse definitions of integration, and then reasons for deciding about integration. I will then discuss research on the quantity and quality of integration and will indicate the way different approaches depend on different definitions. I make no attempt to provide a comprehensive review of research studies but use examples to show how empirical and conceptual matters are linked. I am reporting on some of the developments in my own thinking so please forgive me for the conceit of referencing my own work.

How we research integration depends on how we define it. It is commonly assumed that integration is about disabled students or others categorised as having 'special needs', but then how can it be 'a matter of school reform' affecting all students? Jonathan Solity defines integration loosely as 'the process of teaching children with special educational needs within mainstream settings' (Solity, 1992:20). Some people use the term with greater restriction to imply that a student 'is integrated' when he or she is included in a mainstream school when other 'similar' students might be in a 'special school'. Others distinguish between sham and 'proper' integration. Brahm Norwich adopts this position when he asserts that 'functional integration, which is usually considered as authentic integration, involves children with special educational needs joining and learning in ordinary classes as full participants' (Norwich, 1990:55).

Brahm Norwich's view is a slightly inaccurate recall of one of the 'states' of integration promoted within the Warnock Report (DES, 1978:100–101) with its notions of 'locational', 'social' and 'functional integration', to mean, respectively:

- a presence but little participation in the mainstream;
- involvement with other students socially, but not engaging in shared lessons

on a common curriculum;
- joint, but not necessarily 'full' or full-time, 'participation in educational programmes'.

This way of thinking about integration retains considerable influence in the UK but it is of limited value.

Thinking of three states of integration is an improvement on viewing integration in an undifferentiated way, as a presence in the mainstream, and it does focus our attention on the quality of educational experience. However it is a crude system of categorisation compared with the array of possibilities for participation.

I prefer to think of integration differently, as comprising an unending *process or set of processes* rather than a state or set of states. As a process, integration implies change. To say that integration is occurring means that the participation of some students in mainstream schools has increased. I define integration in the following way:

- It is the process of increasing the participation of students in the cultures and curricula of mainstream schools and communities.
- It is the process of reducing the exclusion of students from mainstream cultures and curricula.

My view of integration merges with the development of a comprehensive, community, non-selective, system of pre-school, primary, secondary and further and higher education. Any simple definition of integration has to be set in the context of a broader view of education. For if students are to be included in 'the mainstream' we need to know not only to which students reference is made but also what form of mainstream education is envisaged.

Students who become categorised as having 'special needs' or who are disabled are only some of those subject to exclusionary pressures from mainstream schools. It makes little sense to me, to foster the inclusion of some students because they carry a label, whilst ignoring the lack of participation of others.

Applying the notion of integration or inclusion to all learners is also a consequence of my analysis of learning difficulties and the deconstruction of the notion of 'special needs'. Learning takes place in a relationship between students, teachers, curricula and resources. Difficulties in learning arise through a break-down in these relationships and can affect any student, as common sense tells us when we reflect on our own learning. Teaching and learning difficulties in school do not arise from, nor will they be improved solely by attention to, the characteristics of students. By thinking of learning difficulties as the property of a special group of students we undermine the learning of all students. This does not mean that we cease to be concerned with the low attainment or disabilities of students but that we recognise the very limited information about education provided by a category of disability or 'special need'.

I include both the fostering of participation *and* the reduction of exclusion in my definition of integration. In fact participation may only be increased by addressing pressures to exclusion. Such pressures are reduced when schools are organised, supported and resourced so that they respond to the diversity of their students. For example, the participation of students who have relatively low attainments is limited by the hierarchy of value attached to attainment in some schools. To change the exclusionary pressures which such devaluations produce, schools have to look at all forms of internal selection in groups, sets and option choices. Now although the reduction of selection, within, as between schools, is highly contentious, according to my definition a realistic programme of integration has to address it.

I am concerned about the reduction of all forms of exclusion, formal and informal. Students who come into school with one label may be excluded under another. There are a disproportionate number of students who are the subject of statements of special educational need in the rapidly growing statistics for formal disciplinary exclusions (DfE, 1995). In fact it may be a matter of chance whether a particular student, excluded under the 1993 Education Act, is subjected to 'special need' or 'disciplinary exclusion' (Booth, 1996). Other groups vulnerable to exclusion include girls who become pregnant while at school, and children of Travellers as well as children of ethnic minorities. The over-representation of Afro-Caribbean boys in the disciplinary exclusion statistics is well known but concern has also been raised at the channelling of Asian-British bilingual students into lower sets in some schools (CRE, 1992). The participation of such students as well as disabled students, and others who experience difficulties in learning are promoted equally by an an approach to education which is about the celebration of and support for a diversity of learners.

Defining segregation

Often, as I have suggested, segregation is identified with attendance at a special school although I identify it with the process of 'exclusion'. Traditionally a special school has been seen as a school physically separate from any other school which includes as students *only* those categorised as having 'special needs'. But is that the way that special schools should be defined in the late 1990s? For such special schools do several things: they centralise resources and students said to experience difficulties *and* they isolate students and resources from the main-stream. You can argue for the centralisation of resources without the isolation of students. The difficulty of arguing for an educational benefit for the isolation of disabled students and others categorised as having 'special needs' has led both legislators and academics into confusion. In the 1993 Education Act special schools are defined as schools 'specially organized to make special education provision for pupils with special educational needs' but realising that this could make any school a special school the writers of the act were forced to exclude 'maintained' and 'grant maintained' schools from the definition. Similarly Gary Hornby has recognised the difficulties of justifying isolation by arguing that:

few special educators would disagree with the suggestion that all children could be educated on the same site – that is locationally integrated. Also that as much social integration as possible should be encouraged, for the benefit of all pupils.

(Hornby, 1992:133)

Such a suggestion would involve getting rid of separate special schools yet he also supports the notions that 'there would always be a need for special schools' and that 'it is necessary to maintain a range of special education provisions...similar to that which exists at present in the UK' (Hornby, 1992:131,134). This wish to maintain the status quo then, must spring from a different motive than a concern with careful and consistent argument and I will have more to say about that below.

Of course there is a difference between compulsory segregation or isolation and voluntary isolation as advocated by some deaf adults to maintain deaf culture and British Sign Language in special schools.

In recent years it has become fashionable to supplant the term 'integration' with that of 'inclusion' or 'inclusive education' and this has gained international currency. Some suggest that this new term implies a new more sophisticated view of education. For example, Mel Ainscow contrasts 'integration' which implies 'additional arrangements...within a system of schooling that remains largely unchanged' with 'inclusive education where the aim is to restructure schools on order to respond to the needs of all children' (Ainscow, 1995:1). I think that this ignores the variety of ways in which either term has been used. Neither word means much without careful definition and the new term is likely to give rise to no less contention than its predecessor. However, I suspect that 'inclusion' and 'inclusive education' are going to survive and that 'integration' will die out. I have argued that because 'inclusion' has the clear opposite of 'exclusion' its adoption may encourage people further to see the connection between both sets of processes.

Deciding about integration

Some researchers would like to believe that the evidence provided by their studies should be pivotal in decisions about policy. They argue, for example, that integration should be supported only if research shows that it improves the education of students. It is easy to see how such a view reflects on the status of research and researchers and is therefore seductive. Yet, as I will show, it faces considerable conceptual and practical difficulties. While research evidence may frequently be invoked in the rhetoric about different educational arrangements, I regard moral and political views as the major determinants of educational decisions. This is not because policy makers, including teachers, are irrational or unsophisticated about the benefits of research or simply recalcitrant, but because different approaches to schooling represent different outlooks on life. The actions of people always have a moral or political dimension and this is obscured if we believe that they are based on research. The academic study of the policy and practice of integration is enhanced when the reasons for action are accurately reported.

The idea that a suggested change in social practices should await the findings of research is a way of concealing opposition to that change. For the current arrangement of special provision did not itself arise on the basis of research. In any case the idea that there is a single status quo which remains unchanged is a myth. Provision varies dramatically from region to region, area to area and school to school and is subject to competing legal, economic and political pressures. The defence of an amorphous status quo avoids the need to confront and make explicit the reasons for making decisions about changes in policy and practice. It also avoids the identification of and commitment to a particular status quo. Precisely what forms of provision should be made available to students? Those existing in Barnsley or those in Lambeth or some other?

In the absence of research evidence it is a commonplace for educational psychologists to argue that integration should be decided according to the needs of students. For example, like Peter Mittler (1985) before him Garry Hornby argues that 'the level of integration...should be decided on the needs of each individual child and the exigencies of each situation' (Hornby, 1992:133), which include the effects on others, the costs and the wishes of parents. I do not think that it makes any sense to say that a child needs a particular form of provision, such as a mainstream class or a special class or a special school, or for that matter a hut in the garden. Such a 'need' isn't something that we discover on the basis of an assessment of a child but is something that we invent and project onto a student as a reflection of the educational system with which we are comfortable or the provision that is currently available in one area.

Such a view also conceals assumptions about the relationship between the severity of need or difficulty and the form of provision. The Code of Practice (DfE, 1994) puts forward the 'principles' that there are continua of need and provision with the implication that a more severe difficulty will require a greater degree of segregation (Booth, 1993). The false move in this argument is to identify the place of education with the amount of support that is required. A student who has a very limited understanding of language and cannot move around on their own may need considerable human support to participate with others in an educational community and if so that would be true wherever they were educated.

Of course some young people do express a preference for a school other than their local one and sometimes this is a special school. Sometimes their parents make similar choices on their behalf. In either case it is important to distinguish between a choice made on pragmatic grounds because it seems to be the best option available, from one which includes a commitment to policy change. Thus it is possible, without contradiction, to choose a special school for one's child as the best available option, whilst campaigning for its resources to be transferred into the mainstream.

Many people, including many disabled people, think that disabled children have a right to attend a local mainstream school (for example, Oliver, 1992; Rieser and Mason, 1990) and the campaign to end compulsory segregation by the Integration Alliance (Mason, 1992), is an attempt to assert this right. Others have difficulty in accepting the relevance of the language of rights to discussions of integration. If decisions are made on the basis of rights then they take away the power of those who have controlled or contributed previously to decisions about integration. In my experience a recognition of rights is easier to contemplate for those in other countries than in the UK. To enable people to reflect on any resistance to considering rights to a mainstream education I have constructed a parallel argument on women's rights, in Figure 13.1, through an imaginary extension of an intervention made by Christabel Pankhurst at a meeting addressed by Winston Churchill.

Research in practice

It should be clear that how we research integration depends on the questions we are trying to answer, how we define it, as well as on often hidden ideological commitments. I have already indicated some of the hidden assumptions behind studies of the effectiveness of integration and segregation. Here I want to look in a little more detail at this and other approaches to research. I will start by assessing attempts to measure the quantity of integration and segregation then look at research comparing integration and segregation and finally at research which documents inclusion and exclusion either of particular groups or as an attempt to understand the processes affecting all students.

A number of studies have documented changes in the proportion of students attending special schools in the UK and elsewhere and such studies can provide important information. I reported the gap between the rhetoric that integration was burgeoning and the reality of the statistics which showed a growth in the proportion of students attending special schools (Booth, 1981) and subsequent studies kept track of the changes showing that after a small downturn in numbers in the middle and late 1980s, in the 1990s the proportion of students in special schools again started to rise (Norwich, 1994; Swann, 1988). Later figures also revealed the large variation in provision in different areas. Thus in 1992 the proportion of students aged 5–15 years in special schools in Barnsley was 0.45% whereas in the London Borough of Lambeth it was 2.98% (Norwich, 1994).

However, such studies have limitations. They encourage a simple view of integration and segregation as representing presence in the mainstream and attendance at a special school respectively. In theory it is possible to employ a more complex view of integration in attempting a statistical answer to the question: 'Is integration occurring?' However no studies to my knowledge have documented the changes in the form and extent of student participation alongside changes in the practices of selection within as well as between schools. No study

Figure 13.1 The integration of women into the democratic process

On Friday 13th October 1905 Christabel Pankhurst attended a meeting at The Free Trade Hall in Manchester where Winston Churchill a prominent member of the Liberal Government was speaking.

Christabel Pankhurst (shouting); Will the Liberal Government give votes to women?

Christabel Pankhurst was ignored by the speaker and was taken from the hall. Determined to get arrested she spat at her escorting policemen. However, for our purposes, we can imagine that a conversation with Winston Churchill proceeded as follows:

Winston Churchill: Madam, can you explain to me in precisely what ways giving women the vote will benefit the women themselves or men or the nation?

C: Women have the same rights as men. They are their equals in every respect.

W: But you have ignored my question. Where is your evidence? Can you show me the improving powers of voting on the female intelligence? Will it make women clever as well as voluble speakers? Will they be better keepers of the household budget or better cooks? Will the rate of female illiteracy drop?

C: These questions are irrelevant. It may be true that the participation of women in the democratic process, in the machine of power, will change the way they view themselves. It may change the way they think and what they learn. But we do not demand the vote for that reason. We demand it because it is right. It is our right.

W: You speak in theory whilst I seek facts. I see no reason to disrupt the status quo of this nation for some nebulous concept of rights. We will leave things as they are until we have compelling evidence that they should be otherwise.

has looked at changes in overall exclusion rates in an area and this is particularly significant in view of the overlap between 'special needs' and 'disciplinary' exclusions mentioned earlier.

I think that the comparative statistics must be treated with particular caution. Pijl and Meijer (1991) compared the rates of inclusion and exclusion of students categorised as having 'special needs' in eight countries. I reproduce a comparison for three of the countries in Table 13.1. As the authors point out the numbers of students as well as the particular students said to have 'special needs' varies so much between countries that comparison between the figures is problematic. The total number of students said to have 'special needs' in England is given as 1.8% which matches the number which at the time of their research were the subjects of statements but departs dramatically from the official view that at any one time, around 1 in 6 or 17% of students have 'special needs' (DES, 1978).

Pijl and Meijer (1991:21) define 'curricular integration' as 'educational settings where handicapped and non-handicapped students work together in curricular activities at the same time, at the same place, with the same teacher'. Leaving aside issues of translation from the Dutch, it is not clear how meaningful 'working together' has to be before it can be labelled curricular integration or how much of the week it comprises. Would one want to say that students who attend lessons but do not appear to participate in them are 'curricularly integrated' whether or not they carry the label 'special needs'?

The authors conclude that since even in those countries with the lowest exclusion rates 1.5% of students are not 'curricularly integrated', then this group must present particular difficulties for integration. But we do not know whether the 1.5% of students not sharing common curricula in England are the same as those in Italy. Further, since there are huge variations in inclusion and exclusion rates within countries national rates of exclusion are of questionable significance. If we are looking for the lowest rates of exclusion from mainstream curricula and schools then we should examine the lowest rates locally rather than nationally.

Table 13.1 Summary of data concerning students with special needs

Country	A Curricularly integrated	B Socially integrated	C Segregated	B+C Hard to integrate curricularly
Italy T=1.7	0.2 %	1.3%	0.2%	1.5%
England T=1.8	0.3%	0.1%	1.4%	1.5%
Holland T=4.1	0.2%	0%	3.9%	3.9%

T= total percentage of recognised students with special needs.
Selected from Pijl and Meijer, 1991:108. All figures and wording are theirs.

Comparing the outcomes of integration and segregation

The comparison of the outcomes of 'integration' and 'segregation' also presume a simplistic definition of integration. Typically comparisons are made between the progress made by students who attend mainstream and special schools or between students who are based in special classes in mainstream schools and those who are not selected in this way. The latter comparisons are more typical of studies in the USA. Garry Hornby (1992) is amongst those who argue that integration should be assessed by such efficacy studies, and like others who take this position he amalgamates the results from different countries. In this way the performance of students that are said to be integrated by some in the UK because they attend a mainstream special class may be contrasted with students said to be segregated in the USA because they attend such a class! Though commonly done there is little justification for amalgamating findings from different countries or even within countries without careful argument. I do not think that schools, teachers, students, cultures and curricula are sufficiently similar within or between countries and over time to make such an approach rational.

While the comparison of outcomes has seemed attractive to many people, it makes little sense. Special schools and mainstream schools do not, of themselves define distinctive educational environments. They represent a vast number of different educational possibilities. The progress of students depends on the quality of the particular teaching and learning approaches that exist in each setting rather than the nature of the setting itself. Helen Keller was born deaf and blind. Her teacher Anne Sullivan worked on her education in a hut in her garden (Keller, 1903). Despite the dramatic educational success of her methods, no one has recommended that a major research programme be conducted into the effectiveness of garden huts in special education.

The search for proof of whether 'integration' or 'segregation' is the more effective form of education can appear like a religious quest. Each new research study is scanned to see if it, finally, can provide the basis for a decision between the two. Thus I was informed by an eminent psychologist that he thought a particular study by Fewell and Oelwein (1990) provided proof of an advantage for segregation in the development of language in children with Down's syndrome. However when I examined the study I found it insubstantial. It is on pre-school children attending segregated pre-school 'programs' and it correlated the length of time spent in an 'integrated environment' with a number of developmental measures. Children were involved in the research for between 3 and 9 months. They were assigned to one of three groups; zero time in the mainstream, between half an hour and 5 hours per week in the mainstream or between 5 hours 10 minutes and 17 hours 30 minutes in the mainstream. The authors do not speculate on what effect half an hour 'in the mainstream' might have nor do they think through the possible disrupting effects of attending two environments and the ethical questions facing such studies. They found only one significant difference in the whole study; the development of expressive language 'favoured children in sites with no integration'.

Now even with my limited knowledge of statistics, I know that where large numbers of correlations are made some are likely to be statistically significant by chance. Further I know that even if such a difference between these settings persisted the interpretation of this result is fraught. The quality of a language environment is not defined by its characterisation as 'integrated' or 'segregated'. If progress in the development of children's expressive language is made in either setting it will be because of the quality of the language environment, the opportunities for expression, the use that is made of human and other resources.

While questions can be raised about why the study was attempted in the first place the authors themselves were aware of some of its methodological deficiencies and urged 'caution in interpreting the results'. For example, in explaining the difference in language progress, they mentioned the greater human resources in the segregated setting. However, I was surprised to discover that these researchers actually interpreted their findings to yield opposite conclusions to those of my informant:

> The curriculum employed and the quality of instruction may have a more powerful effect on developmental outcome and skill acquisition than who is in the class....Given the moral and legal support...the results of this study provide evidence that integrated settings with strong, high quality programs are good choices.
>
> (Fewell and Oelwein, 1990:115)

The authors quote a number of research studies which support the first part of this conclusion like Marten Söder (1989) who claimed that 'research on integration and mainstreaming in schools shows clearly that merely physical placement of a disabled child among non-disabled peers does not lead to positive social contacts'. But do we really need research studies to tell us that 'who is in the class' cannot of itself determine academic or social outcomes? In other contexts a few moments thought might reveal that the proximity of boys and girls is a necessary precondition for the formation of relationships between them, but it cannot guarantee that positive alliances will form or be long-lasting.

Documenting inclusion and exclusion

Comparisons of outcomes are often treated, wrongly in my view, as if they can provide information on 'whether to integrate'. Descriptive case-studies of inclusion are commonly thought to provide evidence about 'how to integrate'. However the idea that what is presented in some way represents 'good practice' can produce an unacknowledged bias if problems of practice are not reported or sought out. Accurate reports and analyses of the practice of others provide a rich source of ideas that can be adapted to one's own circumstances and of how difficulties may be avoided or overcome.

Descriptions of inclusion and exclusion can be divided into two groups. There are those which focus on students characterised by a 'special needs' label or a disability and those which are concerned with describing and analysing the participation of all students and all forms of exclusion. Studies which have focused on categorised groups have been conducted in the UK at least since the early 1970s with Elizabeth Anderson's important work on physically disabled students (Anderson, 1973) and continuing with the studies on Blind and Partially sighted students (Jamieson *et al.*, 1977) and then the major study of integration practice by Seamus Hegarty and Keith Pocklington in the early 1980s (Hegarty and Pocklington, 1982). At the same time we began to document the practice of integration at the Open University in courses and in books such as the *Nature of Special Education* (Booth and Statham, 1982) and in *Integrating Special Education* (Booth and Potts, 1983). Campaigning organisations have been influential in this area, first with the National Association of Mental Health and the Campaign for Mental Handicap (for example, Beresford and Tuckwell, 1979) and then the Centre for Studies of Integration in Education, now called the Centre for the Study of Inclusive Education.

Some studies from the mid-1980s began to set the inclusion of previously excluded groups within the context of the curricula and organisation of the whole school (see, for example, Booth, 1987, 1992). However, very few have managed to look at the development of participation of all students in a school as well as documenting exclusion across schools as a whole. This approach is represented to some extent in Towards Integration (Gilbert and Hart, 1990) and I have discussed the change in conception that such an approach entails as well as elements of a study in Catherine Clark, Alan Dyson and Alan Millward's *Towards Inclusive Schools* (Booth, 1995). Colleagues and I are involved in a further study linked to the approach developed in that book. While this emphasis may be slow to emerge it is only by looking at the way schools can foster the participation of all students and reduce all pressures to exclusion that we can fulfil Seamus Hegarty's request to treat *integration as a matter of school reform.*

Summary

Progress in research on integration may be no more possible than the quest for the definitive comparison of integration and segregation. Ironically both may owe their attraction to the positivist and historicist views of the development of human societies and the contribution of science to them, generated in the nineteenth century. Comparisons of the outcome of 'integration' and 'segregation', although methodologically and conceptually flawed, are connected to a dominant ideology of research in education. Unless the limitations of that ideology are widely accepted, it is likely that such an approach to research will continue to be reproduced, funded and disseminated.

I have discussed a number of ways of conceptualising integration and looked at the consequence for understanding integration once a challenge is made to official notions of 'special need' or 'learning difficulty'. Such a redefinition of integration leads to a redefinition of research so that it focuses on how schools respond to the diversity of all their students rather than on groups categorised by 'special need' or disability. But this notion of an expanded and reconstituted mainstream can also be applied to those who conduct research. It is a relatively simple matter to deconstruct, on paper, the notion of special education as a separate area of study. However, we have an understandable resistance to the reconstruction of the working practices that pay the mortgage. Even if we wish to do so, we have a limited capacity to rewrite our job descriptions.

Nevertheless, I remain optimistic. I think that it will become increasingly difficult to defend research on integration which is conceptually unclear and does not make its assumptions explicit. Nor will practitioners be able to continue to pretend that they are drawing on research or science when they assign children to forms of provision based on the requirements of local bureaucracies. And if change does not come from within these groups, it will become increasingly hard to ignore the political voice of disabled people and groups of parents, who in championing their rights will help to put the contribution of research on integration to policy and practice in its rightful place.

References

Ainscow, M. (1995) 'Education for all: Making it happen', Keynote address at the *International Special Education Congress*, Birmingham, England.

Anderson, E. (1973) *The Disabled Schoolchild*. London: Methuen.

Beresford, P. and Tuckwell P. (1979) *Schools for All*, London: MIND and CMH.

Booth, T., (1981) 'Demystifying Integration'. In Swann, W. (ed.) *The Practice of Special Education*. Oxford: Blackwell.

Booth, T. (1987) 'Extending primary practice: Springfield Junior School'. In Booth, T., Potts, P. and Swann, W. (eds) *Curricula for All: Preventing Difficulties in Learning*. Oxford: Blackwell.

Booth, T. (1992) 'Under the walnut tree: the Grove Primary School'. In Booth, T., Swann, W., Masterton, M. and Potts, P. (eds) *Policies for Diversity in Education*. London: Routledge.

Booth, T. (1993) 'Continua or Chimera?', *British Journal of Special Education*, **21(1)**, 21–24.

Booth, T. (1995) 'Mapping inclusion and exclusion, concepts for all?' In Clark, C., Dyson, A. and Milward A. (eds) *Towards Inclusive Schools?* London: Fulton.

Booth, T., (1996) 'Stories of exclusion; natural and unnatural selection'. In Blair, E. and Milner, J. (eds) *Exclusion from School*. London: Routledge.

Booth, T. and Statham, J. (1982) The Nature of Special Education, London: Croom Helm.

Booth, T. and Potts, P. (1983) *Integrating Special Education*. Oxford: Blackwell.

Commission for Racial Equality (1992) *Set to Fail? Setting and Banding in Secondary Schools*. London: CRE.

Department of Education and Science (1978) *Special Educational Needs, Report of the Committte of Enquiry into the Education of Handicapped Children and Young People*. London: HMSO.

Department for Education (1994) *Code of Practice on the Identification and Assessment of Special Educational Needs*. London: DfE.

Department for Education (1995) *Final Report to the Department for Education; National Survey of Local Education Authorities' Policies and Procedures for the Identification of, and Provision for, Children who are out of School by Reason of Exclusion or Otherwise*. London: DfE.

Fewell, R. and Oelwein, P. (1990) 'The relationship between time in integrated environments and developmental gains in young children with special needs', *Topics in Early Childhood Eduction*, **10(2)**, 104–16.

Gilbert, C. and Hart M. (1990) *Towards Integration*. London: Kogan Page.

Hegarty, S. (1993) 'Reviewing the literature on integration', *European Journal of Special Education*, **8(2)**, 194–200.

Hegarty, S., Pocklington, K. and Lucas, D. (1981) *Education Pupils with Special Needs in the Ordinary School.* London: NFER-Nelson.

Hegarty, S. and Pocklington, K. (1982) *Integration in Action.* London: NFER-Nelson.

Hornby, G. (1992) 'Integration of children with special educational needs: is it time for a policy review?', *Support for Learning*, **(7)3**, 130–34.

Jamieson, M., Parlett, M. and Pocklington, K. (1977) *Towards Integration; A Study of Blind and Partially Sighted Children in Ordinary Schools.* Slough: NFER.

Keller, H. (1903) *The Story of My Life.* London: Doubleday.

Mason, M. (1992) 'The integration alliance; background and manifesto'. In Booth, T., Swann, W., Masterton M. and Potts, P. (eds) *Policies for Diversity in Education.* London: Routledge.

Mittler, P. (1985) 'Integration: the shadow and the substance', *Education and Child Psychology*, **2(3)**, 8–22.

Norwich, B. (1990) *Reappraising Special Needs Education.* London: Cassell.

Norwich, B. (1994) *Segregation and inclusion, English LEA statistics, 1988–92.* Bristol: Centre for Studies on Inclusive Education.

Oliver, M. (1992) 'Intellectual masturbation, a rejoinder to Söder and Booth', *European Journal of Special Needs Education*, **(7)1**, 20–28.

Pijl, S. and Meijer, C. (1991) 'Does integration count for much? An analysis of the practices of integration in eights countries', *European Journal of Special Needs Education*, **(6)2**, 100–111.

Rieser, R. and Mason, M. (1990) *Disability Equality in the Classroom: A Human Rights Issue.* London: ILEA.

Söder, M. (1989) 'Disability as a social construct: the labelling approach revisited', *European Journal of Special Needs Education*, **4(2)**, 117–19.

Solity, J. (1992) *Special Education.* London: Cassell.

Swann, W. (1988) 'Trends in special school placement', *Oxford Review of Education*, **14(2)**, 139–61.

Chapter Fourteen

Trauma in school: The psychology of helping

Chris Best and Charlie Mead

Every day we can switch on the TV news, listen to the radio, or pick up a newspaper and be faced with traumatic events that have happened in all corners of the world. We go to the cinema and, depending on the film, are confronted with traumatic events that assault our emotions. And yet, somehow, we usually remain distant from the horrors. Rarely are we affected unless the magnitude of the event is so enormous that our compassion may come to the fore, such as the genocide in Rwanda, the sinking of the ferry *Estonia* in the Baltic, or the plight of the children in Romanian orphanages.

As Knapman (1993) says: 'There is a paradox in the fact that the world is so often portrayed as full of violence and that children see death on the TV and reported in the media, yet in actual fact they will have less real experience of death than their forebears'.

The *Oxford English Dictionary* defines 'trauma' as 'a morbid condition of body produced by wound or external violence; emotional shock'. The definition of school is an 'institution for educating children or giving instruction'. By definition then, these two words would seem incompatible, yet schools have been the focus for many traumatic events in recent years. Think of the destruction of the school in Aberfan in 1966, think of the schoolgirl killed in a Middlesbrough classroom in front of her classmates, of the pupils held hostage by a gunman in Birmingham. Think of the pupils killed in the Hagley School minibus crash or the children swept away at Land's End.

Trauma does not respect any school boundaries and as Capewell (1992) says, 'trauma may:

- Emotionally and/or physically hurt children and/or staff.
- Disrupt school functioning.
- Leave scars which affect behaviour and school performance and can continue affecting the person through adult life.'

Trauma then, becomes not the distant media version but a harsh reality. Trauma can directly or indirectly involve a school. It can happen inside or outside the school gates. Indeed the school may be part of an affected community such as Hungerford, Hillsborough or Lockerbie.

It would be erroneous to think that all trauma is associated with major incidents. Incidents such as the death of an individual pupil, a teacher or a parent by natural causes, accident, violence or suicide are, sadly, relatively common. In Yule and Gold's (1993) view: 'While large scale disasters may happen infrequently, small scale incidents happen with far greater frequency. Regardless of the size of the incident, the distress caused to the individuals involved can be equally devastating'.

We feel it important to state that in our experience the distress caused to individuals involved happens to both the recipients of large- or small-scale traumatic events and to those who help. For the best humanitarian reasons people often rush to situations where they feel they are needed; but working within any traumatic situation is not easy and should be treated with caution. Ideally it should be carried out by those who are personally robust enough to cope with the pressures, who have examined their own motives for wanting to put themselves in that 'helping' position and who have received some training. Access to professional colleagues for debriefing purposes is essential if further 'casualties' are to be avoided. In other words, we would argue that working with trauma in schools should carry a 'government health warning': if you are confident in your knowledge and can cope with the emotional and practical pressures, you will be able to work effectively; if not, then this area of work may not be for you.

Our purposes in this chapter are to provide the reader with both theory and practice in working with traumatised children and school staff and to outline strategies for planned interventions, including communication systems, support networks and sharing of knowledge. To provide a practical basis, we have divided the chapter into two sections: working with an individual focus and working with a group focus, each with a case example.

Trauma in school – individual focus

In recent years trauma in school has taken on a high profile amongst educationalists. It has become a 'sexy' topic. However, the incidence of trauma affecting a whole-school community is, fortunately, still relatively rare. The same cannot be said for the incidence of loss for the individual child when parents separate or die, friends are killed in an accident or they suffer trauma by abuse. Of all the schools we work in there is not one that has not had to cope with the effects of loss amongst pupils or staff and this causes trauma in itself. School staff do not see this as 'sexy' at all. What they have wanted is a simple explanation of the possible effects of loss on the child, what they can do about it and how it should be done. Whilst the nature of whole-school and individual incidents might be dramatically different, there are many aspects of the effects on children that are remarkably similar. The need for all school staff to be aware of these potential effects, in the classroom and the playground, is therefore paramount. And having become aware of the effects, school staff need to communicate this to each other, to parents and to pupils directly affected.

This next section outlines briefly the main areas of the potential effect loss might have on an individual child and the response a school might make. It should be recognised that some children will not display any of these features and that others might display many of them. They may even display features that are contradictory and confusing to the outside world. There is no conclusive research to suggest why this might be the case, but clearly the age of the child, the support they receive outside school and their ability to adjust to new circumstances are important factors in coming to terms with their loss. Some of these factors are explored in the next section.

Aspects of adjustment

Kendall Johnson (1992) and Elizabeth Capewell (1994) have identified four major aspects of a child's development that might be affected by trauma or loss: cognitive, physical, emotional and behavioural. We would add the psychological, spiritual and practical effects of loss to a child also. These seven aspects of adjustment need to be understood and recognised as the possible effects of trauma before an intervention can be devised and implemented within a school setting. Table 14.1 outlines the main signs associated with each aspect of adjustment.

Table 14.1 The possible effects of trauma or loss on a child

Aspect of adjustment	Signs associated with the aspect
Cognitive	Confusion over the event, difficulty in ordering or sequencing in time, indecisiveness, poor concentration, loss of memory, loss of judgement and reasoning skills, decline in intellectual and academic functioning
Psychological	Obsessive behaviours, loss of concentration and attention skills, change of 'personality', increased dreams/nightmares, fear of recurrence of the event, overconcern for others
Emotional	The need to be looked after (fed, dressed, etc.) depression, anxiety, anger, guilt
Spiritual	Discovery or rediscovery of faith, loss of faith
Behavioural	Any sudden change in behaviour including clinging, reappearance of younger habits, obsessive and repetitive talking, disobedience, decline in self-discipline and responsibility to others, drug or alcohol abuse, dropping out of school
Physical	Headaches, shock, shivering, constriction of the throat, disturbed sleep, tiredness, loss of appetite, loss of physical control, avoidance of others including school refusal
Practical	Inability to cope with regular, established routines at home or school, usually associated with the aspects outlined above

Socio-cultural issues

For school staff to understand the nature of the effect of loss on a child it is important to have some background information. Without this it is possible for school staff to fall into the trap of 'making things worse' rather than providing a positive framework for the readjustment of the child. The child's upbringing, culture, way of life and experience will help determine its attitude to death or loss. Some children may have directly encountered a cultural attitude to death that is both different and challenging to our Western European view. The dying rooms of China, the planned neglect of Indonesia or Romania or the ethnic cleansing of Rwanda or Bosnia may be extreme examples, but they present a view of death to the child that may be in conflict with our own norms. School staff should not put themselves in a position where their advice to a child is in conflict with that of the family or community as a whole. We therefore feel it is important for teachers to have:

- knowledge of the child's cultural and religious beliefs, experiences, ceremonies and rites of passage to the afterlife;
- a working knowledge of the child's philosophy of life, appropriate to their level of development;
- knowledge of any taboos relating to all aspects of death including funerals, wakes, cremation, burial, undertakers, etc;
- knowledge of the involvement of the child in the process of the funeral in the case of death;
- an understanding of the facts in the case of divorce or separation or trauma by abuse.

One of the implications of acquiring this information is that some of it needs to be gathered on a routine basis for all children in a school before an incident occurs as it is difficult for school staff to impinge on family grief after the event. A system for gathering and collating information should be developed by schools so that this aspect of dealing with loss can be effective.

The normal pattern of grief and mourning

In the past few years there have been an increasing number of models of the expected pattern of grief and mourning when experiencing individual loss, from Bowlby (1981), through Katz and Florian (1986) to Dyregrov (1991) and Kleber and Brom (1992). The model that we have found most useful in explaining this process to school staff comes from Baker and Duncan (1992). Whilst most of their work has been centred on the trauma caused by child abuse, it is equally applicable to other traumatic events and to individual loss. Table 14.2 outlines their main findings. The time-scales indicated are approximate and are dependent upon the age of the child and the level of intervention provided for the child from their family and school.

Table 14.2 The possible effects of trauma and loss on a child from the time of the incident onwards

Time of loss to 2 months	1-3 months after loss and ongoing from then	8-9 months after loss and ongoing from then	1-2 years after loss and ongoing from then
Shock Physical and mental pain, shivering, constriction of the throat	*Anxiety* Insecurity Irrational fears Unusual dependency	*Depression* Loss, despair, anxiety, anger, remorse, guilt Personality problems get worse	*Acceptance* Loss no longer felt as an appalling tragedy Can settle to new circumstances Regain and develop interests
Numbness Sense of isolation Indecisiveness Feelings of depersonalisation Irrational behaviours Withdrawal or clinging	*Guilt* Self-recrimination *Anger* 'Why me?' Misplaced anger at anything	*Apathy* Lack of will Purposelessness Denial of anger and other feelings Become unreliable Neglect own best interests Rejection of friends	*Healing* Restructure life patterns Develop deepened maturity and wider compassion Regain equilibrium
Denial 'It can't be true'	*Grief* *Loneliness* Feelings of rejection	*Loss of identity* 'Who am I now?'	
	Yearning Acute emotional pain Nightmares Loss of concentration Self-interest Extreme tiredness	*Stigma* Possible social/cultural ostracism	
	Searching Frustration Wanting to put the clock back Window Shopping Overspending Childhood regression	*Mitigation* Rediscovery of old self and beginning of adjustment if 'grief work' is being done	

The cognitive effects of loss and responses to trauma

In recent years there has been an increase in the level of understanding amongst educationalists about the cognitive effects of loss and trauma on children. There appear to be two main areas of cognitive effect:

1. The age and cognitive development of the child at the time of loss. This includes their ability to understand what is happening to them over a period of time

2. The effect of the incidence of loss on cognitive development, academic and social functioning.

It has been recognised that the age and level of cognitive development of the child will determine the length and form of response to the traumatic incident in their life. Simply put, a 7-year-old child will take longer to come to terms with loss than an adolescent. We would agree with Baker's general argument that a child under 6 years, whilst expressing anxiety, does not appreciate the concept of guilt, self-anger or grief. It is only as they develop do those concepts take on meaning. As they do, it is likely that the child will re-live their trauma in the light of these new realisations. For example, a girl whose mother had died when she was 7 only really appreciated the loss in terms of a lasting relationship when she was developing lasting relationships herself as a teenager. This caused deep depression in the girl and a realisation, not experienced before, that her mother would not be at her wedding nor see her own children.

So, the normal pattern of grief and mourning outlined in Table 14.2 may be extended for many years if the loss occurs at a time when the child does not have the appropriate level of understanding to appreciate the significance of the loss. Baker and Duncan (1992) identify key ages when a child's development will permit this appropriate level of understanding. They also suggest what the needs of the child might be at those key ages and the consequences of these needs not being met. We have added our own experiences and reflections to this model which are outlined in Table 14.3. In our work with schools and individual pupils this matrix has proved a useful tool in enabling a level of understanding to be reached by staff. As with all the models in this chapter we are wary of the ages and time-scales used as each individual will respond differently, but we have found the model to answer more questions than it raises.

Clearly this information is essential to school staff if they are to understand any unusual behaviours in the context of the classroom or playground and help and support the child throughout their school careers. Some staff express the view that children should be better able to cope with loss because they do not really appreciate its significance. The opposite appears to be closer to the truth. Children may appreciate it more and over a much longer period of time. They therefore require more support than many adults. Statements from staff about children who have suffered loss like 'It's been six weeks now. They must be over it surely!' are not uncommon in our experience We hope this section will help dispel such unhelpful myths.

Defences against feelings

Much of the literature concerning loss and trauma and their effects on children touch on the repression of feelings if children are not given an opportunity to explore and express those feelings (Dyregrov, 1991; Johnson 1992; Kleber and Brom, 1992). It is not our intention to re-visit these arguments but to inform or remind readers that the repression of feelings in children can be dangerous for the long-term development of a child. Denial of loss forces a child to take a different route in their life compared with an acceptance of loss. This can lead to unresolved internal conflicts that may surface later in life in emotional responses such as an inability to develop relationships with others.

Table 14.3 Indicating the response of a child to a traumatic incident or loss according to age and cognitive development

Response to loss	Child may need	If needs are not met	Possible consequences
Anxiety – Child under 6 years	Reassurance and explanations of the loss in real world terms, with someone who the child is comfortable and safe with	The child may block out their own memory of the event, relying on the stories and myths of others	Regression, aggression, overactive behaviours, poor sleep patterns, confusion, fears/phobias and a pre-occupation with what they know of the loss
Guilt – Child over 6 years	Honest acknowledgment and confirmation/correction of what they know and what has happened	The child may rationalise their own view of events which may lead to self-deception	Self-isolation, misery, self-delusion, passivity, apathy, poor concentration, low self-esteem, obsessional and dominating behaviours
Anger – Child over 8 years	The child may need help in expressing their own feelings	Anger may be focused on self or on others who are equally not to blame	Self-harm, taking risks, overcontrol, eating disorders, power games and cheating. Older children may also suffer sexual difficulties, become involved in crime and arson
Grief – Child over 12 years	A listener, an advocate and a witness, preferably well known to the child. Someone who will help them come to terms with their expressions of grief	Denial of grief	The child may become stuck at denial and is unable to resolve their grief leading to further difficulties with their aspects of adjustment

Unresolved emotional responses

Many of the types of unresolved responses to loss have been identified in Table 14.3. However, we felt it would be beneficial to spend some time reviewing unresolved grief. Denial of grief is the psychological response to the finality of death (Baker and Duncan, 1992). We cannot replace the one we loved but we cannot accept their going either. Our response is to search for surrogate emotions that will give us some hope for a rekindling of what we feel we have lost. This invariably takes on a negative aspect and involves revenge or similar destructive emotions (Dyregrov, 1991). These emotions tend not to satisfy the need for acceptance we are looking for. For school staff who recognise this response in pupils we suggest an initial discussion with a prime carer and referral to a support agency that has some expertise in this field. We would be hopeful that the pupil would be helped to acknowledge and accept their denial which might lead to a re-evaluation of the events surrounding the trauma or loss and a re-discovery of themselves in the process.

School and staff response to trauma

School staff have many responses to trauma and loss in their own lives as well as that of the children in their care. Many draw on that experience to help them cope with trauma at work but their experiences do not always allow them to be as effective as they might. Table 14.4 is a simple list of do's and don'ts that have been developed by ourselves over the past few years. These should be seen within the context of the possible consequences of trauma in children as identified above.

Table 14.4 Guidance to school staff responding to trauma and loss

Do	Don't
Accept the reality of the loss	Be patronising
Be honest	Tell mistruths about where the dead person
Be prepared to talk about anxiety, anger, guilt	has gone
and grief	Avoid them
Be available for talks or hugs	Say you know how they feel
Encourage pupils to be patient with themselves	Say 'you ought to be feeling better now'
Let your concern and caring show	Tell them what they should do or feel
Talk about the event of loss if they wish	Change the subject if they want to talk about their
Explain what might happen in years to come	loss
Keep them busy	Avoid mentioning their loss (they won't have
	forgotten about it)
	Try to find something positive about the loss
	Point out that they at least have other parents etc.
	Say they can always have another mother etc.
	Make them feel guilty about their loss by making
	comments which suggest the loss is their fault

Example 1. The murder of the father of a Year 4 child, age 9

The incident
In the summer term of 1994 the father of a Year 4 pupil, John (a pseudonym) was murdered outside his home on a Friday night. He was stabbed to death by a known acquaintance. The incident was not witnessed directly by John but he arrived on the scene soon after. The murder was reported in the local press and featured on local television naming both the father and the pupil. The circumstances surrounding the murder and the ensuing publicity caused the family to go into hiding for some weeks where they were not able to be contacted directly.

The response
On the following Monday the Headteacher of John's school contacted the school psychologist (one of the authors), to seek advice on how best to handle the situation. They were unsure how to proceed, especially as John did not appear to be returning to school in the near future. They were already aware of gossip and rumours amongst the children, especially in John's class. They felt that they needed to do something quite soon but did not know what or how.

Wagner (1990) identified practical strategies for schools to adopt in helping a bereaved child:

- Gaining as much knowledge as possible about the child's beliefs.
- Gaining as much knowledge as is reasonable about the loss.
- Letting the child know that the school knows about the loss.
- Encouraging the child's friends to be supportive and helpful.
- Providing the remaining family members with information about how the child is coping once they have returned to school.

All of these strategies require effective communication within the school and between school, family and child. For outside agencies such as a Psychological Service it is important to help the school establish these networks and to maintain them over time.

The first response was to visit the Headteacher and class teacher at school to find out what they knew and devise a strategy. The facts of the death were reasonably well documented. The difficulty that the school had was:

- the absence of a whole-school strategy for dealing with loss in the school;
- a lack of expertise in coping with this type of incident amongst the staff;
- a variety of reactions from John's class and the rest of the school, from hostile to tearful.

The Headteacher was clear that he wanted to create an environment which made it as easy as possible for John to return and settle back into the school routine. To do this effectively it was agreed that the educational psychologist would:

- Address John's class about the murder of his father.
- Address the school staff about the likely effect on John of the murder, over a period of time (this was done by introducing the main points in Tables 14.1–14.3 to all staff in the school).
- Talk to John on his return to school (this was rejected by the family as they were already receiving support through their GP).

The Headteacher let the whole school know that the staff were aware of what had happened to John's father, that John would not be returning for some time and that when he did return it was expected that all pupils would be supportive. Making this very public statement, without dramatising or dwelling on the incident, enabled the staff and pupils in the school to acknowledge the incident and prepare them for the implementation of any strategies thought necessary to help support John.

The purpose of addressing John's class was to help them clarify the facts around the murder, let them share their thoughts and feelings about death and this death in particular, and have them suggest ways in which they might best support John on his return to school. As a group of 8 and 9 year olds it might be thought that they would not have much to say about death or not want to say it. To the surprise of the class teacher this discussion went on for nearly an hour and all members of the class contributed at some stage. The class teacher commented that some children contributed who did not normally volunteer any information in class, and that other pupils who usually found it difficult to concentrate were attentive for most of the time. Involving pupils in a participatory way with the process of dealing with trauma is a cornerstone to the successful re-integration of pupils suffering from trauma or loss. They were able to articulate their thoughts, some sad, some funny; develop a collective truth about the incident; devise positive strategies for John's return and suggest ways in which the school could help John and themselves in coping with their feelings. In particular they suggested:

- That the Headteacher talk to John and his mother about what they wanted when John returned to school.
- A re-organisation of the classroom to give privacy to John or others needing time out.
- Access to the Headteacher or Special Needs Coordinator (SENCO) should pupils want to talk to someone in private about their feelings.
- Formally letting their parents know that they had this discussion and what the results of it were.

The Headteacher and class teacher, who were present during this session, also suggested that the class might like to take on the responsibility of letting other pupils in the school know what had happened to John's father and the family. As the class had agreed on the facts of the murder and developed a shared understanding of the school's response it was felt they were able to correct false rumours about the incident and be seen to be actively supportive of John. After a short discussion the class agreed to take on this role on the understanding that if they found it difficult to challenge older pupils they would have the support of the staff. This sophisticated form of negotiation was new to the class but not to the Headteacher or ourselves. They took their responsibility very seriously but had little cause to challenge others' misunderstandings. They were mainly involved in letting other pupils know how John would be supported on his return.

This open form of discussion with the class proved beneficial to John, the class and the whole school. Staff reported a positive attitude from pupils to the way that the school was seen to have helped John when he returned 3 weeks after the murder. The pupils responded positively and openly to John, letting him know they were aware of what happened and the systems set up to help him. Staff were, on the whole, able to adhere to the Do's and Don'ts outlined earlier in the chapter and help John face the reality of life without his father. Clearly there is the potential for John to experience many of the complications associated with loss in the remainder of his life, but whilst he is at his present school he will have support and understanding to help to cope with those difficulties.

The school now has a system for coping with trauma. It is an ongoing system and will be evaluated yearly as part of the school development plan. It is not possible to impose such a system on a school, but where they find it necessary, beneficial and able to be implemented it will help staff and pupils cope with the tragedy of trauma and loss. There are many pitfalls in coping with loss but if schools are willing to address trauma, from whatever cause, they will be better equipped to meet the needs of the children in their care.

Trauma in school – group focus

Research into major traumatic incidents in schools appears to be in its infancy. In the UK Yule and his colleagues (1990, 1991a,b, 1993) have pioneered work from the Traumatic Stress Clinic at the Maudesley Hospital in London, focusing particularly on children's fears, depression and anxiety following incidents such as the sinking of the cruise ship *Jupiter*, screening children for post-traumatic stress disorders and advice for schools on coping with crises. The text *Wise Before the Event* (Yule and Gold, 1993) has been distributed to most schools in the country to help them in developing their critical incident management plans.

Capewell (1992, 1994) has developed systems for managing critical incidents in schools following her extensive work looking at trauma management worldwide. Mallon and Best (1995) provide an outline of the response provided by a school psychological service to a major incident in a secondary school plus investigation of children's response to the trauma. Parker, Watts and Allsopp (1995) have looked at post-traumatic stress symptoms in children and parents following a school-based fatality concluding that without professional guidance most parents are able to respond to their children's problems, and that this ability does not seem to be affected by the symptoms that the parents are suffering themselves.

Overseas, the literature focuses largely on intervention, research and treatment. Authors such as Blom (1986), Klingman (1987), Toubiana *et al.* (1988) and Wenkstern and Leenaars (1993) give illustrations of major situations involving accidents in and outside schools and emphasise the importance of applying basic crisis intervention principles, supervising intervention and implementing therapeutic procedures. Terr (1983, 1989) and Johnson (1989, 1992) outline methods of treating trauma in children through hypnosis, play and psychotherapy and outline possible lay interventions that parents, teachers and others can use following traumatic events. Terr concludes that the treatment of childhood trauma will probably rely on several different approaches used simultaneously or in tandem.

Bonenberger (1991) and Markwood (1988) give advice in implementing institutional crisis response plans where school travel, bomb threats, etc. are involved. Similarly, Shrestha (1990) and Zakariya (1985) examine the senior management role in effective crisis intervention giving experiences from a variety of school districts and crises ranging from murder to flood. These provide very similar models to those outlined by Yule and Gold (1993).

Management of the outcomes of natural disasters where the school is part of an affected community are given by Galante and Foa (1987; Italian earthquake), McFarlane (1989; Australian bush fires) and Ponton and Bryant (1991; Loma Prieta earthquake). Again the emphasis is on planning, co-ordination and communication.

In all the research there is a clear view that there is a need for education departments and schools to have a policy and action plan in place to meet traumatic events and disasters. Coupled with this there is a need for awareness and training for staff to meet the needs of those in school suffering the effects of trauma. In the UK this is being fostered mainly by TACT (Trauma After Care Trust), a registered charity which aims to educate professionals on all aspects of dealing with the aftermath of trauma (see Useful addresses at end of chapter).

In the research literature it is well documented that many of those who experience traumatic events can develop a distinct set of physical signs and symptoms which tend to fall into three clusters that can lead to what is called post-traumatic stress disorder (PTSD):

- Recurring intrusive recollections of the traumatic event such as in dreams and flashbacks.
- Persistent avoidance of stimuli associated with the trauma.
- Persistent symptoms of increased arousal, characterised by hyper-vigilance, increased startle responses, sleep difficulties, irritability, anxiety and physiological hyperactivity (Yule and Gold, 1993).

These symptoms appear to be exacerbated by exposure to stimuli associated with the original event (Perry, 1991). Traumatic incidents also appear to facilitate disclosure of previous trauma. Terr (1983) and Famularo (1990) conclude that children who suffer exposure to repeated traumatic events exhibit more avoidance-type symptoms than those exposed to isolated trauma. Children suffering severe post-traumatic stress have reactions similar, both in type and severity, to adults with some additional features, including sleep-walking, withdrawal, enuresis, academic failure and personality change (Udwin, 1993).

Given the research, how then can we translate it into practice? The next section outlines, by linking the two concepts, a practical example involving a major incident.

Example 2. A hostage taking in a girl's secondary school (adapted from Mallon and Best, 1995)

The incident

On 5 July 1993 at about 2.50 p.m., a young man aged 17 entered a Birmingham secondary school for girls, apparently following an argument with his girlfriend, a pupil at the school. The man was armed with a machete, a meat cleaver and a firearm which later proved to be an air pistol.

The man went into a Year 7 classroom, held a knife at the class teacher's throat, while brandishing the pistol in his other hand and demanded to see the Headteacher. Seeing a group of Year 9 girls emerging from another classroom, he ordered them back inside. Some of these girls escaped into a cupboard whilst the others were ushered into the Year 7 classroom. The young man then proceeded to cause considerable damage, including smashing windows and computer monitors, and then threatened the girls, at one stage asking, 'Who wants to die first?' The fire alarm was triggered by a staff member resulting in the evacuation of all other pupils in the school and the police were called.

During the next 30 minutes the intruder released pupils individually and in small groups before surrounding himself with a group of girls, fearing he would be shot by the police, and gave himself up.

The response

To assist smooth response to a crisis Yule and Gold (1993) suggest the school assign responsibility for the following 12 tasks. These are followed by a description of the action taken by this particular school:

1. Obtain factual information
2. Senior management meet with support personnel
3. Establish an intervention team
4. Contact families (all within hours)
5. Call a staff meeting to give information
6. Inform pupils in small groups
7. Arrange a debriefing meeting for staff involved in traumatic event.
8. Debrief pupils involved in the trauma.
9. Identify high-risk pupils and staff
10. Promote discussion in classes.
11. Identify the need for group or individual treatment
12. Organise treatment

The Headteacher contacted the local education department and outside agencies including the School's Adviser who in turn contacted the School Psychological Service, the Child Advisory Social Work Service and Education Welfare Service. She was concerned that there were a large number of pupils and staff who appeared deeply upset at what had happened and asked for help and support.

Good communication in the early stages was considered vital. Uncertainty would breed rumour which could add significantly to distress. A phone line was cleared for outgoing calls. Other phone lines were used for taking inquiries and calls logged. Although not used in this event, a 'telephone tree' where some parents telephone others to ensure speedy transfer of accurate information proves highly effective.

The needs were isolated into two areas by the Headteacher, those of the pupils and those of the staff. Given the gender and ethnic concerns it was agreed that only women would be involved in the debriefing of pupils with male and female professionals working with staff. Debriefing serves the purpose of clarifying what happened, allows for a sharing of reactions and gives reassurance that reactions are normal not abnormal. Experiencing trauma, people often feel numb and almost as if the event is not really happening to them. Afterwards they are often in a state of shock for a few days. Debriefing is a method of talking about not only what happened but of sharing the sometimes terrifying reactions to the event. It is usually carried out by experienced outside agencies (in this case educational psychologists and social workers) and allows not only for the expression of feelings but education in coping strategies for the time to come.

Initially, police restrictions curtailed primary debriefing sessions. Pupils and staff were only allowed to be seen individually rather than in groups – which presented logistical difficulties as there were over 50 pupils and 30 staff directly or indirectly affected and a maximum of five professionals for any one session. The situation was one of conflict between the evidential needs of the police and the personal needs of those involved. Additionally, media attention and pressure proved intrusive and required firm handling.

Priorities for debriefing needed to be established. Some pupils appeared in a state of acute shock whilst others displayed symptoms ranging from withdrawn behaviour to nonchalance and bravado. Ultimately the Heads of Year decided who should be seen and in what order. A spreadsheet was constructed as a practical method of recording which pupils had been seen by outside agencies and any additional comments.

After 2 days police permission was granted to undertake group debriefing in groups of 4–6 pupils. This resulted in much more efficient use of time with positive benefits for pupils in terms of the process of normalisation. Two weeks after the incident the Year 9 group were brought together for debriefing with the teacher who had been with them when the incident occurred (she had been absent on medical grounds until that date).

Careful note had been kept of observed post-traumatic stress reactions. Debriefing sessions had elicited from pupils 'fright and flight' reactions on seeing a kitchen knife in their own home, fear of leaving home or school alone, 'jumpiness' at the slightest noise such as doors banging, cars coming up the school drive and persistent vigilance and anxiety regarding intruders. The latter was only slightly alleviated on the day after the incident when the school employed a security guard to check everyone entering the school building.

In class teachers noted that pupils lacked concentration, talked to each other more frequently and rarely completed set tasks. In a science lesson one of the authors noted excessive joke telling, out-of-seat behaviour and the crescendo of a 'Mexican wave' – from a class of normally quiet, diligent pupils.

Desensitisation proved difficult. Girls were refusing to walk up the stairs to the classrooms where the incident occurred. With sensitive handling, this was eventually achieved and the pupils entered the classrooms where they were allowed to explore and to some extent re-enact the events in detail. Recall was vivid and gross hostility to the perpetrator much in evidence.

At the beginning of the next term, a full staff meeting was held at which outside agency input to date was described. Staff were alerted to pupils thought to be at high risk of suffering from PTSD.

Happily the school has made a successful return to normality and appears to be functioning well as do the majority of pupils who witnessed this incident. Whilst the incident reported here was clearly disturbing and frightening, no lives were lost and no physical harm befell pupils. However, there is no doubt that the lives of some pupils and staff have been profoundly affected and some of these individuals may require continuing support.

Conclusion

In this chapter we have provided practical suggestions and examples of how schools might manage traumatic events that effect the school population. The main themes that we would highlight are the policies that schools develop, how an effective system of communication is implemented, how they develop a network of people to help support the school or individuals in it and a means of reviewing and changing their practice in the light of actual events. We hope that this chapter may contribute to this process.

Acknowledgements

The authors wish to thank the following for their help: colleagues in the Birmingham Psychological Service and Child Advisory Social Work Service, particularly Francis Mallon and Sheila Finlayson, and the Headteachers, staff and pupils of the schools involved.

References

Baker, T. and Duncan, S. (1992) *Emotional Responses to Trauma, a Developmental Perspective.* (Personal correspondence).

Blom, G. (1986) 'A school disaster: Intervention and research aspects', *Journal of the American Academy of Child Psychiatry*, **25(3)**, 336–45.

Bonenberger, L.M. (1991) 'Remain in your seats: Crisis management for the Alumni Travel Director', *Currents*, **17(2)**, 38–41.

Bowlby, J. (1981) *Attachment and Loss.* Vol. 3. Harmondsworth: Penguin.

Capewell, E. (1992) 'Disaster: The role of education', *Home and School*, **March**, 3–12.

Capewell, E. (1994) *Systems for Managing Critical Incidents in Schools*, Newbury: Centre for Crisis Management and Education.

Dyregrov, A. (1991) *Grief in Children. A Handbook for Adults*. London: Jessica Kingsley Publishers.

Famularo, R. (1990) 'Symptom differences in acute and chronic presentation of childhood post-traumatic stress disorder', *Child Abuse and Neglect, The International Journal*, **14(3)**, 439–44.

Galante, R. and Foa, D. (1987) 'An epidemiological study of psychic trauma and treatment effectiveness for children following a natural disaster', *Annual Progress in Child Psychiatry and Child Development*, **1987**, 349–64.

Johnson, K.(1989) *Trauma in the Lives of children*. Basingstoke: Macmillan.

Johnson, K. (1992) *School Crisis Management*. London: Hunter House.

Katz, S. and Forian, V. (1986) 'A comprehensive theoretical model of psychological reaction to loss', *International Journal of Psychiatry in Medicine*, **16**, 325–45.

Kleber, R. and Brom, D. (1992), *Coping with Trauma; Theory, Prevention and Treatment*. London: Jessica Kingsley Publishers.

Klingman, A. (1987) 'A school-based emergency crisis intervention in a mass school disaster', *Professional Psychology Research and Practice*, **18(6)**, 604–12.

Knapman, D. (1993.) 'Supporting the bereaved child in school – feeling at a loss?' In Alsop, P. and McCaffrey, T. (eds) *How to Cope with Childhood Stress*. Harlow: Longman.

McFarlane, A.C. (1989) 'The prevention and management of the psychiatric morbidity of natural disasters: An Australian experience', *Stress Medicine*, **5(1)**, 29–36.

Mallon, F. and Best, C. (1995) 'Trauma in school: a Psychological Service response', *Educational Psychology in Practice*, **10(4)**, 231–38.

Markwood, S.E. (1988) 'When the television cameras arrive', *NASPA Journal*, **25(3)** 209–12.

Parker, J. Watts, H. and Allsopp, M.R. (1995) 'Post traumatic stress symptoms in children and parents following a school based fatality', *Child Care Health and Development*, **21(30)**, 183–89.

Perry, B.D. (1991) 'Neurobiological sequelae of childhood trauma:post-traumatic stress disorders in children'. In Murberg, M.(ed.) *Catecholamines in Post Traumatic Stress Disorder: Emerging Concepts*. Washington, D.C.: American Psychiatric Press.

Ponton, L.E. and Bryant, E.C. (1991) 'After the earthquake: Organizing to respond to children and adolescents', *Psychiatric Annals*, **21(9)**, 539–46.

Shrestha, B.K.(1990) 'Crisis management in schools: New aspects of professionalism', *OSSC Bulletin*, **34(2)**, 32.

Terr, L.C. (1983) 'Chowchilla revisited: the effects of psychic trauma four years after a school bus kidnapping', *American Journal of Psychiatry*, **140**, 1543–50.

Terr, L.C. (1989) 'Treating psychic trauma in children: a preliminary discussion', *Journal of Traumatic Stress*, **2(1)**, 3–20.

Toubiana, Y.H., Milgram, N.A., Strich, Y. and Edelstein, A. (1988) 'Crisis intervention in a school community disaster: Principles and practices', *Journal of Community Psychology*, **16(2)**, 228–40.

Udwin, O.(1993) 'Annotation: Children's reactions to traumatic events', *Journal of Child Psychology and Psychiatry*, **34**, 115–27.

Wagner, P. (1990) *Children and Bereavement Course*. London: Schools Psychological Service, London Borough of Kensington and Chelsea.

Wenkstern, S. and Leenaars, A. (1993) 'Trauma and suicide in our schools', *Death Studies*, **17(2)**, 151–71.

Yule, W. and Williams, R.M. (1990) 'Post traumatic stress reactions in children'. *Journal of Traumatic Stress*, **2**, 279–95.

Yule, W. (1991a) 'Work with children following disasters'. In Herbert, M. (ed.) *Clinical Child Psychology: Social Learning, Development and Behaviour*. Chichester: John Wiley.

Yule, W. (1991b) 'Screening child survivors for post traumatic stress disorders: experiences from the *Jupiter* sinking', *British Journal of Clinical Psychology*, **30**, 131–38.

Yule, W. (1993) 'Post traumatic stress disorder. In Rutter, M., Hersov. L. and Taylor, E. (eds) *Child and Adolescent Psychiatry: Modern Approaches*, 3rd edn. Oxford: Blackwells.

Yule, W. and Gold, A. (1993) *Wise Before the Event*. London: Calouste Gulbenkian Foundation.

Zakariya-Banks, S. (1985) 'Flood, ruin, murder, strike: How four boards confronted crisis', *American School Board Journal*, **172**, 29–32.

Useful addresses

Trauma After Care Trust (TACT), Buttfields, The Farthings, Withington, Glos. GL54 4DF. Tel: 01242 890306/890498.

If you require OHTs of tables, please contact the authors at: Psychological Service (South area), 74 Balden Road, Harborne, Birmingham B32 2EH.

Chapter Fifteen

Auditing special educational needs: A case study of problem solving using educational psychology

Michael Hymans, Trevor Bryans and Alison Pinks

This chapter describes a system for auditing special educational needs within one local education authority. It attempts to depict both the process by which the system came to be adopted and the procedures involved, highlighting the role of psychology. The audit came about as a consequence of:

1. National developments in special educational needs service delivery, for by the end of the 1980s it was clear that a major overhaul of special educational needs planning and provision was overdue

2. A local Audit Commission report into special educational needs within the borough.

At a national level, in Britain, provision for pupils with special educational needs has moved through three distinct phases since the passing of the 1944 Education Act and the 1945 Regulations (Cline, 1992).

In the first phase public attention focused on categories of handicap or within-child deficits so that the task for professionals was to identify the handicap and move the child to specified provision. In the second phase there was a growing consensus that categorisation was reinforcing and maintaining a segregationist view of disability and impairment and that the rapid expansion of separate provision in segregated environments was disenfranchising substantial cohorts of the school population (Wolfsenburger, 1972). This phase was also increasingly affected by equal opportunities drives in both the USA and the UK resulting in early intervention programmes which focused on the timing, content and presentation of tasks (Cicirelli *et al.*, 1969). Special education labels began to break down as the awareness of 'normative' and 'non-normative' special education labelling became more clearly established.

The last stage and the one currently in evidence, is that of the so-called interactionist view of special needs, taking account of the learner's total environment and circumstances so that learning support in a variety of resourced forms is delivered to the learner, irrespective of location.

Within the UK, the passing of the 1981 Education Act formalising the intentions and recommendations of the Warnock Report (Department of Education and Science, 1978) signalled a new era where it was acknowledged, for the first time, that the majority of pupils with special educational needs are in ordinary schools, not special schools, and that the majority will have learning difficulties (i.e. non-normative difficulties) – not medical conditions or impairments. The 1993 Education Act and the Code of Practice (Department for Education, 1994) simply reinforced this intention.

The abolition of categories enshrined in the 1981 Act did have a number of effects, however, which were to cause administrative problems within a few years. Briefly these were:

1. A rise in parental expectation about levels of service to be delivered by local education authorities and schools to individual pupils in a variety of settings determined, or at least influenced by, parental choice (Mason, 1992).

2. A rise in single issue lobbying, e.g. dyslexia.

3. Confusion over the use of labels (Kirkman, 1992) with respect to individual children's difficulties.

4. A rise in statementing and great variability across the country in local education authority criteria for triggering formal assessment (Audit Commission 1992a,b).

5. Great uncertainty over what constitutes special educational needs.

6. Confusion over the role and deployment of support services, especially after the passing of the 1988 Education Reform Act.

7. A legislative requirement for local education authorities to delegate a greater percentage of central funds to budgets managed by schools themselves.

The main findings of a study of special educational needs within the borough in 1992 were in line with national trends stated above, but other specific issues emerged. These were that:

- There were no clear reasonable criteria of what constituted a special educational need.

- The local education authority was taking too long, on average, to complete statements of special educational needs once it had been agreed to statutorily assess a child.
- Criteria for deploying support services, including educational psychologists, were unclear. Rather each of the support services appeared to have its own referral networks, criteria and *modus operandi* irrespective of what any of the other support services were doing.

This report confirmed that inconsistencies between and among schools was adding further to the need for concerted action at borough level.

The whole audit initiative could therefore be considered within a 'problem solving paradigm', involving alliances between and among different professionals, with the intention of delivering support to individual children within a rational framework (Sigston, 1992).

This notion of the 'organisational imperative' is a consistent feature of all public service delivery. As was noted above in the discussion of variable support service delivery, it seems that sub-organisations (such as individual support services in education) do tend to drift into routines and activities which increasingly diverge. The necessity for periodic rationalisation is therefore a natural part of organisational development (Cohen *et al.*, 1972).

Within the audit framework, the educational psychologists were viewed as the process consultants (Phillips, 1990) who would have a lead role in redefining organisational objectives and as a by-product, reshape how teachers and others would justify the resourcing of special educational needs for all pupils within borough schools.

The two National Audit Commission Reports (1992a,b) proposed that, as both the number of Grant Maintained (GM) Schools (i.e. schools not under local authority control) and financial delegation of budgets increases, schools should be viewed as the contractor (or provider) meeting the individual needs of pupils, with the local education authority acting as the purchaser of those services for pupils.

The Code of Practice (Department for Education, 1994), arising out of the 1993 Education Act (Part III), introduced a five-staged model of assessment to ensure that responsibility for meeting special educational needs was given to schools in the first instance (i.e for the first three stages) with support coming from the local education authority at the end of the third stage. The principles of the Code of Practice suggest:

- that there is continuum of need and provision;
- most children with special educational needs will be in mainstream schools with no statement;
- there should be early action in meeting a child's needs relating to both age and stage of assessment;
- there should be a partnership with parents;

- there should be active links between schools, local education authority and other agencies (e.g. Child Health, Social Services).

It is within this context above, that Brent's Special Educational Needs Audit Team sought to devise a rational, equitable and flexible system for distributing resources for pupils with special educational needs. For this to be achieved it would require more than workable procedures, for the local education authority could not simply dictate a policy to self-governing schools. At social and psychological levels the perspectives and goals of different professional groups would need to be integrated to create an alliance committed to ensuring that these procedures were wholeheartedly implemented.

Ownership of the audit process

Earlier work done in the borough had suggested that there were common concerns about the identification and resourcing of special educational needs. Two key superordinate groups of professionals could be identified: those working centrally for the local education authority who would be mainly involved in managing and using information the system provided, and those working in schools who would supply the information and use the resources allocated to them as a result of the audit. The system would need to meet the needs of both for it to be jointly 'owned'.

A team of two LEA Officers and three LEA Educational Psychologists was established in November 1992 to design and manage the SEN audit. Its draft proposals were discussed (and agreed) with headteachers and special needs coordinators at a series of cluster meetings in early January 1993. These meetings had many of the characteristics of group problem solving described in Chapter 2 of this book. The proposals included:

- the development of criteria and definitions for levels of SEN to be shared across the authority;
- methods of identification of SEN which could be rigorously and consistently applied across all schools;
- procedures for delegating funds to schools relating to level and incidence of need and allowing maximum flexibility of deployment within the purpose specified;
- systems for moderating schools' own identification of SEN, and for monitoring allocated provision;
- a clarification of the respective responsibilities of schools and LEA for meeting SEN and structures for accountability;
- programmes of in-service education to develop further schools' capability for providing for pupils with SEN.

The evolution of the audit

Toward a pilot exercise

A key psychological issue in conducting the Audit concerned assessment. On the one hand an effective system had to provide information on all pupils that was comparable across schools (otherwise the allocation of resources would be unfair); on the other hand an interactive definition of special educational needs implies considering children's needs within the particular contexts in which they are apparent. Comparability is most easily attained by normative assessment – the use of tests administered in a standard way to all children. Context specific assessment relies heavily on the knowledge and skills of individual teachers. To attempt to reconcile these approaches it seemed important to find ways of anchoring teachers' judgements through giving them broad criteria (hereafter called descriptors – see Table 15.1 for those used in the first full run of the audit) to interpret children's needs accompanied by ranges of scores that might typically describe children with these difficulties.

Table 15.1 Summary of descriptors

Descriptor number	Definition of descriptor
One	Access to a differentiated curriculum and/or materials in one or two curriculum or developmental areas
Two	Additional opportunities and/or support for consolidation of specific skills
Three	Extra support to overcome global learning difficulties
Four	Access to individual behaviour management programmes
Five	Access to technical aids or supplementary facilities or support for physical difficulties and/or medical and/or sensory needs

The results of the consultations described earlier heralded a research phase. The aim was to collect data on a number of fronts, which included the practical implications of operating the Audit and an estimation of the number of children who might be considered to have special educational needs. Most importantly it sought to establish the range of interpretation teachers gave to broad descriptors and what might be termed the 'typical' performance of children within groups identified by the teachers as having special educational needs.

The pilot study

In April 1993 the pilot audit was carried out to identify unstatemented pupils with special needs within mainstream schools. A 'banding' system of identification was used. Children were defined as having band 1 (or marginal difficulties) if they required, probably in the short term, occasional specific interventions in order to access the National Curriculum adequately.

Band 2 (or marked difficulties) are where children require, probably in the longer term, regular and intensive interventions in order to access the National Curriculum.

Thirteen schools were selected to reflect the range of pupil characteristics in the borough. All the schools agreed to take part and were asked to list pupils with special educational needs in Years 2, 3, 4, 6, 7, 9 and 10 by band. Once these lists were complete each school was visited by an educational psychologist from the audit team who selected for further assessments matched groups of band 1 band 2 and control pupils. A battery of standardised tests was chosen for ease of administration because they covered a wide age range. These comprised tests of reading, spelling, vocabulary and basic number skills. In addition class teachers were asked to complete a Behaviour Questionnaire for each child. In total 300 children were tested in their matched groups to cover a sample from each of the specified year groups in each school.

From a qualitative analysis of the pilot process the aspect of the descriptors which was most welcomed was the dialogue prompted within the school about what is meant by special educational needs and interventions/strategies being used to meet such needs. Where time was not given to drawing out issues from the descriptors, there were problems of inconsistency across the school, anxieties about the exercise and demands from teachers for written guidance and exemplars arose.

The greatest difficulties in using the descriptors were experienced where children were bilingual and/or transient in the school. The ethnic categories currently used by the borough were considered inappropriate to the diversity of ethnic groups now in Brent schools. This includes long-established Gujerati, Caribbean, West African and Irish communities as well as newly arrived communities and refugees from North Africa, the Horn of Africa and Eastern Europe.

Small size of school and relatively small numbers of children in the control group sometimes made matching difficult, as did absenteeism, transience of pupils and occasional suspected false dates of birth. Teachers were not always certain who to include in the control group. Some schools had problems making an ethnic and/or gender match across one or more year group samples. One or two schools had large numbers of children fitting one category of special educational need and not the other.

From the psychologists' point of view, there were very few problems administering the test battery. All children were assessed 'blind' in that the examiner did not know which category the child had been allocated by teachers at the outset of the test session.

All scores obtained on the tests, except the behaviour questionnaire, were converted to attainment/achievement ages and they were entered on a database.

Results of the pilot study ·

The main conclusion of the pilot study were:

1. More finely tuned descriptors were needed for the early years (i.e. Year 2 and below).

2. Teachers appeared primarily to use reading and spelling judgements about whether or not a particular child had marked or marginal special needs.

3. The picture vocabulary and maths tests, although useful to the moderating educational psychologists, did not concur as well as the other measures with the descriptors as used by the teachers. The picture vocabulary test produced a large number of very low scores across all bands and ages.

4. It was possible to build up a profile of pupils in each band and category, using the test battery.

5. Teachers in Year 7 (i.e. first year of secondary school) showed less certainty of discrimination of banding than in any other year group.

6. An analysis of every individual pupil's scores reveals only a handful in the band 1/band 2 categories who were mis-categorised by teachers in reading or spelling, i.e. placed in the 'wrong band'.

7. It was difficult to know precisely how many pupils were included primarily for behaviour or adjustment problems.

8. Boys showed significantly more over-reactive behaviour than girls but girls are more inclined to display significantly greater under-reactive behaviour than boys. This is a well-established observation (Department for Education, 1989).

The pilot also highlighted the need for guidance for teachers in distinguishing between those children with language needs as a result of English being their second language from those with additional special educational needs. This is in line with findings from other research (e.g. Cummins, 1984; Saunders, 1988).

The pilot exercise required Special Needs co-ordinators to identify children by their characteristics/difficulties who ought to be given some form of 'additional' provision. Subsequent data collection attempted to clarify these characteristics or difficulties via a sampling exercise. A possible systemic problem with emphasising identification by low attainment is that it would inevitably divert schools' attention from providing for children, toward testing that will stand up to external scrutiny, reframing the role of the special needs co-ordinator as mainly concerned with identification rather than intervention. Given that resources are at stake (allocations of funds for band 1 and band 2 children) it would be expected that senior managers in schools would seek to ensure this emphasis.

Extending and clarifying the descriptors – linking them to both level of difficulty as well as arrangements to meet children's needs – was considered as a balanced method of resolution to the problem. The school would need to demonstrate both severity of the child's difficulties and the implementation of plans to assist the child. It was also decided to expand the descriptors relating to social, emotional and behavioural difficulties and to further differentiate medical, physical and sensory descriptors.

However, before making these changes, more accurate levels of difficulty (for reading and spelling) were required, in order to establish 'thresholds' for each band and to compare these calculations with teacher judgements. A 'hybrid' method for calculating the thresholds was chosen. This method involved using both the *mean* attainment levels for each year group in the pilot and *test* standardisation data norms. The thresholds obtained for band 1 and 2 provided a unique borough profiling system which was used to extend the descriptors to provide information about the pupils' levels of difficulty. It was also possible to look back at the test data from the pilot schools and find the percentage agreement between the teachers' banding judgement and the borough thresholds using expectancy tables. The percentage agreement varied from school to school and ranged from approximately 20% to 70%. As would be expected, some schools had consistently over-included and others under-included pupils into bands.

This information was fed back to schools so that they would have perceptions of the special needs within their school in comparison with the rest of the borough. This information would thus assist staff with future audits. Schools with the highest agreements were generally those where a considerable amount of time had been set aside by the staff for audit training and discussions between staff. An analysis of feedback from the pilot schools illustrated a need to clarify and expand the descriptors to ensure that they would be interpreted in the same way by each school.

Implementing the audit

In January 1994 schools carried out their audits by completing a banding record sheet for each identified child. School summary sheets listed the initials of all banded pupils by year group and all the sheets were sent to the local education authority.

Real data about real children

For the first time there was authority wide, valid information about the numbers and difficulties of children with special educational needs. A few snapshots of this data are presented here. Every school was visited by an educational psychologist to clarify any outstanding issues about the audit and schools welcomed this opportunity for discussion and confirmed ownership. To ensure consistency across the borough, moderation was an essential part of the audit procedure to verify the schools bandings. Schools were asked to make available for the moderators one or more of the following six types of evidence:

1. Unaided samples of children's work.

2. Contextual observational notes over time on children's learning or behaviour.

3. National Curriculum levels, SATS results.

4. Records of arrangements to meet children's needs.

5. Test results/teacher assessments.

6. Evidence of reports from other professionals (e.g. educational welfare officer, social worker, doctor).

A randomly selected sample of pupils was chosen for moderation by the audit team. Seven teams of moderators were chosen with at least one member being an employee of the local authority (e.g. educational psychologist, head of a support service or an audit officer) and one or more other members being a headteacher, special needs co-ordinator or borough support teacher.

Training the moderation teams was an important aspect of this stage of the procedure and involved discussions of the types of evidence that would be acceptable. Case studies were presented for the teams to discuss so that consistency between the moderating teams was achieved.

An analysis of the entire audit sample of children revealed that:

- 64% were in band 1 of whom 61% were boys and 39% were girls
- 36% were in band 2 of whom 64% were boys and 36 % were girls
- For both bands 1 and 2, 62% of the sample were boys and 38% were girls
- 26% of sample used one descriptor; 24% used two descriptors; 27% used three descriptors; 17% used four descriptors and, 6% used five descriptors
- of the 26% using a single descriptor, 35% used descriptor 4 and 27% used descriptor 1 (see Table 15.1).

Table 15.2 extends this analysis by comparing, by year group, the percentages of children in each band.

Table 15.2 Band 1 versus Band 2

Year	Band 1*	Band 2*
One	68	32
Two	60	40
Three	63	37
Four	69	31
Five	64	36
Six	62	38
Seven	59	41
Eight	68	32
Nine	69	31
Ten	65	35
Eleven	61	39
ALL	64	36

* As a percentage of the sample.

Table 15.2 shows that the percentage of band 1 children is one-and-half times to twice that of the band 2 children – that is, with the exception of Year 7, which confirms the suggestion (point 5) in the pilot study data mentioned earlier. This trend also supports the concept of a continuum of special educational needs with more children being at the lower (marginal) end.

The analysis can be further extended to include numbers of children included in the audit by gender, as well as year group, for each descriptor, and for both bands of children – as a percentage of all children in Brent (Table 15.3).

Table 15.3 Gender/year bias in the use of descriptors, for both band 1 and band 2 children, as a percentage of all children in Brent

Year	Descriptor 1		Descriptor 2		Descriptor 3		Descriptor 4		Descriptor 5	
	Boy	Girl	Boy	Girl	Boy	Girl	Boy	Girl	Boy	Girl
I	15.3	10.7	14.6	9.3	12.6	7.1	11.5	4.5	3.2	2.2
2	18.1	10.3	21.3	11.7	15.8	8.5	11.3	4.7	2.9	1.7
3	21.5	14.5	22.5	14.9	17.7	11.5	15.2	9.5	5.6	1.9
4	16.7	13.6	17.8	14.9	13.8	12.6	13.8	9.8	5.4	2.8
5	17.1	11.3	16.8	14.8	12.1	11.0	12.4	7.8	5.2	2.6
6	19.3	12.7	17.6	12.7	13.9	9.6	9.4	4.0	2.0	1.0
7	16.2	11.0	17.1	12.1	14.8	7.0	9.5	2.8	0.8	0.2
8	12.8	7.1	10.4	4.9	7.0	2.5	13.6	1.8 *	0.8	0.2
9	12.5	5.1	11.1	3.7	8.0	1.8	8.9	2.1	0.9	0.4
10	10.1	5.9	8.8	4.4	5.3	2.3	10.7	3.9	0.6	0.5
11	8.1	5.1	6.7	3.4	4.0	2.3	5.2	2.7	0.8	0.3
All	15.9	10.4	15.7	10.3	12.0	7.5	11.3	5.2	2.8	1.4

Table 15.3 shows that more boys than girls were identified by all five descriptors in all 11 year groups. This fits with the general consensus that boys are more frequently described than girls as having special educational needs – both learning needs (descriptors 1–3) and behavioural difficulties (descriptor 4), even though the latter descriptor included descriptions such as: 'isolated, obsessive, unresponsive and unreactive behaviour (e.g. anxiety, passivity) (Department for Education, 1989).

Such differences were fairly consistent, overall (see bottom row of table) for the most heavily used descriptors: 5.5 (for descriptor 1); 5.4 (for descriptor 2); 5.5 (for descriptor 3) and, 6.1 (for descriptor 4). The largest single difference (12) occurred in Year 8 for descriptor 4 (behaviour) – no explanation can be offered, other than perhaps the onset of adolescence. Other large differences occurred in Year 2 and particularly with descriptors 1 (difference of 8) and 2 (difference of 9). It is also interesting to note that Year 11 had the lowest differences for all five descriptors and that the general trend is for larger differences in Years 1–3 and Years 7–9 with a gradual increase as one moves up each of these triads: Year 6 sees a rise on Years 4 and 5 and Years 10 and 11 sees a progressive drop on Years 8 and 9. Clearly then, gender differences become more marked during the early years of schooling and that primary secondary transfer and the first 3 years of secondary education highlight such differences too. The drop in Years 10 and 11 is interesting especially in the light of recent research on how girls have overtaken boys in GCSE results.

Evaluation and reflections

One danger with close team working is that members can find themselves in a cosy consensus where assumptions and decisions are not sufficiently challenged. Janis (1972) has described a phenomenon he called 'groupthink' drawing on the way close advisers of President Kennedy became convinced of the probable success of the 'Bay of Pigs' assault on Cuba – which in reality turned out to be a debacle. To ensure that the audit arrangement stood up to outside scrutiny, as well as to seek suggestions for its improvement an independent psychologist was commissioned to carry out an evaluation. The evaluation, via questionnaire and interview, assessed the process of developing audit arrangements; materials used; training and the process of moderating the audit.

There was a 45% response rate to the questionnaire and, in relation to:

- *The process of developing the audit* – Overall there was a high level of satisfaction and that the dissemination of information was most highly regarded.
- *The materials used* (the audit pack) – The audit pack had a very strong vote of confidence while at the same time there were clearly expressed views about how it could be improved.
- *The training* – Ratings were again very positive, particularly with regard to the content of the training with the main reservations being expressed in relation to the amount of training and to a lesser extent the way it was organised.
- *The process of moderating* – Procedures were on the whole regarded as efficient but there was a substantial view, but *not* a majority view, amongst primary schools, that the moderation was less successful in achieving fairness and comparability between schools.

The interview data revealed:

- *Positive aspects of the way the audit was planned and conducted:*
    - schools and officers viewed the audit positively;
    - it was generally perceived to be a fairer way of allocating resources;
    - the audit had raised the profile of special educational needs in schools and across the borough;
    - long-term planning and meeting of deadlines seemed active and purposeful;

- consultation and co-ordination between the audit team and practitioners were felt to be a strong feature;
- information about the progress of the project had been appreciated and had helped maintain interest and motivation;
- the audit pack was felt to be very well thought through;
- on the whole the process of moderation was felt to have gone well.

- *Problem areas identified:*
- achieving greater consistency across moderators due to:
  - variable or inadequate evidence provided for moderation,
  - the size of moderation samples being too small,
  - moderators training requiring development,
  - concern over the use of tests,
- improving the clarity of the audit materials;
- developing schools' systems and accountability:
  - the relative development of school systems for identifying Special Needs,
  - mismatch between schools' systems for identifying Special Needs and audit arrangements,
  - time pressures,
  - accountability for the use of money following the audit.

This evaluation made a number of recommendations all of which have been acted upon in carrying out the second main audit (January 1995):

- Between the moderation sample being selected and the moderation visit schools should prepare common information *for children in the sample only.*
- Development of a screening checklist for early years/Key Stage 1.
- Moderation should begin to take more account of schools' planning and provision in addition to the level of difficulties shown by students.
- Moderation sample in each school should be increased to 20% of each school return and be representative in respect of gender and types of difficulty experienced by children.
- Amending administration required of special educational needs co-ordinators.
- Moderation of behaviour difficulties should focus primarily on evidence concerned with schools' response to behaviour where this is the students' main area of difficulty.
- Amending the layout of the audit pack (now called an audit handbook).
- Assisting special needs staff/class/subject teachers in making reference to National Curriculum and common curriculum materials under 'Likely level of difficulty.'
- Providing additional guidance on the inclusion of bilingual students:
  - Has the student sustained opportunities to learn English?
  - Do students show similar levels of competence when using their first language?

- Do the students' difficulties stem from understandable trauma or loss due to relatively recent events?
- Publishing a time-line and maximising the time between notification of the moderation sample and the moderation visit.
- Cascading audit training to class and subject teachers and providing informal support for special educational needs co-ordinators.
- Inviting schools to contribute copies of their special educational needs policies and annual reports to governors for a borough compendium.

The successful implementation of the audit of unstatemented pupils achieved a number of secondary aims by:

- clarifying the Code of Practice Stages of Assessment;
- identifying commonly agreed descriptions and thresholds of need with schools across the borough;
- clarifying respective responsibilities between schools and the local education authority for meeting the needs of the child;
- setting out explicit criteria by which children and young people are referred for statutory assessment.

The extension of the audit into statemented pupil categories was therefore a natural follow-on. The process of piloting and developing the arrangements began in 1995 and builds on our experience of the model described here. A detailed analysis of all statemented pupils' needs and the provision in place to meet these was carried out first of all. This gave a comprehensive overview of all arrangements currently in place for all statemented pupils.

Summary

It should be apparent from this detailed discussion of the audit process and its evaluation, that the problem-solving paradigm was a key component at each stage of the implementation. Furthermore, the information gathered at each stage could not necessarily have been predicted in its entirety. Each preceding stage of the audit provided the 'scaffolding' for developing the next stage of the process. And as a consequence of this auditing system there is now a clear and precise delineation of the continuum of special educational needs within a local context, including criteria for initiating statutory assessments. There is also greater clarification over responsibility for the identification and assessment of special educational needs.

The ultimate aim of the audit is to improve the quality of experiences of needy children in school. Throughout the development and implementation of the audit arrangements psychological knowledge and skills have been to the fore in group problem solving, promoting ownership of the process of change and in conducting field research and evaluation. We believe these contributions have been significant to assuring the success of the venture so far.

References

Audit Commission/HMI (Her Majesty's Inspectorate) (1992a) *Getting in on The Act: Provision for Pupils with Special Educational Needs.* London: HMSO.

Audit Commission/HMI (1992b) *Getting the Act Together: Provision for Pupils with Special Educational Needs.* London: HMSO.

Caplan, G. (1969) *An Approach to Community Mental Health.* London: Tavistock.

Cohen, M.D., Marsh, J.G. and Olsen, J.P. (1972) 'A garbage model of organisational choice', *Administrative Science Quarterly,* **17**, 1–25.

Circirelli, V. *et al.* (1969) *The Impact of Head Start: An Evaluation of the Effects of Head Start on Children's Cognitive and Affective Development.* Westinghouse, Ohio: Report for the Office of Economic Opportunity, US Department of Commerce.

Cline, T. (ed.) (1992) *The Assessment of Special Educational Needs: International Perspectives.* London: Routledge.

Cummins, J. (1984) *Bilingualism and Special Educational Needs: Issues in Assessment and Pedagogy.* Avon: Multilingual Matters.

Department for Education (1989) *Discipline in Schools: Report of the Committee of Enquiry chaired by Lord Elton.* (The Elton Report), London: HMSO.

Department for Education (1994) *Code of Practice for the Identification of and assessment of Children with Special Educational Needs.* London: DfE.

Department of Education and Science (1978) *Special Needs Education* (The Warnock Report). London: HMSO.

Janis, I.L. (1972) *Victims of Groupthink.* Boston: Houghton Mifflin.

Kirkman, R. (1992): 'Blood, sweat and many tears', *Times Educational Supplement,* **17 July**, 20.

Mason, M. (1992) *The Inclusive Education System.* London: The Integration Alliance.

Phillips, P. (1990) 'Consultative teamwork in secondary schools: a training exercise', *Educational and Child Psychology,* **7(1)**, 67–77.

Saunders, G. (1988) *Bilingual Children: from Birth to Teens.* Avon: Multilingual Matters.

Sigston, A. (1992) 'Making a difference for children: The educational psychologist an empowerer of problem-solving alliances'. In Wolfendale, S. *et al.* (eds) *The Profession and Practice of Educational Psychology: Future Directions.* London: Cassell Education.

Wolfsenburger, W. (1972) 'The principle of normalisation in human services', *Education and Child Psychology,* **3(3)**, 19–28.

Index